AF677002

Misapplying Globalization

Misapplying Globalization: Jordan and the Intellectual Property Policy Challenge

By

Faris K. Nesheiwat

CAMBRIDGE SCHOLARS
PUBLISHING

Misapplying Globalization:
Jordan and the Intellectual Property Policy Challenge,
by Faris K. Nesheiwat

This book first published 2014

Cambridge Scholars Publishing

12 Back Chapman Street, Newcastle upon Tyne, NE6 2XX, UK

British Library Cataloguing in Publication Data
A catalogue record for this book is available from the British Library

Copyright © 2014 by Faris K. Nesheiwat

All rights for this book reserved. No part of this book may be reproduced, stored in a retrieval system, or transmitted, in any form or by any means, electronic, mechanical, photocopying, recording or otherwise, without the prior permission of the copyright owner.

ISBN (10): 1-4438-5163-9, ISBN (13): 978-1-4438-5163-3

To my family
Karim, Jacqueline, Mara, Fadi, Reem, Manar, Owen and Karim

TABLE OF CONTENTS

LIST OF TABLES

LIST OF ABBREVIATIONS

ACTA	Anti-Counterfeiting Trade Agreement
ARPO	Author's Right Protection Office at the National Library
ASEZA	Aqaba Special Economic Zone Authority
CBJ	Central Bank of Jordan
CCPA	United States Court of Customs and Patent Appeals
CIF	Cost, Insurance and Freight
CRC	United Nation's Committee on the Rights of the Child
DSB	Dispute Settlement Body
DSU	Dispute Settlement Understanding
EFTA	European Free Trade Area
EU	European Union
FAO	UN Food and Agriculture Organization
FCIA	Federal Courts Improvement Act
FDI	Foreign Direct Investment
FOB	Free on Board
FTA	Free Trade Agreements
GAO	United States Government Accountability Office
GATS	General Agreement in Trade in Services
GCC	Gulf Cooperation Council
GCR	Global Competitiveness Report
GDP	Gross Domestic Product
GSD	General Statistics Department
ILO	International Labour Organization
IMF	International Monetary Fund
IP	Intellectual Property
IPIC	Treaty on Intellectual Property in Respect of Integrated Circuits
IPPD	Industrial Property Protection Directorate
IPRs	Intellectual Property Rights
IPRS	Intellectual Property Rights Section within the Jordanian Customs
JAPM	Jordanian Association of Manufacturers of Pharmaceuticals and Medical Appliances
JIB	Jordan Investment Board
JD	Jordanian Dinars
JEUAA	Jordan–European Union Association Agreement

JFDA	Jordanian Food and Drug Administration
JIPA	Jordan Intellectual Property Association
JISM	Jordan Institute of Standards and Metrology
JUSFTA	Jordan–US Free Trade Agreement
MCA	Millennium Challenge Account
MENA	Middle East and North Africa
MERCOSUR	Mercado Comun del Sur
MNC	Multi-national Corporation
MoIT	Ministry of Industry and Trade
NAFTA	North America Free Trade Agreement
NGO	Non-governmental Organizations
NL	National Library
OECD	Organization for Economic Cooperation and Development
OHCHR	United Nations Office of the High Commissioner for Human Rights
PCT	Patent Cooperation Treaty
PhRMA	Pharmaceutical Manufacturers Association
QIZ	Qualified Industrial Zones
QIZA	Qualified Industrial Zones Agreement
RBT	Regional and Bilateral Treaty
R&D	Research and Development
SPLT	Substantive Patent Law Treaty
TRIPS	Agreement on Trade Related Aspects of Intellectual Property
TRRM	Trade Policy Review Mechanism
UPOV	International Convention of the Protection of New Varieties of Plants
USAID	United States Agency for International Development
USTR	United States Trade Representative
WCO	World Customs Organization
WCT	WIPO Copyright Treaty
WHO	World Health Organization
WIPO	World Intellectual Property Organization
WPPT	WIPO Performance and Phonograms Treaty
WTO	World Trade Organization

PREFACE

The advent of the twenty-first century brought dramatic changes to the global governance of intellectual property (IP). The seeds of this change were sown in the 1980s and 1990s, as the United States and the European Union championed the establishment of universal rules to govern IP practices. Their goal was and remains the globalization of OECD-style IP regimes, which emphasize greater protection of intellectual property rights (IPRs) at the expense of more public access to those rights. The most significant milestone towards harmonizing national IP standards with OECD standards was the inclusion of TRIPS in the World Trade Organization (WTO), which was the result of intense lobbying by corporate executives, backed by the trade negotiators of the developed countries.

Studies had concluded that, notwithstanding the limitations on setting national IPRs policies imposed by TRIPS, countries could still exhibit diminished variations in their IP laws in accordance with their specific economic and social conditions. Such early assessments, however, did not take into account the advent of regional and bilateral treaties (RBTs), which pushed the compliance pendulum towards higher IPRs protection. RBTs were introduced by the United States and the European Union as they realized that the ultimate goal of IPRs harmonization was not being fully achieved through TRIPS, and because they were increasingly aware of the blocking power that developing countries enjoyed by virtue of the requirement of consensus for any amendment to TRIPS. As a result, the United States and the European Union moved to an RBT approach, aimed at achieving IPRs harmonization outside the multilateral approach of the WTO.

RBTs were presented to developing countries as yet another piece of the contemporary landscape of trade agreements intended to provide them with a heightened degree of integration into the international economy. Specifically, they offered developing countries the trade-off of exclusive entry conditions to the US and EU markets in return for amending the legal and administrative frameworks governing IPRs such that they became similar to those in the United States and the European Union. Thus, the price to be paid for increased market access under RBTs was the relinquishing of many of the very tools that historically were used by developing countries to attain the developmental benefits of integration in the international economy.

Although many scholars have been critical both of TRIPS and the increasing integration of intellectual property into RBTs, little of that criticism is country-specific; rather, it is focused on general rules and legal provisions.[1] While the criticism of the increased integration of IP into RBTs has at times been based on the RBTs' threat to eliminate the national capacity to tailor IP management to national conditions, it has not progressed into an analysis of country-specific local political and cultural frameworks. I argue that without such an analysis, it is not possible to understand the tensions between the technologically advanced countries' push for higher rights protections and the less-developed countries' resistance to the resulting increased cost of regulation. What is at stake is the impact that IP policies and laws can have on country-specific human development programmes and allocation of limited resources.

Jordan has attached its strategies for IPRs integration to the multilateral framework of the WTO, and the RBTs it has entered into with the United States and the European Union. This is having a range of effects on Jordanian law, institutions, and cultural attitudes. However, one should not consider this shift towards greater IPRs as the final word in the overall historical discussion of IPRs, because the tension between the desire for maximum exclusivity and the desire for maximum access cannot be resolved for the benefit of one over the other. Such a one-sided approach

---

[1] There are some notable exceptions. An analysis of the effect of RBTs on the Arab world in general, but without a specific focus on Jordan, is provided in Hamed El Said and Mohammed El Said, "The European TRIPS-Plus Model and the Arab World: From Co-Operation to Association—A New Era in the Global IPRS Regime?" *Liverpool Law Review* 28, no. 1 (2007): 143–174; Mohammed El Said, "The Implementation Paradox: Intellectual Property Regulation in the Arab World," *Journal of International Trade Law and Policy* 9, no. 3 (2010): 221–235. Malkawi has provided an analysis of the JUSFTA, but only in the context of deciding whether its terms can serve as a template for a proposed US–Middle East FTA, not to examine the local context of those terms. See Bashar H. Malkawi, "The Intellectual Property Provisions of the United States–Jordan Free Trade Agreement: Template or Not Template," *The Journal of World Intellectual Property* 9, no. 2 (March 1, 2006): 213–229. El Said and El Said have also examined the terms of the JUSFTA, cautioning against the negative effects of TRIPS with respect to access to medicines, but not looking at the larger picture of compliance and enforcement. See H. El-Said and M. El-Said, "TRIPS-Plus Implications for Access to Medicines in Developing Countries: Lessons from Jordan–United States Free Trade Agreement," *The Journal of World Intellectual Property* 10, no. 6 (2007): 438–475.

will result in either severely restricting access to knowledge or eroding the economic incentive to innovate. The discussion over IPRs must inevitably address the tension between the interests of rights holders, who want to maximize the control they exert over their works in hopes of maximizing the profits gained thereby, and the interests of those who are not right-holders but need access to these works with the aim of using them to create other innovations.

We need a fair and balanced system of IP laws that provides for a suitable degree of exclusivity while also allowing a level of access consistent with the broader public interest. A balanced system should be dynamic and adaptive to new technologies, as well as to economic shifts and global developments. Importantly, an adaptive system is an open system that is able to alter its behaviour according to changes in its socio-legal environment precisely because it is closely linked to that environment. For IP, creating such a system requires that governments and legislators have a better understanding of the specific nature and local needs of the societies in which those IP systems are implemented. This book attempts to provide such understanding for the specific case of Jordan.

CHAPTER ONE

INTRODUCTION

It is justifiable to wonder why any developing country – or any developed country, such as Canada, that is a net intellectual property importer – would agree to join TRIPS. After all, the World Bank estimated in 2002 that TRIPS implementation would cause annual losses of \$530 million for Brazil, \$5.1 billion for China, \$903 million for India, and \$15.3 billion for South Korea. Proponents of TRIPS have argued that stronger IP protection is a prerequisite for technology transfer, yet this is belied by the work of various scholars, and indeed the subsequent history of TRIPS vindicates the concerns of developing countries that they do not stand to gain much from implementing higher intellectual property standards. Nevertheless, as the promises of global trade and economic empowerment through globalization took root in the collective political consciousness, TRIPS became a reality, and, despite any misgivings they might have entertained, developing countries within the WTO embarked on IP reforms of varying magnitude and scope.[1]

---

[1] There is a great deal of literature which criticizes TRIPS and the increasing integration of intellectual property into RBTs, but most of it concerns general rules and legal provisions as opposed to country-specific analysis. See, for example, Peter Drahos, "Information Feudalism in the Information Society," *The Information Society* 11, no. 3 (July 1995): 209–222; Christopher May and Susan K. Sell, *Intellectual Property Rights: A Critical History* (Lynne Rienner, 2005); Susan K. Sell, *Private Power, Public Law* (Cambridge University Press, 2003); Keith Eugene Maskus, *Intellectual Property Rights in the Global Economy* (Washington, DC: Peterson Institute, 2000); C. M. Correa, *Intellectual Property Rights, the WTO, and Developing Countries: The TRIPS Agreement and Policy Options* (New York: Zed Books, 2000); Duncan Matthews, *Globalising Intellectual Property Rights: The TRIPS Agreement* (London: Routledge, 2002); Kenneth C. Shadlen, "Exchanging Development for Market Access? Deep Integration and Industrial Policy Under Multilateral and Regional-Bilateral Trade Agreements," *Review of International Political Economy* 12, no. 5 (2005): 750–775. For a discussion of the danger that RBTs would undermine the national capacity to tailor IP management to national conditions, see, for example, Kenneth C. Shadlen, "Intellectual

Jordan's accession to TRIPS and the various amendments it made to its IP laws can be attributed to two major and broad drivers. First, the perception that Jordan's attempt to shift to a knowledge-based economy could not have gone far without input from the multinational companies who are the purveyors of knowledge and innovation, and who in turn requested tighter and more stringent protections for their IP assets. Jordan did not have much negotiating power to deny such requests. The economic bubble of the first decade of the twenty-first century meant that there were many countries standing in line to comply with multi-national companies' requests for IP asset protection in return for their investment in the local economy. Thus, the promises of attracting greater flows of foreign investment played a significant role in Jordan's accession to TRIPS, for all that the data cast doubt that such promises would be fulfilled.

Second, Jordan is heavily dependent on foreign aid, and the provision of such aid became increasingly linked to meeting the commercial and legal demands of the donors. Policies relating to IP protection have become infused into the aid culture within Jordan. Whole programs and projects are now vetted for their compliance with the IP politics of the developed countries, including TRIPS and TRIPS-plus standards. In general terms, "capacity development" is the new gateway for the penetration into developing countries' decision-making circles, and the creation of a monolithic point of view, mainly that of the donor country, as regards the role and importance of IP.[2] For example, US Government-financed technical assistance programs were designed explicitly to implement IP standards that in fact exceeded the obligations under TRIPS.[3]

In practice, these two dynamics were expressed in terms of requirements that Jordan meet certain goals and so-called growth and development criteria, mainly focused on the existence of sufficient IP laws, the

---

Property, Trade, and Development: Can Foes Be Friends?" *Global Governance* 13 (2007): 171.

[2] See Benjamin Fordham and Victor Asal, "Billiard Balls or Snowflakes? Major Power Prestige and the International Diffusion of Institutions and Practices," *International Studies Quarterly* 51, no. 1 (2007): 31–52; Kristian Skrede Gleditsch and Michael D. Ward, "Diffusion and the International Context of Democratization," *International Organization* 60, no. 4 (2006): 911–933; Beth Simmons and Zachary Elkins, "The Globalization of Liberalization: Policy Diffusion in the International Political Economy," *American Political Science Review* 98, no. 1 (2004): 171–189.

[3] See Carolyn Deere, *The Implementation Game: The TRIPS Agreement and the Global Politics of Intellectual Property Reform in Developing Countries* (Oxford: Oxford University Press, 2008).

availability of enforcement agencies, and the compilation of a statistical indicator of the minimum number of raids and confiscations of pirated and counterfeit products. Within all this, little attention was paid to the actual compatibility of those measures and indicators with Jordan's local economic, social, and developmental needs.

The new IP laws were introduced into the Jordanian legal framework with remarkable haste. Parliament was suspended for the period when the new IP laws were enacted, and the process was deprived of a full debate by the legislative branch. The laws enabling WTO accession and the entering into a free trade treaty with the United States were passed under the executive authority of the king while parliament was dissolved, without much public debate or involvement. Additionally, civil-society organizations were not involved in their enactment, which limited the consideration of the economic and social costs associated with their implementation. Jordan now has thirteen laws that deal directly or indirectly with IP, some of which contain drafting mistakes. As chapter five will show, the administrative agencies charged with enforcement are marked by overlapping and confused responsibilities, and Jordan is under constant pressure to take on new enforcement roles geared towards defending the interests of multinational corporations. Meanwhile, the Jordanian private sector and public are increasingly disaffected with the strengthened IP regime, from which they have seen few benefits.

An account of the forces at work here which treats either the donors, or the recipient country, as monolithic, will miss a crucial layer of rich analysis. It is important to examine the domestic politics and setup of the enforcement agencies, as well as the socio-economic factors which impacted upon Jordan's decision to accede to TRIPS and other associated treaties. Without understanding those factors, one will not be able to suggest ways either to reform or better enforce those laws. This book attempts to take on this task.

The book is structured as follows. The remainder of the present chapter provides a general background on TRIPS and an overview of pertinent aspects of Jordanian society, while chapter two introduces the Jordanian legal system particularly as regards to IP. Chapter three examines those pressures on Jordan to reform its IP legislation which stem from the international legal and political framework, looking first at those which are rooted in the WTO, and then at those bound up with the regional and bilateral treaties (RBTs) to which Jordan is a signatory. We will see that the relatively minor flexibilities allowed under TRIPS are largely foreclosed under the RBT system. Chapter four looks at the wider ideational and economic pressures which were brought to bear to persuade

Jordan to join the TRIPS and TRIPS-plus frameworks. Chapter five discusses the effects of the heightened standards on economic development in Jordan, as well as the impacts on the administrative institutions charged with enforcing Jordan's new laws. Chapter six reflects on ways forward.

TRIPS and the developing world

The Agreement on Trade Related Aspects of Intellectual Property Rights (TRIPS) is a multilateral agreement on the regulation of intellectual property rights, negotiated through and administered by the World Trade Organization (WTO). Historically this issue has been dominated by the developed countries, and they included their proposal for TRIPS in the Uruguay Round (1986–1994) as a means to regulate IP protection within the GATT rules.[4] As such, TRIPS represents one particular view of IPRs; but it is a view that came to be marketed by developed countries as the *only* acceptable form – excluding from consideration the various processes by which IPRs have been developed and formulated at national levels throughout the history of IP. Jordan was not a party to TRIPS negotiations, as it was not yet a member of the WTO, and its acceptance of TRIPS was a *fait accompli* within the WTO accession process, as opposed to a debated and properly negotiated agreement. It also marked Jordan's sliding from a centrist approach to IP regulation and enforcement, dating from the Ottoman era, which balanced the public and private interests, to the more monopolistic end of the IP enforcement spectrum, where right-holders are given precedence over public interest.

Prior to Jordan's amending its laws in preparation for its accession to the WTO on April 11, 2000, it possessed no substantive legal body that focused on issues of IP. IP was marginalized for the majority of the period from the creation of the Jordanian state in 1921 until the 1990s, but that changed with the increased prominence of IP in the early 1990s resulting from a major overhaul of laws and regulations. The main two catalysts for that overhaul were Jordan's goal of securing membership in the WTO, and

---

[4] For an examination of the lobbying by the corporate interests of developed countries in the process of including TRIPS in the WTO, see, for example, P. Drahos, "Global Property Rights in Information: The Story of TRIPS at the GATT," *Prometheus* 13, no. 1 (1995): 6–19; Matthews, *Globalising Intellectual Property Rights*; Sell, *Private Power, Public Law*; C. May, *The World Intellectual Property Organization: Resurgence and the Development Agenda* (Abingdon: Taylor & Francis, 2007).

the new liberalized economic outlook, which focused on market liberalization, economic openness, and the attraction of foreign investments.

Pursuing WTO membership was mainly a political rather than an economic decision, and it was an outlook influenced by the principles advocated by the International Monetary Fund (IMF) during its program of support for the Jordanian economy and currency, which began in 1989 and ended in 2004. The economic impact and value of such decisions were not evaluated beyond the promises made by the developing countries of more access to world markets, increased foreign direct investment (FDI), and the improvement of the Jordanian standard of living.[5]

Shortly after the WTO accession, Jordan embarked on negotiations with the United States to conclude the Jordan–US Free Trade Agreement (JUSFTA), and with the European Union to conclude the Jordan–EU Association Agreement (JEUAA). The JUSFTA was signed on October 24, 2000 and entered into force on December 17, 2001, and the JEUAA entered into force on May 1, 2002. Both treaties have a strong IP component which extends the requirements on Jordan beyond those incorporated in TRIPS. It is common to refer to such standards, which lack a unified institutional basis such as the WTO but are no less potent, as "TRIPS-plus" standards. While the TRIPS regime allowed developing countries to retain a certain degree of flexibility in how they established their IP laws, these flexibilities are being removed by these new agreements.[6] These regional and bilateral treaties (RBTs), which drove Jordan into the TRIPS-plus era, are also having corrosive effect on the multilateral trade system, as will be discussed in chapter five.

A brief review of the situation with patents and copyright illustrates themes that this book will study more closely. The first Jordanian patent law No. 22 (1953) provided for process patents but did not allow for product patents (art. 4). It further allowed for a sixteen-year protection

---

[5] On this point I am indebted to various members of Jordanian public and private institutions who agreed to be interviewed for the purposes of this study. For more information on these interviews, see appendix one.

[6] See, for example, C. Correa, "Intellectual Property Rights and the Use of Compulsory Licenses: Options for Developing Countries," Trade-Related Agenda, Development and Equity (T.R.A.D.E.) Working Papers 5 (South Centre, October 2001); The Commission on Intellectual Property Rights, *Integrating Intellectual Property Rights and Development Policy* (London: CIPR, 2002); Kenneth Shadlen, "Exchanging Development for Market Access? Deep Integration and Industrial Policy Under Multilateral and Regional-Bilateral Trade Agreements," *Review of International Political Economy* 12, no. 5 (2005): 750–775.

period, which would not be extended in the event of any modifications or amendments made to the original patent (art. 16). While the law allowed the patent registrar at the Ministry of Industry and Trade (MoIT)[7] to approve a patent, it placed the responsibility for the veracity of the patent's information on the applicant rather than the registrar (art. 4(2)), effectively ensuring that Jordan never developed patent examination expertise. A new Patent Law granting twenty years of protection was enacted in 1999, incorporating TRIPS-consistent standards into its language (Patent Law No. 32). The language of the 1999 law presented a significant departure from the language in the previous law; it clarified the criteria for awarding a patent, listed the areas outside patentability domain, detailed the rights and obligations of a patent holder, and outlined specific sanctions that can be requested by a patent holder in the event of a patent infringement. The law was amended twice, in 2001 and 2007, to reflect other concepts and to put it in line with Jordan's obligations and international best practices.

Under the new patent law, product patents were allowed, an examination process was required, and several ways to extend the life of a patent were provided, including marketing exclusivity periods for data protection. The law puts forth the following patentability conditions that must be met for a patent to be issued: novelty, non-disclosure, non-obviousness, and industrial utility (art. 3). These requirements restrict the universe of what can be patented under Jordanian law. The new patent law was modelled after similar laws in developed countries; thus, it was not suitable for a country which, for historical reasons, had a virtually non-existent patent law practice, and whose patent examination duties were delegated to the WIPO. By expanding the terms of patentability and enlarging the sphere of patent protection, the patent law of 1999 drastically limited imitation and therefore failed to address the needs of the Jordanian people for technological and innovation incentives. This is shown by the patent ownership numbers in Jordan, which are predominantly foreign-based, and by the negligible rate of technology transfer. Up until mid-2010, around 80% of patents granted were for foreign holders, and 87% of the patent applications were by foreigners.[8] The patent law of 1999 also failed to encourage foreign companies to transfer their technologies to their Jordanian counterparts, although those

---

[7] In April 2013 the Ministry of Industry and Trade was renamed the Ministry for Industry and Trade and Supply.

[8] Data until March 2010. See "MoIT Department of Industrial Property," http://www.mit.gov.jo. The researcher relied on the data within the tables and not the totals provided, as the numbers within the tables do not add up to the totals provided by the tables.

foreign companies had benefited from the protections granted to them under the Patent Law. Similarly, Jordan's levels of research and development are less than half a percentage point of the GDP, and much of that amount is allocated to the military.[9] The net result so far is that Jordanian industry is not benefiting from any significant levels of technology transfer, is still dependent on importing technology products, and must pay high prices for those products.

Similar observations can be made with regards copyright laws. Prior to the 1992 law on copyright, Jordan used the Ottoman-era copyright law, and the Supreme Administrative Court confirmed such usage in opinions (for example, Opinion No. 76/81). The older copyright law's denial of any protection for copyrighted material that was not registered with the National Library was an acceptable compromise for Jordanian citizens, as intellectual works by local individuals had not played an important role in the cultural or educational development of the economy. Material that would otherwise be considered copyrighted material, such as books and audio-visual works, were produced by non-Jordanians; thus, because they were not usually registered with the National Library, they were not offered protection under the older copyright law. Conversely, the 1992 copyright law (sec. 45) granted automatic copyright protection to any published work whether or not it was registered by the Jordanian National Library (henceforth NL).[10] In addition to expanding the level of protection granted, it clarified as exclusive to the author rights that were previously thought to also belong to publishers, editors, and the public at large (sec. 8).

The 1992 law improving copyright protection, corresponding to the concerns of the major donors, brought mostly Western standards for protection and significantly improved protection in areas mostly dominated by Western products, such as sound recordings, audio-visual products, and computer software. Considering the lack of any local products or substitutes in those areas, as well as the lack of any alternative pricing scheme for original products in the local markets, those products were placed out of the reach of the vast majority of the local population. That helps to explain the proliferation of pirated audio-visual products and other copyrightable material.[11]

---

[9] Jomana Amara, "Military Industrialization and Economic Development: Jordan's Defense Industry," *Review of Financial Economics* 17, no. 2 (2008): 130–145.

[10] The National Library is the governmental agency in charge of registering copyrightable material.

[11] Naseem Tarawnah, "Steal This Article!," *Jordan Business*, May 2008.

Because the idea of copyright is not fully compatible with the Jordanian society's economic realities and the Jordanian culture, which considers knowledge-sharing and pursuit of education rather than author's rights to be paramount, it will continue to prove extremely difficult to enforce. Significantly, the law's value in improving creativity in Jordan is in doubt. The Jordanian audio-visual industry, for example, which was in reasonably respectable shape in the late twentieth century, is on the verge of collapse, with the number of its productions greatly reduced. This situation might not be solely related to IPRs, but it proves that the promises of increased copyright innovation with the enforcement of tighter copyright protections were greatly exaggerated if not unfounded.[12] Any enforcement activity in the copyright area will impact low-income citizens, operators of kiosks, and street vendors depending on such products for economic survival.

For Jordan, as indeed for any developing country, enforcement is a balancing act between three competing concerns. On the one hand, there is the need to show ample and sufficient compliance with obligations and commitments resulting from the international agreements and treaties it has signed. On the other hand, there is the significant challenge of limited resources and ever-increasing economic pressures, which makes it difficult to allocate limited financial and economic resources to enforcement. Third, there is the government's own assessment of the legitimate needs of the population, and how these are to be respected in the face of demands stemming from a different cultural and political milieu, such as the WTO. This balancing act is thus further complicated by the governmental realization that lax enforcement, especially in the copyright field, may represent the only financially feasible way for an important segment of the population to access those works. Our understanding of the legal aspects of IPRs therefore needs to be complemented by an account of relevant socio-economic aspects of local culture.

Jordanian culture and IPR

Historically and culturally, Jordanian society is anchored to traditional communal values that favour collective effort and knowledge over individual ownership and monopoly. These values were sustained by the agrarian nature of Jordanian society for the majority of the twentieth

---

[12] Nedal Burqan, "Ministry of Culture Conference: Jordanian Drama in Danger," *Addustour Daily Newspaper*, March 5, 2010.

century. Jordan's religious background also supports such a position, as reflected in the absence of any developed sense of IPRs during the history of the Islamic state, which lasted until the fall of the Ottoman Empire at the end of World War I. Sophisticated IP concepts, therefore, do not originate from within Jordanian society; rather, these concepts were introduced by interaction with developed countries through colonialism.

According to the cultural indicators developed by Hofstede,[13] Jordan and the Arab world can be described as conservative, masculine, power-distant, and collective. On this schema, "masculine" cultures are seen as more assertive than "feminine" cultures, and value achievement and materialism. In power-distant cultures, the authority of superiors is accepted, inequalities among people are both expected and desired, less powerful people are dependent on the more powerful, and the hierarchy in organizations reflects the inequality between higher-ups and lower-downs.[14] Collective countries have little personal freedom, because the groups and organizations to which one belongs invade one's private life.

Hofstede's power distance index measures the extent to which the less powerful members of organizations and institutions (like the family) accept and expect that power is distributed unequally, resulting in inequality (those who have more versus those who have less). Hofstede suggests that the followers endorse a society's level of inequality as much as the leaders do. For example, Germany is positioned at 35 on Hofstede's scale. Compared to Arab countries where the power distance is very high (80) and Austria where it is very low (11), Germany falls somewhat in the middle. German society does not have a large gap between the wealthy and the poor, and German citizens have a strong belief in equality. German citizens have the opportunity to rise in society. By contrast, the Arab world has a large gap between the wealthy and the poor, and its residents do not have a strong belief in equality.

---

[13] Hofstede developed a typology of cultural attributes by analyzing data obtained from surveys conducted among individuals in fifty-three nations in 1968 and 1972. Since all 116,000 respondents were employees of the same firm, IBM, Hofstede was able to hold constant the influence of industry and corporate culture. Based on the data obtained, he classified countries along four dimensions: power distance, uncertainty avoidance, individualism/collectivism, and masculinity/femininity. Hofstede rated each of the fifty-three countries in his study by these cultural dimensions. See "Power Distance Index," n.d., http://www.clearlycultural.com/geert-hofstede-cultural-dimensions/power-distance-index/.

[14] S. S. Robbins and A. C. Stylianou, "A Study of Cultural Differences in Global Corporate Web Sites," *Journal of Computer Information Systems* 42, no. 2 (2002): 3–9.

The strong collectivist culture of the Arab world, of which Jordan is part, results in little personal freedom, which leads to a weak individual assumption of responsibility. This collectivist orientation is expressed in ideals that scholars associate with Arab culture, such as solidarity, cooperation, commitment, mutual trust, support, and a sense of belonging.[15] The literature suggests that collectivist cultures place strong cultural restrictions on the self, resulting in a low need for uniqueness and a strong motivation not to break away from the aforementioned values.[16] In a society where individuals sacrifice their personal ambitions for the good of the collective, the spread of IP piracy is more likely, as individuals motivated by solidarity, cooperation, trust, and support are likely to share property with others and expect them to do the same, without much regard for the notion of IPRs.[17] A survey of Jordanian students conducted by this author and detailed in appendix two of this book, bears out these expectations: 89.9% of the respondents had knowingly engaged in buying counterfeit products or using cracked software on at least one occasion, and 71.9% of the respondents asserted that buying counterfeit products was not unethical, since counterfeit products provide people with access to goods, software, and books that they otherwise could not afford.

IP piracy is also related to power distance, which is high in Arab countries.[18] The greater a culture's power distance (i.e., the further individuals feel from their superiors, such as law enforcement officials), the greater the propensity to pirate IP products.[19] Arab culture, therefore, scores high on collectivism and power distance, both of which have been

---

[15] A. Cohen, "The Relationship Between Multiple Commitments and Organizational Citizenship Behavior in Arab and Jewish Culture," *Journal of Vocational Behavior* 69, no. 1 (2006): 105–118.

[16] J. Kurman, "Why is Self-Enhancement Low in Certain Collectivist Cultures?" *Journal of Cross-Cultural Psychology* 34, no. 5 (2003): 496–510.

[17] Donald B. Marron and David G. Steel, "Which Countries Protect Intellectual Property? The Case of Software Piracy," *Economic Inquiry* 38, no. 2 (2000): 159–74. Trevor T. Moores and Jasbir Dhaliwal, "A Reversed Context Analysis of Software Piracy Issues in Singapore," *Inf. Manage.* 41, no. 8 (November 2004): 1037–1042; Jia Lu, "Chinese Culture and Software Copyright," *New Media & Society* 11, no. 8 (December 1, 2009): 1372 –1393; Fang Wang et al., "Purchasing Pirated Software: An Initial Examination of Chinese Consumers," *Journal of Consumer Marketing* 22, no. 6 (January 10, 2005): 340–351.

[18] Bryan Husted, "The Impact of National Culture on Software Piracy," *Journal of Business Ethics* 26, no. 3 (2000): 197–211.

[19] C. A. Depken and L. C. Simmons, "Social Construct and the Propensity for Software Piracy," *Applied Economics Letters* 11, no. 2 (February 10, 2004): 97–100.

correlated in the literature with increased piracy rates and low enforcement of IPRs. Notably, 75.1% of respondents to the student survey said that they believed that counterfeit products infringe on the rights of companies, while 63.5% indicated that they personally did not care about the companies' losses.

Religious factors and IPR

Religion is an important moral and cultural force in Jordan, where 95% of the population is Muslim.[20] However, although religion directs citizens' behaviour in Islamic countries, it is difficult to ascertain a clear position in Islamic jurisprudence towards IP concepts.[21] On the one hand, those who adhere to the position of classical scholars reject the idea of intellectual property, arguing that knowledge should be available for all humans to use and share with each other and that no one should be deprived access to it.[22] On the other hand, some Islamic scholars have accepted the premise that ideas and/or methods can be owned under the rubric of IP but have based their prohibition of copying on the need to have a "legitimate ruler" approve such a prohibition.[23] The issue of who is a legitimate ruler under Islamic law is not a clear one; sharia, which is considered God's law and to supersede the laws of the state, is expected to be the sole criterion of behaviour, and the authority of the temporal ruler as the representative of God is derived from and designed by that law.[24]

Jordan, like all Arab countries, has adopted a hybrid legal system that takes sharia into account only in certain areas. This is a key factor in leading observant Muslims to believe that laws pertaining to IPRs should

---

[20] Quintan Wiktorowicz, *The Management of Islamic Activism: Salafis, the Muslim Brotherhood, and State Power in Jordan* (New York: SUNY Press, 2001).

[21] Salah Al-Fadhli, "The Ethical Dilemma of Software Piracy in Islamic Societies: The Case of Kuwait," *The Electronic Journal of Information Systems in Developing Countries* 39 (2009).

[22] The main principles here do not constitute a complete negation of IPRs, rather (i) the rejection of plagiarism, and (ii) the permissiveness of personal use. See, for example, "حقوق التأليف والاختراع والابتكار محفوظة لأصحابها - إسلام ويب - مركز الفتوى," n.d., http://www.islamweb.net/fatwa/index.php?page=showfatwa&Option=FatwaId&Id=161059 (a fatwa stating that one should not claim for themselves that which they did not produce, but that personal use of knowledge is permissible).

[23] "www.Sistani.org," n.d., http://www.sistani.org/local.php?modules=nav&nid=5&cid=131.

[24] N. J. Coulson, "The State and the Individual in Islamic Law," *The International and Comparative Law Quarterly* 6, no. 1 (January 1, 1957): 49–60.

not be observed from a religious point of view – since the ruler who approved them is not technically a "legitimate ruler" according to Islam because he is not applying sharia in *all* areas.

Since there is no single unified Islamic position on IP, any claims that Islam supports the enforcement of TRIPS-style IP are questionable. The problem of establishing a unified religious position on IP is further complicated by the fact that Islam does not acknowledge the role of a universal legal authority with the power and right to make laws applicable to *all* Muslims; rather, the authority of even a legitimate ruler is no greater than that of any other qualified *mujtahīd* (one who possesses the power of *ijtihād* – the interpretation of problems not precisely covered by the Qur'an, *ḥadīth* (traditions concerning the Prophet's life and utterances), and *ijmā* (scholarly consensus)).[25] Therefore, since the default position under Islamic jurisprudence is to allow an activity unless it is specifically prohibited, the position of one legal scholar opposed to piracy is considered only that scholar's personal opinion and cannot be given any more weight than another scholar's opinion which might contradict it. IPRs is not addressed under the Qur'an, *ḥadīth*, or *ijmā*; thus, it is an area that will likely never be treated uniformly by legal scholars, resulting in inconsistent approaches that allow for individual interpretation on whether a Muslim should observe IP laws. Those studies which suggest that Muslims will abide by IPRs laws if piracy is prohibited by Islam[26] should be interpreted in the light of this lack of treatment of IPRs under Islamic law, always bearing in mind that any Islamic legal opinion on piracy will be limited in impact and is unlikely to have a universal jurisprudential weight.

The complexity of the role of Islam and sharia with respect to Jordanian attitudes to IPR is reflected in the results from the survey of students. A majority of respondents (65.9%) believed that counterfeit products are not prohibited by religion, while only 28.6% thought that religion prohibited them. A larger majority of respondents (81.1%) indicated that they would stop buying counterfeit products if prohibited by religion, while a smaller majority (64.8%) indicated that they would stop buying counterfeit products if prohibited by state law. However, these results require a nuanced interpretation. In follow-up questions, only 52.8% said they would always follow the guidance of their main religious authority on the prohibition of counterfeit products, while 46.7% said they would either never or only sometimes follow such guidance, indicating that the effect of religion on the respondents' choice to use counterfeit

[25] Coulson, "The State and the Individual."
[26] Al-Fadhli, "The Ethical Dilemma."

products may not be as strong as first appears, and underscoring the complexity of the relation between sharia and the laws protecting IPR. (For more details of the survey, see appendix two.)

Another potential rationalization for disregarding IPRs is that counterfeiting data provided by multinational companies is accused of being heavily overestimated, with some research concluding that piracy is an externality to multinational corporations (MNCs) – meaning that it has little to no negative monetary impact on MNCs.[27] MNCs have been accused of making false claims of massive economic losses in order to divert attention from the real harms of counterfeiting, such as the use of IP piracy to fund organized crime, and the MNCs' role in perpetuating these harms by aggressively marketing their expensive brands as status symbols.[28] The literature points out that people look for ways to rationalize their behaviour when considering decisions such as whether to make pirate copies of software.[29] A monetary rationalization posits that most IP companies are large corporations that make large profits and can therefore afford the loss of pirated copies. A religious one might be based on any of the religious positions under Islamic law that oppose the enforcement of IPRs.

A note on the empirical data

This book is concerned with the implementation and enforcement of IP laws. Laws do not exist in a vacuum; rather, they derive their value and significance from the impact they have on their environment and surroundings. One of the guiding themes of this book is the idea that a law that does not have such an impact is destined to be no more than a passive text. To this end, this book draws on empirical data as part of the analysis to gauge the impact of IP laws. However, obtaining data in Jordan is difficult for the following reasons.

---

[27] See, for example, Simon Mackenzie, "Counterfeiting as Corporate Externality: Intellectual Property Crime and Global Insecurity," *Crime, Law and Social Change* 54, no. 1 (July 2010): 21–38. Daniel Chow, "Counterfeiting as an Externality Imposed by Multinational Companies on Developing Countries," *Virginia Journal of International Law* 51, no. 4 (2011).

[28] Chow, "Counterfeiting as an Externality."

[29] Robert A. Strikwerda and John Minor Ross, "Software and Ethical Softness," *Collegiate Microcomputer* 10, no. 3 (1992): 129–36; C. A. Depken and L. C. Simmons, "Social Construct and the Propensity for Software Piracy," *Applied Economics Letters* 11, no. 2 (February 10, 2004): 97–100.

First, there is no unified repository of information on most issues, including legal topics. In addition, statistics have not been made publicly available in all areas (including important economic information like FDI, as has been noted by the US Government accountability office),[30] and available information is usually lacking in detail. Even though Jordan has a General Statistics Department (GSD), statistics and data on several areas are compiled by other agencies and sources (e.g., GDP and FDI numbers are compiled by the Central Bank of Jordan (CBJ)). Similarly, data on court activities are compiled and published by the Ministry of Justice and the Judicial Council, and data on specific enforcement agencies like the Customs Department and the MoIT are available almost exclusively through those agencies. This problem is not unique to the economic or legal sector and even extends to social sectors. For example, there are three different figures for the percentage of individuals with disabilities in Jordan,[31] and unemployment numbers are similarly disputed. The end result is that in order to secure data or statistics on almost any social, legal, or economic area, one must perform a great deal of research to determine the source of those figures and to reconcile their disparate values, often by examining their differing definitions, areas of measurement, and measurement mechanisms.

Second, the quality of the available data is not uniform. For example, the imports and exports numbers compiled and published by the CBJ are usually presented in the form of a press release that states the relative breakdown of a few major categories of imports and exports but stops well short of a detailed analysis or even a complete listing. FDI numbers as presented by the CBJ represent another major problem because they are not broken down by category, which meant that this researcher could not find a specific number for the IP component of FDI figures and instead had to deduce that component from other numbers pertaining to the sources of the FDI and the areas to which the FDI was targeted. In some instances, as with the numbers pertaining to investments benefiting from incentives by the investment promotion laws, which are compiled by the Jordan Investment Board (JIB), it was found that projects were counted more than once in order to artificially increase the value of projects

---

[30] US Government Accountability Office, *International Trade: Four Free Trade Agreements GAO Reviewed Have Resulted in Commercial Benefits, but Challenges on Labor and Environment Remain*, 2009, http://www.gao.gov/products/GAO-09-439.

[31] The GSD estimates the percentage of disabled persons on Jordan to be 1.2% (GSD 2004 census), the Higher Council for Handicapped Persons puts it at 4%, and the World Bank estimates that 4–6% of the population is disabled.

benefiting from those incentives.[32] This researcher therefore relied on CBJ data rather than JIB data when examining the impact of IP laws on economic development and investment. This lack of uniformity, which continues to be perpetuated by the many competing sources of data and the absence of full statistical analysis, is particularly dangerous because the public tends to be easily manipulated by statistics. An old adage describing the persuasive power of numbers rings true in the case of obtaining data in Jordan: "There are three types of lies – lies, damned lies, and statistics."

Third, the various agencies and departments are largely reluctant to offer figures related to their work, especially if those numbers pertain to areas that are considered problematic or in which the official data could be used in potentially unflattering ways, such as IP laws.[33] Jordan does have a law (Access to Information Law No. 47, 2007) which stipulates that citizens have the right to access written, recorded, and photographed governmental information and basic government records. Actual access, however, is restricted by agencies' obfuscation and by other laws like the Press and Publication Law and the Government Secrets Law, in addition to ten exceptions within the Access to Information law itself that place certain data outside its purview. It is worth noting that these agencies' reluctance seems to disappear when communicating with foreign governmental officials or local staff of foreign embassies. Correspondence between the Jordanian Government and foreign agencies and information released through Wikileaks demonstrates that Jordanian officials are very willing to share information with foreign agencies.[34] The Access to Information Law Request Form also demands that the seeker explain why the information is needed, thus allowing the request to be refused if the reviewer does not approve the intended use. There are no mechanisms to force the government to explain its denial of the request; while the law states that each denied request must be justified, the refusal to provide an

---

[32] Hiba Issawi, "Values of Projects Benefitting from Investment Promotion Laws Do Not Reflect Improvement in Data," *Alghad Daily Newspaper*, April 8, 2010, sec. Markets & Finance.

[33] "The Center for Defending the Freedom of Journalists (CDFJ) issue[d] a statement to the Jordanian government, calling for wider support of freedom of the press and its right of access to information. The statement comes after a news report posted on the Amman news website, which included a copy of a circular signed by Prime Minister Nader Dahabi warning public employees against handing over copies of documents to the media related to alleged administrative and financial corruption." *Jordan: 2009* (Global Integrity, 2009).

[34] Wikileaks website, n.d., http://wikileaks.org/origin/187_0.html.

answer to a request is considered an implied denial under the law which does not require justification (art. 9). It is not clear how would one exercise a judicial review option under such a *de facto* denial, as the requester is not provided with any reasons to include in its claim before a court of law. On the other hand, Jordan's willingness to provide information to international agencies was clearly indicated by considerable data often found by this researcher in filings by the Jordanian government to the WTO, or to the US Trade Representative (USTR) and the US Congress, when attempts to obtain similar data from the local sources were futile.

CHAPTER TWO

IP AND THE JORDANIAN LEGAL SYSTEM

The Jordanian legal system evolved throughout the twentieth century, moving from a system based on Ottoman and Civil Law legal traditions to one which incorporated TRIPS standards. Historically, IP had been tangential to the Jordanian legislative concerns, and while patents, trademarks, and copyright were acknowledged as distinct areas of jurisprudence in the Civil Code, the small role they played in practice reflected their generally minor economic roles. Nonetheless, Jordan had the necessary legal infrastructure in place, with various levels of courts, including a Supreme Administrative Court dedicated to challenges of the governmental administrative decisions, and legislation that covered the basic areas of IP. Intellectual property areas not covered in specific legislation were dealt with, if needed, under the general principles of civil liability in various other codes such as the Civil and Commerce Codes.

Trademarks were the most legally defined IP area prior to TRIPS, since the courts had produced a sizable body of jurisprudence. Meanwhile, the lack of research and development within the Jordanian commercial and industrial environment gave patent law little practical relevance. Copyright protection was linked to actual registration at the National Library, automatically placing any foreign-registered material outside the scope of protection in Jordan.

This situation changed with the WTO accession talks and Jordan's growing openness to the global economy. The adoption of TRIPS as part of the WTO accession resulted in sweeping changes to IP laws. A new patent law (Patent Law No. 32, 1999) granting twenty years of patent protection was enacted in 1999, incorporating TRIPS-consistent standards into its language. A new copyright law (Copyright Law No. 22) was enacted in 1992, while the law on trademarks (Trademarks Law No. 33), which dates back to 1952, was amended several times throughout 2007. Additionally, in the span of three years (2000–2003), Jordan went from having only four IP laws to having twelve. The laws covering Copyright (Law No. 22 (1992)), Patent (Law No. 32 (1999)), Trademarks (Law No.

33 (1952)), and Service Marks (Law No. 19 (1953)), were joined by an additional eight items of legislation covering various aspects of IP.[1]

These developments were not made without controversy. Parliament was suspended for the period when the IP new laws were enacted, and thus the process was deprived of a full debate by the legislative branch. Additionally, civil society organizations were not involved in their enactment, which limited the input of economic and social costs associated with their implementation.[2] This process did not foster conditions for accountability, transparency, or rule of law, all of which are key factors for the development of good governance and political sustainability.[3] The overriding rationale for the adoption and implementation of IP standards was embedded in the social, economic, political, and cultural relationship envisioned with the United States in particular and the West in general. In that sense, Jordan has not been notably different from other countries in the region, which exhibit similar dependence on those entities.

Thus, in the span of a half a decade, Jordan transformed its IP legal framework into one that is in compliance with the requirements of accession to the WTO. Areas of protection that had previously existed were augmented and modernized, and areas like integrated circuits, plant breeding, and geographical indications were provided with their own specific legislations with explicit protections. This chapter sets out the basic framework of the Jordanian legal system, particularly as applied to IP.

Foundations of the Jordanian legal system

From the fourteenth century until the end of World War I, greater Syria, which consists of present-day Jordan, Lebanon, Syria, Palestine, and Israel, was under the rule of the Ottoman Empire.[4] After the end of the

---

[1] Industrial Forms and Drawings Law No. 14, 2000; Integrated Circuits Law No. 10, 2000; Geographical Indications Law No. 8, 2000; Unfair Competition and Trade Secrets Law No. 15, 2000; New Plant Varieties Law No. 24, 2000; Instructions for Border Points Regarding the Protection of Intellectual Property No. 7, 2000; E-Transactions Law No. 85, 2002; Competition Law No. 49, 2002; National Products Protection Law No. 50, 2002.

[2] I am indebted on this point to members of Jordanian public and private sector organizations who agreed to be interviewed for this study. See appendix one.

[3] Deborah Brautigam, "Governance, Economy, and Foreign Aid," *Studies In Comparative International Development* 27, no. 3 (September 1992): 3–25.

[4] See William L. Cleveland, *A History of the Modern Middle East*, 2nd ed. (Westview Press, 1999), 157–158. "For the Arab people who have lived within the

war, the Ottoman Empire lost its political control over the region, partly because of a revolution led by Hussein bin Ali, the Sharif of Mecca.[5] The revolution was supported by Britain to undermine the Ottoman Empire's rule in Hejaz, the western part of modern-day Saudi Arabia.[6] In return, the Sharif asked the British for a pledge of financial and political support for his movement, with the ultimate goal of establishing an independent Arab government in the Arabian Peninsula and most parts of greater Syria.

The revolt never fulfilled its ultimate goal of a pan-Arab state headed by the Sharif. While Great Britain was promising the Sharif independence should he continue to press his revolt against the Turks, Great Britain and France entered into the 1916 Sykes–Picot agreement, dividing the region into political bodies representing their respective spheres of influence. Thus, Great Britain and France assumed the Ottoman Empire's control of the region. The current geopolitical map of the Middle East was drawn as a result of this process and has remained practically unchanged ever since.

One of the Sharif's sons, Abdullah, headed the newly created political entity, called Trans-Jordan. Trans-Jordan proclaimed its independence from the British Crown on May 25, 1948, and was re-named the Hashemite Kingdom of Jordan.

A modernization movement was created in the nineteenth century due in large measure to the contact between the Islamic world and the West.[7]

[Ottoman] domains, the dismemberment of the Ottoman Empire marked more than just the end of a particular state; it also marked the end of a political, social, and religious order that had shaped their patterns of public behavior for 400 years. Ottoman rule had applied with differing degrees of intensity in various regions of the Arab provinces. That kind of adaptability was the very essence of the Ottoman system: It governed directly the areas that could be efficiently controlled and allowed a certain degree of latitude to chieftains and feudal amirs in more remote locations."

[5] See Cleveland, *History*, 148. The Sharif of Mecca was an honorary title granted by the Ottoman Caliph to his representative in Arabia. Usually it was awarded to the head of a family that claims to be a direct descendant of the Prophet Muhammad.

[6] See Arthur Goldschmidt and Lawrence Davidson, *A Concise History of the Middle East*, 9th ed. (Westview Press, 2009).

[7] See Matthew Lippman, Sean McConville, and Mordechai Yerushalmi, *Islamic Criminal Law and Procedure: An Introduction* (Praeger Publishers, 1988), 100. "The first sectors affected by the modernization movement were criminal and civil justice, the economy, and the military. In these fields the deficiencies of traditional Islam were most apparent to modernists. The gap between new conditions and traditional law was unbridgeable, and thus the rulers opted for the Western approach."

The movement was initiated by two factors; the Ottoman government's adoption of the French Commercial and Penal Code and the establishment of a system of secular courts. The *Majalla*, a publication issued between 1869 and 1876, encompassed the newly created Ottoman civil law, which was an amalgam of French law and the Hanafi School of Islamic law.[8]

The Jordanian legal system is based on a civil law approach. *Stare Decisis* – the legal principle under which precedent plays a significant role in the creation of legal facts – is not well-defined or a forceful element in the formulation of legal code or in the code's interpretation by the courts, as it is in the common law tradition. Consequently, courts of the same level are generally not bound by one another's rulings, and the rulings of the highest (Cassation) court are binding only if issued *en banc*.[9]

Under the colonial effects of Great Britain, elements of the common law were introduced to the various legal areas, most notably the first Jordanian Commercial Code.[10] In the midst of all those legal traditions that affected or influenced the Jordanian legal system, Islamic law's most notable impact was in the area of personal status, such as family affairs and inheritance. Islamic law does not have any impact on IP laws in Jordan.

Jordanian law

The major non-IP laws that have an impact on the enforcement of IPRs in Jordan are as follows:

The Constitution

Enacted in 1952, the Jordanian constitution was a novelty in the Middle East in its time because it explicitly granted rights to the citizens (citizenship, property, assembly, travel, etc.) and instituted a parliamentary monarchy. It contains a clear delineation between the executive,

---

[8] Noel J. Coulson, *A History of Islamic Law* (Edinburgh University Press, 1995), 151–152.

[9] The issues of disseminating the holdings of the Cassation Court, and the introduction of modern technology, including the posting of past and present holdings on a dedicated website for the court, are among the most urgent, yet easily achievable, modernization requirements of the Jordanian legal system.

[10] The first Companies Law in Jordan was enacted with British experts' assistance in 1964 and reflected many Common law ideas. More recently, a clear effect of the Common law can be detected on procedural laws and those dedicated to creating alternative dispute-settlement mechanisms.

legislative, and judicial branches, and a role for the monarch as the head of the executive branch, guardian of the constitution, and enforcer of the separation of powers. In line with the accepted practice for Arab and Islamic nations, the constitution declares Islam as the state religion and Arabic as its official language.

The Civil Code

The Jordanian Civil Code was twenty-two years in the making, from February 4, 1952, when the initial draft was submitted to parliament, until the 1964 royal letter requesting the drafting of a "Civil Code based on Islamic law and broad enough to govern the various areas of daily life," culminating in the Code's actual enactment in 1976.[11]

The Civil Code contains rules, which mainly organize private financial relations, and types of rights – personal rights that include, *inter alia*, contracts and injurious acts, and real rights like property rights. It also organizes contracts.[12] The Civil Code's clauses are binding when a private law does not address a specific point that is otherwise addressed by the Code.

Commercial laws

Commercial laws in Jordan encompass several laws and legislations all revolving around the same concept of organizing the commercial sector. The most important commercial laws in Jordan are the Trade Law, Companies Law, Banking Law, Securities Law, and Trading in Foreign Exchanges Law. The Civil Code has rules to be applied in commercial cases, particularly in the interpretation of contracts; however, as stated earlier, such rules are of a general nature and are pre-empted by any specific laws where applicable.[13] Trade Law, being the oldest of the group, reflects a more traditional perspective of commerce. The other legislations

[11] Royal letter to then Prime Minister of Jordan Hussein Bin Naser, dated April 1964. The committee that delivered the law on January 5, 1976 stated that it based its work on four resources: (1) Islamic jurisprudence in all its schools, (2) effective Jordanian legal code, (3) draft Civil Code law presented by the upper house of parliament, (4) all modern legislations, which are based on Islamic law.

[12] The Jordanian Civil Code recognized the freedom of contractors in establishing any legitimate contracts.

[13] The general rule is that all the articles of the Civil Law can be applied on commercial cases provided they are consistent with the basic principles of the Law of Commerce.

are more modern, as they were either promulgated or updated after Jordan's accession to the WTO in 2000.[14] They also reflect the constant evolution of the legal framework of doing business in Jordan, and in that sense share the features of evolution and development with IP laws in Jordan.

The legislative process

Jordan's legislative branch is represented by Parliament, in which legislative authority is vested by the Constitution. Parliament consists of two chambers, often referred to as the upper and lower houses. The lower house, also referred to as the House of Representatives, consists of elected members whose term is for four years. The upper house is also known as the Senate. There are twice as many seats in the House of Representatives as in the Senate, and the Senate seats are appointed by the King for two-year terms.

In addition to laws, which can be passed only through Parliament, Jordan also has other types of regulative documents, including Systems, which are promulgated by the council of ministers, and Regulations, which are promulgated by a minister and impact only that specific ministry. This hierarchy is further illustrated in table 2-1, below. Any legislation proposed to Parliament must be approved by both houses and then ratified by the King.

[14] The most recent of the commercial laws is the Trading in Foreign Exchanges Law No. 50, 2008, which came into effect as a result of the increased sophistication of dealers and middlemen attempting to market and promote investments in foreign exchanges. As it became clear that a substantive portion of those investment opportunities were nothing more than Ponzi schemes, the law was enacted in late 2008 in an attempt to regulate an area that was as of that time unregulated.

Table 2-1. The hierarchy of the Jordanian regulative documents

The Constitution
The law of the land and the foundation upon which all other legislations must be based and with which they must conform.

Laws
Enacted exclusively by Parliament based on drafts from the government, members of the House of Representatives, or the Senate. Provisional laws can be passed by the government but must be confirmed by Parliament once reconvened. Must be in compliance with the Constitution.

Systems
Enacted by the Council of Ministers to clarify, augment, or execute a law or portions thereof. Can be mandated sometimes by the law itself, which can request that one or several clauses be further detailed by a system to be issued by the government. Must comply with the text of the law they are meant to clarify, augment, or execute, as well as with the Constitution.

Regulations
Are issued by the minister or by a senior official of the ministry who is empowered by the minister. Enforceable only on the executive agency for which they were issued and must comply with relevant systems and laws, as well as with the Constitution.

The judicial system

Civil and criminal conflicts in Jordan can be legally resolved through the court system or through arbitration. The court system consists of several tiers with laws outlining the duties and responsibilities of each, as well as the limits of their jurisdiction.[15] This multi-tier system applies to the three types of courts in Jordan, namely regular, religious, and special courts.[16]

[15] Article 27 of the Constitution vests the judicial authority in the courts and authorizes them to issue verdicts in the name of the King. Article 100 of the Constitution states that the way and manner that all types of courts are to be set up will be outlined in a special law, which must include the formation of a Supreme Court. It is not clear if the term "supreme court" as used in the Constitution is meant to be the Supreme Administrative Court in the format in which currently exists as a review of administrative law, or the creation of the Cassation court.
[16] Article 99 of the Constitution authorizes the creation of three types of courts: (1)

Table 2-2, below, illustrates the three types of courts and their different tiers, along with a brief description of each. Of special importance to IP conflicts and disputes is Jordan's Supreme Administrative Court.[17]

Regular courts

These courts handle commercial, civil, and criminal cases. Regular Courts are classified into three different types: Courts of First Review, the Court of Appeals, and the Court of Cassation.

There are two types of courts within the category of **Courts of First Review**: the Small Claims Court and courts of First Instance. Small Claims Courts have jurisdiction over claims under 7,000 Jordanian Dinars (JD) and criminal cases in which the penalty does not exceed two years the imprisonment.[18] Verdicts from Small Claim Courts can be appealed to courts of First Instance if their value is less than JD 1,000 or if the penalty is less than three months' imprisonment. Original jurisdiction is vested in the courts of First Instance over all cases, but jurisdiction for Small Claims Courts is carved out and specifically provided for in the law creating First Instance Courts.[19]

There are three **Courts of Appeal** in Jordan, located in the cities of Amman, Irbid, and Ma'an. They have appellate jurisdiction over certain decisions by Small Claims Courts and all decisions by the courts of First Instance (Courts Formation Law No. 17, 2001, art. 8). An appellate panel

regular, (2) religious, and (3) special. Article 110 of the Constitution stated that special courts would be organized based on laws to be passed for that purpose.

[17] The Supreme Administrative Court's jurisdiction over final copyright, trademark, and patent administrative decisions is based on article 9(9) of the Supreme Administrative Court Law No. 12, 1992, giving the court jurisdiction over the appeal of final administrative decisions issued by governmental agencies. The origins of the Supreme Administrative Court are in Article 100 of the Constitution, which calls for the creation of the courts and specifically mentions a "Supreme Court" by name. Pursuant to that constitutional mandate, the first law organizing courts was issued in 1952, the Courts Formation Law No. 26, 1952. It, however, did not include a designation for a Supreme Court. This constitutional oversight was rectified when the Cassation Court exercised its role as a final arbiter for judicial opinions in its capacity as a Cassation Court, and for administrative opinions in its capacity as a Supreme Administrative Court. This dual-hat anomaly continued till the enactment of the Supreme Administrative Court Law No. 12, which created a separate court named the Supreme Administrative Court.

[18] Small Claims Courts Law No. 15, 1952, arts. 3 and 5, as amended in 2008.

[19] Courts Formation Law No. 17, 2001, art. 3, as amended in 2008.

usually consists of three judges, whereas First Instance and Small Claims Courts consist of one judge (or two in some criminal cases). Evidence Law governs the type of evidence that may be used before the courts as well as the method by which it can be used (Evidence Law No. 30, 1952).

The **Cassation Court** is the highest non-administrative court in Jordan. It usually sits in panels of five judges, but it can sit in panels of eight to review novel legal points, or to review decisions that represent a split between the courts of appeal.[20] Monetary thresholds also govern the appellate process; cases not exceeding JD 10,000 in value require written permission from the Cassation Court to file an appeal. If this written permission is denied, cases are deemed settled and decided by the Appellate Court that last reviewed them. This makes Appellate Courts the final arbiter in IP cases valued at less than JD 10,000 and denied written permission by the Cassation Court.

Arbitration and other alternative methods of dispute resolution

The first Arbitration law was enacted in 1952 and amended in 2001 (Arbitration Law No. 31, 2001). To further facilitate the proceedings of trials and to maximize settlement possibility, the Civil Procedure Law was amended to create a Case Management position to be held by a judge within the lower courts. The Case Management judge is charged with ensuring speedy legal notice to the parties, completeness of the docket, and (failing settlement) transferring the complete docket to the assigned trial judge.[21]

IPRs under Jordanian laws

The notion of what constitutes a "right" under Jordanian law is delineated by the Civil Code, which allows for three types of rights: personal, material, and incorporeal (Civil Code No. 43, 1976, art. 67). The Code defines a personal right as a legal bond between a debtor and a creditor (art. 68). That bond must relate to transferring a material right, executing an act, or abstaining from one. The reference to abstinence from certain acts as one of the components of personal rights refers to injurious acts, or torts.[22]

---

[20] Small Claims Courts Law No. 15, art. 9, as amended in 2008.

[21] Civil Procedure Law No. 24, 1998, as amended by law No. 16 (2006).

[22] Anis Al-Qasem, "The Injurious Acts under the Jordanian Civil Code," *Arab Law Quarterly* 4, no. 3 (August 1989): 183–198.

Table 2-2. Courts in Jordan

Specialized Courts Have jurisdiction over issues specifically outlined in the laws creating them. Have the narrowest jurisdiction of all types of courts.	*Regular Courts* Have general jurisdiction over all civil, commercial, and criminal cases.	*Religious Courts* Have jurisdiction over issues related to personal status such as marriage, divorce, and inheritance.
Supreme Administrative Court Primarily reviews final procedural and administrative rules issued by the various governmental agencies. Is the final arbiter for administrative law.	*Court of Cassation* The country's highest court for all non-administrative law issues. Reviews appeals from all lower courts as the jurisdictional rules allow. Automatically reviews certain criminal rulings, regardless of whether an appeal is filed, if the penalty is more than ten years imprisonment or capital punishment.	
Various Appellate Courts –Court of Appeals for the Customs Department: Receives appeals from the Customs Court of First Instance. Its decisions may be appealed to the Court of Cassation. –Court Appeals for the Tax Department Receives appeals by and against the department of income tax in income tax issues. Its decisions may be appealed to the Court of Cassation –State Security Court: Deals with issues related to terrorism, threats to security, and narcotics trafficking. Its decisions may be appealed to the Court of Cassation.	*Courts of First Review* Include the courts of First Instance as well as the Small Claims Courts. Have jurisdiction over commercial, civil and criminal cases. Municipal Courts: Deal mainly with traffic violations.	

A material right, which can be original or subsidiary, is the direct authority given by the law to an individual (Civil Code No. 43, art. 69). An original material right arises out of legal, direct, physical control over personal or real property. A subsidiary material right is one that is derived from an original right (e.g., a building owner's secondary material right to collect rent arises out of the original material right of ownership) (arts. 69 and 70).

The Civil Code defines incorporeal rights as those rights exercised over intangible or non-material things (art. 71(1)). IPRs including copyrights, patents, and trademarks, are explicitly mentioned as examples of incorporeal rights (art. 71(2)).

Overall, there are thirteen laws regulating aspects of IP under Jordanian law.[23] The Civil Code laid the theoretical foundation for IPRs by incorporating them within incorporeal rights, and it also laid down the rules governing civil liability and contracts.

Patents

The first Jordanian Patent law was enacted in 1953 (Patent Law No. 22, 1953). A new Patent law extending the protection period to twenty years was enacted in 1999, incorporating TRIPS-consistent standards into its language (Patent Law No. 32). The 1999 law clarified the criteria for awarding a patent, areas outside patentability domain, and the rights and obligations of a patent holder. It also outlined some specific sanctions that can be requested by a patent holder in case of a patent infringement. The law was amended in 2001 and 2007 to reflect ever-evolving concepts and to synchronize it with Jordan's obligations and international best practices. It puts forth patentability conditions that include novelty, non-disclosure to the public, non-obviousness, and industrial utility (art. 3).

The first patentability requirement, novelty, is set forth in article 3(a). It represents a codification of the doctrine of anticipation (i.e., whether a claim is anticipated if each and every element in it was shown, described, organized, and functioned in substantially the same way as in prior art). Essentially, article 3(a) requires the applicant for the patent to demonstrate

---

[23] Copyright Law No. 22; Patent Law No. 32; Trademarks Law No. 33; Servicemarks Law No. 19, 1953; Industrial Forms and Drawings Law No. 14; Integrated Circuits Law No. 10; Geographical Indications Law No. 8; Unfair Competition and Trade Secrets Law No. 15; New Plant Varieties Law No. 24; Instructions for Border Points Regarding the Protection of Intellectual Property No. 7; E-Transactions Law No. 85; Competition Law No. 49; National Products Protection Law No. 50.

that the invention is new and is different from prior art in the sense that they are not identical. It has yet to be tested in a court of law, as there have not yet been any cases addressing it.

Claim analysis and determination of obviousness, which are key aspects of patent prosecution and litigation, are non-existent because Jordan lacks a developed patent prosecution mechanism/apparatus, and is dependent on the WIPO for expertise in this regard.[24] A clear sign of the embryonic stage of development of patent prosecution in Jordan is that legally it is the patentee's responsibility to assure patentability (Patent Law No. 32, art. 16), whereas this would be the responsibility of the governmental agent in charge of issuing the patent (i.e., the Patent Registrar) in a developed patent prosecution system.

Non-obviousness, set forth in article 3(b) of the Patent Law, requires the applicant to show that the invention is not trivial. In order to determine whether an invention is trivial it is necessary to investigate whether any prior art contains the exact same elements, or whether a number of sources would combine to produce the claimed invention (art. 3(b)). A patentable invention is required to have non-obvious differences from prior art; in other words, it is necessary that a person with ordinary skill would not have thought the subject matter of the invention to be obvious at the time the invention was made (art. 3(b)). This makes this area of examination highly factual and technical. There is also a very strong element of subjectivity in this test, and combining fact-based examination with a deep technical knowledge of the subject area is key for its fair and balanced application.[25]

Technical knowledge in the invention's subject area is key because it allows the examiner to differentiate between the prior art and the proposed claims, to assess what level is considered *ordinary skill* in the field, and to determine what would be considered obvious based on that level of ordinary skill.[26] A combination of all of the above is the only guarantee that the examiner will be able to produce reasonable and objective evidence of obviousness or non-obviousness. It is the level of technical

---

[24] I am grateful to interviewees for comments on this point; see appendix one.

[25] T. J. Chiang, "Cost-Benefit Approach to Patent Obviousness, A," *John's L. Rev.* 82 (2008): 39; M. Astorino, "Obviously Troublesome: How High Should the Standard Be for Obtaining a Patent," *J. Pat. & Trademark Off. Soc'y* 89 (2007): 239; G. N. Mandel, "Patently Non-Obvious: Empirical Demonstration that the Hindsight Bias Renders Patent Decisions Irrational," *Ohio St. LJ* 67 (2006): 1391.

[26] Astorino, "Obviously Troublesome."

expertise in the patent's subject area that allows a seemingly purely subjective test to be made objectively.[27]

The third patentability requirement, industrial utility, is set forth in article 3(c). It requires the patentee to demonstrate that the claimed invention is "useful" for some purpose. It is not clear whether this statement of utility has to be made explicitly or implicitly. Typically, for a claimed invention to violate the utility requirement it must be incapable of achieving a useful result, which could occur if the inventor fails to disclose enough information to convince an examiner of the claimed invention's utility or makes a demonstrably non-credible utility claim.[28]

Nondisclosure is not a strict requirement. Disclosure occurring up to twelve months prior to the filing date is tolerated, as long as it is either made by the inventor or erroneously or maliciously made by others. Although the law grants the right to a patent to the inventor or his or her successor(s) and allows joint ownership in the case of joint efforts, it is clearly a first-to-file system, and priority can be established either by directly filing with the Jordanian patent office or by proving that a patent was filed with a foreign patent office within the past twelve months.

The patent protections provided under the law are twofold. If the subject of the patent is a product, the holder is granted the right to exclude others from making that product. If the subject of the patent is a method, the holder is granted the right to exclude others from utilizing that method. This exclusionary power is in line with the classical protections granted to patent holders under Western laws, especially the US patent code. The Jordanian law also grants the right to use a patent without a license for purposes of research and development; however, the law does not specify whether such a purpose is insufficient if there is a commercial objective in mind, nor is any case law available to illuminate that point. The law also gives the Minister of Industry and Trade the right to issue a compulsory license in the following four situations:[29]

---

[27] Astorino, "Obviously Troublesome"; Chiang, "Cost-Benefit Approach."

[28] N. Machin, "Prospective Utility: A New Interpretation of the Utility Requirement of Section 101 of the Patent Act," *Cal L. Rev.* 87 (1999): 421. A perpetual motion machine is a classic and often-cited example.

[29] Patent Law No. 32, art. 22. According to the TRIPS Agreement, foreign patentees are not obliged to provide their patents locally, thus, compulsory licenses could have a limited application. Article 31 of the TRIPS Agreement permits compulsory license if the patentee refuses to authorize the use of the invention on reasonable commercial terms. In other words, a compulsory license shall be allowed only when negotiating a license on fair commercial terms has failed.

1. For national security purposes
2. If the patent is not exercised or is not sufficiently exercised by the patent holder within three years of the patent issuance or four years from the date of filing
3. If a court of law decides the patent is being used in a way that restricts competition
4. If the compulsory license will be used to export the subject of the patent to disease-plagued regions to fulfil Jordan's obligations under the World Trade Organization.

The language is broad enough to create a compulsory license when the state deems it necessary, yet narrow enough to protect the patent holder from haphazard governmental decision-making. To add a layer of judicial supervision, the minister's decision is not absolute and is subject to review by the Supreme Administrative Court (Patent Law No. 32, art. 26).

A summary of the main elements of the protections provided under the Jordanian Patent law is illustrated in table 2-3 below, while table 2-4 provides a brief characterization of other laws related to patentable subject matter, including the Industrial Forms and Drawings Law No. 14 (2000), the Integrated Circuits Law No. 10 (2000), the Geographical Indications Law No. 8 (2000), the Unfair Competition and Trade Secrets Law No. 15 (2000), and New Plant Varieties Law No. 24 (2000).

Copyright

Prior to the copyright law enacted in 1992 (Copyright Law No. 22), Jordan used the Ottoman-era copyright law, and the Supreme Administrative Court confirmed such usage in opinions (Opinion No. 76/81). In cooperation with the World Intellectual Property Organization (WIPO), Jordan amended the law twice, in 1998 and 1999, to bring it in line with the requirements of accession to the WTO.[30] One of the most significant changes made in these amendments was the automatic grant of copyright protection to any published work, whether or not it was registered with the Jordanian National Library (Copyright Law No. 22, art. 45).

[30] Amending laws No. 14 (1998) and No. 29 (1999).

Table 2-3. Patent protections

	When Element is Effective	Components of the Element
Pre-award Protection	Prior to issuance of a patent	Temporary protection can be granted to an item that can be patentable in Jordan, for the purpose of protecting the item during an exhibition. Temporary protection license is granted, officially registered, and is valid for six months from the start date of the exhibition (Patent Law Regulations No. 97, 2001).
Criminal Penalties	After granting the patent	Jail terms and/or monetary fines are imposed for: 1. Replicating a patented invention for commercial or industrial purposes. 2. Selling, offering for sale, or importing products patented in Jordan. 3. Labelling or documentation for a product that leads the public to believe that a patent was issued for the product.
Injunctive Relief	In case of an infringement civil or criminal action	If the patent holder provides a bank guarantee, he or she can ask a court for: 1. An injunctive order to stop the allegedly infringing activity. 2. Precautionary seizure of the allegedly infringing products. 3. Preservation of all evidence related to the alleged infringement.
Foreign Patents Registration	Upon approval by the patent Registrar at the MoIT	The holder(s) of the foreign patent can file for a Jordanian patent. If the Jordanian patent is granted, the holder has all the rights and responsibilities of a Jordanian patent.

Table 2-4. Other patentable subject matter laws

Laws	Elements
Industrial Forms & Drawings Law No. 14 (2000)	• Provides protection for designs and models related to the aesthetic appearance of a product, which are registered at the Ministry of Industry and Trade. • Requires novelty, non-disclosure, and a purely aesthetic function for registration. • Period of protection is fifteen years from the date the application is filed. • Provided the registration holder provides a bank guarantee, he or she can ask a court for: –An injunctive order to stop the allegedly infringing activity. –Precautionary seizure of the allegedly infringing products. –Preservation of all evidence related to the alleged infringement.
Integrated Circuits Law No 10 (2000)	• Provides protection for three-dimensional designs of integrated circuits registered in the Integrated Circuits Register at the Ministry of Industry and Trade. • Requires novelty and non-obviousness for registration. • Provides for an R&D use exception. • Grants protection from the date a request for registration is filed. The duration of protection after registration is ten years from the date of first use anywhere in the world, but the total period of protection cannot exceed fifteen years. • Provides for compulsory licensing for national security reasons, pubic non-commercial use, or to counter an emergency. The registration holder is entitled to fair compensation, and can challenge the compulsory license before the Supreme Administrative Court. • Right-holder can ask a court for an injunctive order to stop the allegedly infringing activity.
New Plant Varieties Law No. 24 (2000)	• Provides protection for plant varieties registered in the New Plant Varieties Register at the Ministry of Agriculture. • Requires the plant variety to be novel, non-disclosed, distinguished, homogenous, and stable.

Currently the Copyright Law provides protection to the following works (art. 3):

1. Any written documents
2. Any verbally delivered words like sermons, lectures, and speeches
3. Any theatrical productions, including musicals and mime acts
4. Any musical productions, whether accompanied by words or not
5. Any cinematic, audio-visual, or broadcasted productions
6. Paintings, photography, carvings, sculptures, and architectural and ornamental works
7. Maps, designs, blueprints, and 3-D models, including those related to geography
8. Computer programs in any programming language
9. Titles, except those which have other common usages
10. Compilations of any sort.

Moral rights granted exclusively to the author (art. 8) include the right to:

1. Be identified as the author on all produced copies
2. Modify the work in any form
3. Prevent any change to the work
4. Remove the work from circulation altogether, provided equitable restitution is made to the entities that would otherwise have financial rights to the work.

The financial rights granted to the author under the law (art. 9) clearly identify areas of exploitation that are exclusively within the author's purview, which include the right to:

1. Duplicate and reproduce the work in any form, including photographic, cinematic, or digital reproduction
2. Translate the work to any other language, quote it, or produce it musically
3. Lease or rent copies of the work to the public
4. Distribute the work, give permission for copying it, or any other form of action that would otherwise create ownership rights in copies of the work
5. Import the work
6. Offer the work in a public form such as reading, projection, acting, audio-visual broadcasting, or any other form.

The law also grants licenses for the unauthorized use of the work (e.g., translation of the work with official approval from the Minister of Culture), provides for financial compensation to the copyright-holder, and limits the use of the translated work to educational or research-related activities.

The duration of protection granted under the law varies with the type of work protected, as illustrated by table 2-5 below.

Table 2-5. Copyright protection periods

Type of Work	Duration of Protection
Audio Performance	50 years
Audio Producers	50 years
Audio Broadcasters	20 years
Author's Financial Rights	Duration of author's life plus 50 years after death of all authors
Cinematic and TV works, works authored under a pseudonym, and works not authored by individuals	50 years from the year of publication
Applied Arts (paintings, manuscripts, sculptors, photos, architectural, topographical, or geographical maps, computer programs)	25 years from the year of completion
Author's Moral Rights	Not specifically mentioned in the law, but a Cassation Court decision stated these rights continue with the heirs after the author's death, presumably for the duration of the financial rights (Opinion No. 2003/2648).

While the law is notable for providing universal protection without a requirement for registering the work with the National Library, it does mandate such registration for works published in Jordan and/or by a Jordanian author (arts. 38–41), with failure to register resulting in a monetary fine. Jordanian publishers are also required to file a bi-annual report with the National Library of all titles published during that six-month period.

The mandatory registration requirement before distribution gives the NL implicit authority to exercise a pocket veto over any work should the author decline to register it. Article 38 extends that authority to any work published or distributed in Jordan even if the author is not Jordanian. The overall effect is the limitation of the right to legally distribute foreign works in Jordan without a National Library registration number.

Trademarks

Trademarks occupy a significant place in the Jordanian IP jurisprudence because the trademark law was created in 1952. It has since been amended several times. Along with the 1952 trademark legislation, regulations were enacted that outlined in considerable detail the mechanism and process by which a trademark can be registered as well as how a registration can be renewed, disputed, amended, or revoked (Trademarks Regulations No. 1, 1952). The law and the regulations give the office of the Trademark Registrar the responsibility to perform those tasks (Trademarks Law No. 33). Disputes with the Registrar's decision can be appealed to the Jordanian Supreme Administrative Court. A more recent addition to the panoply of trademark-related laws is the Trade Names Law No. 9, of 2006, which covers the actual names used with goods and services. Similar to trademarks, the law for Trade Names creates a Registrar at the Ministry of Industry and Trade and gives that office the duty of approving and officially recording Trade Names. Decisions by the Trade Names Registrar can be appealed to the Supreme Administrative Court.

In the interpretation of the trademark law, the courts established certain tests for examining whether a common, non-distinguishing mark can be registered. The trademark law explains that a mark can be registered if it has a distinguishing feature (e.g., a name, letter, number, shape, colour, etc.) such that the feature can distinguish the goods or services from those provided by others.[31] The Supreme Administrative Court held that if a suggested mark was common and used by many people, then it lacked distinct associative value and could not be registered (Opinion No. 6/53).

Another area where the courts helped clarify the legislative text was in the area of defining "similarity" as a condition for registration. The court asked the Registrar of Trademarks to consider the:

---

[31] Article 8 of the Trademarks Law No. 33 also lists several features that would render a mark non-registrable, including: marks similar to monarchy, governmental, official, religious, foreign and international symbols, slogans, and flags; marks containing any word or number which may cause the public to believe that the goods enjoy a privileged position with an entity which it does not have actually, or because these words and numbers are used in trade to distinguish that kind of goods from other similar kinds; marks containing a person or entity's name or image without the consent of that person or entity; marks that contravene public order and public morals and confuse the public or encourage unfair competition; and marks which are identical or very similar to other registered marks such that it might confuse the public.

1. General idea of the mark
2. General features of the mark as more important than its detailed parts
3. Kind of goods for which the mark is intended
4. Possibility that the consumer will not carefully examine the mark and compare it to other similar marks to establish their distinctiveness
5. Possibility of visual or auditory confusion between the mark being examined and other similar marks (Opinion No. 108/65).

The courts have upheld the Registrar's refusal to register marks which contravened public order (Opinion No. 87/72, Opinion No. 6/53), promoted unfair competition and confused the public (Opinion No. 163/84), or were similar or identical to registered marks (Opinion No. 128/88).[32]

The law only protects marks registered in Jordan, but it does provide for some protection to non-registered foreign trademarks by denying registration in Jordan for the same type of goods or services by someone other than the holder of the foreign mark (Trademarks Law No. 33). In the case of famous foreign trademarks, the law denies registration for all goods or services, even if not of the same type as the famous mark (art. 8). Famous marks do not need to prove that their foreign registration pre-dates the registration requirement in Jordan by someone other than the famous mark owner, and can, therefore, obtain registration in Jordan even if their application is contested by a similar non-registered mark in Jordan. The law considers the letter of registration of a trademark to be *prima facie* proof that the holder of the letter is the owner of the mark, unless evidence to the contrary can be presented, thus shifting the burden of proof to the person challenging the registration (art. 28). Table 2-6 below outlines the

[32] But the court's refusal to link a trademark to the distinctiveness of the good or service for the sake of avoiding confusion in the mind of the public led it sometimes to issue opinions that came across as parochial, and lack the broad economic understanding of the value of the mark as property, albeit an intangible one. This was clear in the courts' decision to waive the criteria for similarity for pharmaceutical products. The court's rationale was that the dispensing of pharmaceuticals is the purview of physicians and pharmacists who are not likely to confuse pharmaceutical products even if they have similar trademarks or trade names. It is important to note, though, that this opinion of the court pre-dates the accession of Jordan to the WTO, and the subsequent IP rights obligations that were part of that accession, including the protection of foreign trademarks. It also pre-dates the amendment of the trademark law, which prohibited the registration of a foreign-registered trademark in Jordan for a similar product, by other than the owner of the foreign trademark. It is expected, therefore, that should the court revisit this issue again that the distinctiveness and non-similarity criteria will be applied.

Table 2-6. Trademark prosecution and appeal

Step	*Procedure*	*Appeal*
Application	• File a written request with the Registrar of trademarks at the Ministry of Industry and Trade. • Acceptance of the filed application does not mean the trademark registration is approved.	
Application Prosecution	• Registrar can accept the application, accept the application with modifications, or deny registration. • Acceptance of the trademark must include the clear delineation of any restrictions or conditions of use associated with the acceptance.	Applicant can appeal Registrar's final decision to the Supreme Court, but the law does not set a time for filing the appeal.
Opposition	• Opposition to the registration of a trademark can be filed within ninety days of the registration's announcement. • The Registrar resolves the opposition after soliciting responses from the holder of the registration and allowing the entity opposing the registration to respond accordingly	• The Registrar's resolution of the opposition can be appealed to the Supreme Administrative Court within twenty days. • Points other than those presented to the Registrar cannot be presented to the court without the court's permission.
Post-registration	• Trademark is registered for ten-year intervals, which can be renewed indefinitely. • If the owner of the trademark does not request its renewal then it expires within one year of the end of the ten years for which it was originally registered. Others can register an expired trademark. • Requests can be filed to remove the registration of trademarks not used for three consecutive years. • Owner can amend a registered trademark if the Registrar approves.	Registrar's decision to remove a trademark can be appealed to the Supreme Administrative Court.
Rights of Trademark	• Exclude others from using the registered trademark. • Exclude others from using an unregistered famous trademark for the same products.	

main steps for trademark registration. In this connection, we may note that the Supreme Administrative Court had a role in expounding who has standing to file a trademark opposition claim by decreeing that such a claim can be filed by any person, even if that person does not have a direct economic interest in the trademark. The court's rationale was based on the indirect economic interest all citizens have to prevent confusion between brands, and to promote the distinctiveness of high-quality trademarks.

Jordanian trademark law also recognizes collective registration, which allows the Registrar to grant a registration for a single trademark to one or more entities or individuals at the same time if they were using the trademark for the same services or products; the Registrar can impose any conditions it sees fit to guarantee equitable use of the trademark by all (Trademarks Law No. 33, art. 18). The Registrar's decision on this issue can be appealed to the Supreme Administrative Court within thirty days.

The law provides for civil and criminal remedies and outlines several punishable violations, including counterfeiting a registered trademark, illegal use of a registered trademark, and knowingly selling goods with a counterfeit registered trademark.

The owner of a registered trademark can file a civil or a criminal case against the alleged infringer(s), and, subject to the provision of a financial bond, can ask the court for injunctive relief, including a cease and desist order against the infringer, the placing of all goods under protective custody, and/or the safeguarding of any related evidence. If the injunctive relief is granted, the moving party must file a lawsuit against the alleged infringer within eight days from the date of its approval. Failure to file a lawsuit within the eight-day window results in the automatic termination of the injunctive relief measures instituted by the court, thus allowing the accused party to claim equitable compensation for damages caused by the terminated injunctive relief.[33]

The trademark law allows for a trademark to be transferred or sold in conjunction with or separately from the entity that holds it (Trademarks Law No. 33, art. 19). Alternatively, the Registrar can, without affecting the corporate registration of the trademark holder, cancel a registration if it is not used or if the registration process was found to contain violations of the necessary requirements (art. 19).

---

[33] The Court of Cassation in Opinion No. 72/56 (n.d.) opined that for a criminal prosecution against a trademark infringer to move forward, the trademark should be registered and it should be used on the same type of goods associated with the registered trademark. The court effectively added an extra dimension to the requirements of the trademark criminal or civil claim.

The Protection of New Plant Varieties Law

The Protection of New Plant Varieties Law is the result of the accession to the WTO, which required a specific law that gives clear and comprehensive protections to this area of technology (New Plant Varieties Law No. 24). The Ministry of Agriculture is the entity charged with maintaining a public register of the protected plant varieties, which can only include "varieties" of plants which occupy the lowest ring in plant taxonomy. The law therefore does not protect any element of plant taxonomy other than a variety which the law defines as a plant group with specific and reproductively stable genetic characteristics distinguishing it from other plant groups. The main features of the law are outlined in table 2-7 below.

The variety's stability is regarded as the salient feature for continued registration, and any evidence that would call into question the variety's stability is cause for cancellation of the registration, even if the variety was stable at the time of filing.

The breeder has the power to sell, transfer, or place a lien on the registration; all such actions must be recorded with the official Registrar at the Ministry of Agriculture. Furthermore, the registration grants the holder the power to exclude all others from using or cultivating the registered variety for commercial purposes. However, the law does provide for a fair-use exception for research and development and other non-commercial purposes. In the same vein, compulsory licensing is allowed for the public good, and the Minister of Agriculture can make such a determination based on a recommendation from the Registrar. Compulsory licensing does not negate the registration holder's right to equitable compensation for the duration of the compulsory licensing (sec. 21). The law contains an interesting omission in that it does not subject the Minister's decision to grant compulsory licensing to judicial review, though it does subject the Registrar's recommendation to judicial review by the Supreme Administrative Court.

Table 2-7. Elements of the Protection of New Plant Varieties Law

	Requirement	*Notes*
Registration	• A new variety not sold for more than one year inside Jordan or four years outside Jordan prior to the date of filing. • An uncommon variety that clearly differs from any other known variety. (Any filing for any variety, inside or outside Jordan, makes it a common variety as of the date of filing, if a registration is eventually given.) • A variety whose main characteristics are homogenous. • A variety whose main characteristics are stable throughout repeated reproduction and breeding.	• The right to register belongs to the breeder(s) or to the employer if the work was done as part of an employment or contractual duty. • All Registrars' final decisions can be appealed to the Supreme Court.
Priority	• The date of filing with the Jordanian Ministry of Agriculture is the priority date in Jordan. • The foreign filing date is accepted as a priority date in Jordan, if the foreign country and Jordan are part of a treaty that stipulates such action and the filing in Jordan is done within twelve months of the foreign date.	The applicant has up to two years if filed based on a foreign priority date, and six months if filed based on a Jordanian priority date, to meet all the technical examining requirements set forth in article 10 of the law.
Opposition	Any person can oppose the registration of a new plant variety within ninety days of the grant of the preliminary registration.	If no opposition is filed after the preliminary registration is announced in the official gazette, or if an opposition is rejected, a final registration is issued.
Duration of Protection	• Period of protection for registered varieties is twenty years from date of filing. • Period of protection is twenty-five years for trees and grapevines.	
Cancellation of Registration	• If variety is common, not new, not homogenous, or not stable at the time of filing for registration. • If filing for registration is made by someone other than the true breeder. • If variety is initially stable but later becomes unstable.	All Registrar's decisions on cancellation of registration can be appealed to the Supreme Administrative Court.

This law does not provide for any criminal penalties for the unauthorized use of a registered variety. It does, however, provide for procedural protections, which allow the holder of the registration, subject to the provision of a bank guarantee, to ask the court for one or all of the following measures:

1. Injunctive order to stop the allegedly infringing activity
2. Precautionary seizure of the allegedly infringing products
3. Preservation of all evidence related to the alleged infringement.

The owner of a registered variety can obtain injunctive relief without serving notice to the potential infringer if the owner proves to the court that there is a high probability of immediate and significant damage. The court's approval of injunctive relief must be followed within eight days by case filing; otherwise, the injunctive relief measure will automatically terminate, thus allowing the accused party to claim equitable compensation for any damages caused.

Trade secrets and unfair competition

Prior to the enactment of the Unfair Competition & Trade Secrets Law No. 15 (2000), Jordanian laws did not address unfair competition and trade secrets in a specific item of legislation. Table 2-8 outlines the main elements of the relevant components of the law.

Table 2-8. Elements of the Trade Secrets & Unfair Competition Law[34]

Unfair Competition	*Trade Secrets*
DEFINITION: Any act that contravenes fair commercial and industrial practice, including acts leading to: • confusion as to the origin of goods • false accusations against another facility or product	DEFINITION: Any information: • whose final form or detailed components are not known to the public, or are not readily available to those who usually handle such information • that has commercial value by virtue of not being publicly known • that has had reasonable precautions taken by its owner to prevent its disclosure

[34] Unfair Competition and Trade Secrets Law No. 15. Note that this law, like others dealt with in this section, was passed in order to comply with TRIPS provisions on protection of undisclosed information, which itself incorporates the Paris Convention's treatment of unfair competition; see Ch. 3, p. 67 of the present work.

• false labelling as to nature, method of manufacturing, properties, quantities, or expiration dates of products	Acts that result in violating this law: • divulging contractual information • divulging information one under a fiduciary duty to keep secret • obtaining information from a third party that one knows, or could have known, was obtained against fair commercial and industrial practice Acts that are not in violation of this law: • independently arriving at the information • reverse engineering
PROTECTIONS: A court can, upon the request of an allegedly injured party and the provision of a bank bond: [35] • stop that allegedly illegal practice • order the precautionary seizure of related products • preserve all related evidence If the allegedly injured party does not file a lawsuit within eight days, the court orders automatically expire and the accused party is entitled to file for equitable restitution for any incurred damages.	PROTECTIONS: A court can, upon the request of an allegedly injured party and the provision of a bank bond” [36] • stop that allegedly illegal practice • order the precautionary seizure of related products • preserve all related evidence If the allegedly injured party does not file a lawsuit within eight days, the court orders automatically expire and the accused party is entitled to file for equitable restitution for any incurred damages. If an official entity requests, for the purpose of approving pharmaceutical or agricultural products, information pertaining to a trade secret, that entity must: • Agree to protect the trade secret from use by others for up to five years from the date the approval is granted • Not divulge the information unless necessary to protect the public

[35] The law does not restrict the ability to file a complaint with the court to an economically injured party; rather the language refers to any “interested” party injured by the unfair competition. This implies that any concerned citizen can file such a request.

[36] Note 35 applies here also.

While the law provides protections to the holders of trade secrets, it also seems to penalize them for not filing a patent. The period of protection for a trade secret for a pharmaceutical or agricultural product, once shared with a governmental agency, is five years, compared to the twenty-year protection period provided under the patent law (Unfair Competition and Trade Secrets Law No. 15). The law declares as null and void any clause in an IP licensing agreement that might negatively impact commerce or impede the spread of technology. Three situations are mentioned and specifically prohibited (art. 4):

1. Preventing the licensee from sharing improvements on licensed technology except with the licensing party
2. Contractually prohibiting the licensee from litigating or administratively disputing the right to the licensed IP
3. Forcing the licensee to accept, through an adhesion licensing agreement, a package of licensed products, instead of individually selected ones.

Geographical Indications Law

The Geographical Indications Law, passed in order to comply with articles 22 to 24 of TRIPS, creates a central registry for the approved geographical indications, located at the Ministry of Industry and Trade.[37] The main criterion for gaining entry into the registry is whether the product exhibits a trademark that correctly indicates the geographical origin of the product and is not misleading to the public. The law, therefore, requires the geographical reference used to be technically correct and not misleading as to what the geographical region actually is known for internationally. The law emphasizes that the geographical reference for wines and spirits must be technically correct regardless of whether confusing the public is a concern, effectively reducing the test, in the case of wines and spirits, to only its first element.

The law adds another dimension to the analysis by listing two actions that are not considered to be violations of its provisions, namely (1) the filing of an application, in good faith, for a trademark that matches a geographical indication, or (2) the use, in good faith and prior to the geographical indication's registration in its home country, of a trademark that matches the geographical indication.

[37] For further discussion of TRIPS articles 22 to 24, concerning geographical indications, see Ch. 3, p. 60 of the present work.

A Registrar's final decision can be appealed within sixty days to the Supreme Administrative Court, and a registration's revocation does not impart any criminal liability to the violators. Instead, the law provides for a range of administrative and procedural protections under which a court can, upon the request of an allegedly injured party and the provision of a bank bond, stop the allegedly infringing practice, seize related products, and preserve all related evidence. If the allegedly injured party does not file a lawsuit within eight days, the court's order automatically expires and the accused party is entitled to file an action for equitable restitution.

Protection of Integrated Circuits Designs Law

The Protection of Integrated Circuits Designs Law was passed in order to comply with the TRIPS standards for topographies and integrated circuits.[38] For an integrated circuit design to be registered in the designated central registry at the MoIT, it must be novel and non-obvious to practitioners of the art, and an application must be filed within two years of its first commercial exploitation anywhere in the world (Integrated Circuits Law No. 10, art. 4). Once all formalities are presented to the Registrar at the MoIT, a decision can be made as to the eligibility to a license, and then other rules are applied to sort out situations such as joint ownership of a design and the effect of employer–employee relationship. Final decisions by the Registrar can be appealed to the Supreme Administrative Court within sixty days.

Protection for the design begins from the application's filing with the Registry; the protection duration is ten years from the date of the design's first commercial use anywhere in the world, not to exceed fifteen years from the date of its invention. The law emphasizes that all legal dispositions over the protected design should be registered at the Registry at the Ministry of Industry and Trade.

The law also provides for compulsory licensing if required by national security, emergency, or public non-commercial use, which can be based on a judicial or administrative order after a showing that the right-holder's rights are being exercised in a way that stifles lawful competition. Such compulsory licenses are non-exclusive and non-assignable, must afford the owner of the original license equitable compensation, and each application must be dealt with separately.

There are no criminal penalties to violations of the Integrated Circuits Law, but the law allows for injunctive relief measures. It gives a range of

---

[38] See Ch. 3, p. 65 of the present work.

administrative and procedural protections under which a court can, upon the request of an allegedly injured party and the provision of a bank bond, stop the allegedly infringing practice, seize related products, and preserve all related evidence (Integrated Circuits Law No. 10, sec. 22). If the allegedly injured party does not file a lawsuit within eight days, the injunctive relief expires automatically, allowing for claims of compensatory damages by the accused party.

Anomalies in the patent and trademark filing systems

This chapter has set out the basic elements of the Jordanian legal system with particular reference to IPRs, giving an indication of the ways in which the laws were revised in order to bring them in line with TRIPS. As we have noted, this legal transformation took place rapidly and without the normal level of parliamentary or public scrutiny. This lack of scrutiny has led to anomalies, most notably with regards the treatment of national versus international trademarks and patent applications.

Under standard usage definitions, an international patent or trademark application is one that is filed under either the Patent Cooperation Treaty (PCT)[39] or the Madrid Protocol,[40] respectively. The Madrid Protocol offers a trademark owner the opportunity to have a trademark protected in several countries by simply filing one application directly with his or her own national or regional trademark office. An international mark so registered is equivalent to an application for a registration of the same mark made directly in each of the countries designated by the applicant. If the trademark office of a designated country does not refuse protection within a specified period, the protection of the mark becomes effective as if that office had registered it.[41]

The PCT, meanwhile, makes it possible to seek simultaneous patent protection by filing a single "international" patent application instead of several separate national or regional patent applications. The granting of a patent license remains under the control of the national or regional patent offices in what is called the "national phase."

---

[39] The PCT is an international treaty, concluded in 1970 and administered by the WIPO, between more than 125 Paris Convention countries. It provides a unified procedure for filing patent applications in each of its contracting states.

[40] The Madrid system for the international registration of marks (the Madrid system), established in 1891, functions under the Madrid Agreement (1891), and the Madrid Protocol (1989). It is administered by the International Bureau of the WIPO, located in Geneva, Switzerland.

[41] See http://www.wipo.int/madrid/en/ (last visited September 3, 2009).

The use of the term "international application" under either a patent or a trademark application therefore effectively means a filing under the PCT or the Madrid Protocol as described above. Jordan, however, is not a member of either the PCT or Madrid Agreement; therefore, the term "international application" in this context refers to applications filed by foreign companies directly with the Jordanian patent or trademark registrars rather than to a PCT or Madrid Protocol filing. A more appropriate and accurate description, therefore, would be "foreign application," but the use of the term "international application" is consistent with the term used by the Jordanian authorities.

Many local practitioners in Jordan still confuse the foreign applications made directly with the Jordanian patent and trademark registrar with those made under the PCT and Madrid Protocols,[42] and to a certain extent this misplaced presumption is justified, because both the Jordanian trademark and patent laws contain several articles that do in fact allow for the process of filing a trademark and a patent application under the PCT and the Madrid Protocol.

The trademark law, for example, defines an international application as one that is filed under the Madrid Protocol and designates articles 42, 43, 44, and 45 to cover such a filing. Article 46 of the trademark law, however, states that those articles shall not come into effect until three months after Jordan joins the Madrid Protocol. Since Jordan has yet to join the Madrid Protocol, none of those articles is yet in force, even though they are incorporated into the text of the law. Local practitioners usually assume that Jordan has already joined the Madrid Protocol without checking the validity of that assumption and, as a result, wrongly advise as to the possibility of filing an international trademark application.

The situation under the Jordanian Patent Law No. 32 is equally confusing. Similar to the trademark law, the patent law defines an international application as one filed under the PCT and contains several articles that explain the process for filing such an application. It does not contain language that prevents such articles from coming into effect until Jordan joins the PCT (i.e., language similar to article 46 of the trademark law discussed above). This is a glaring omission, and discussions with Jordanian officials indicate that it was an inadvertent omission by the legal team that drafted the patent law. Jordanian law, therefore, allows for the filing of an international patent application under the PCT, even though Jordan is not party to that agreement.

---

[42] I am grateful to my interviewees for observations on this point. See appendix one.

Under the PCT, an application can be filed with the WIPO or the national office, but the Jordanian patent registrar currently refuses to accept such applications. The fact that such a mistake occurred is indicative of the haste with which the legal code on IP was amended to accommodate the requirements of joining the WTO, thus resulting in many of these laws being translated into Arabic from English. The Jordanian government would be strongly advised to remedy this by introducing an amendment to the patent law that excludes the articles on international patent applications from coming into effect until Jordan joins the PCT.

These drafting mistakes are not isolated events; rather, they are emblematic of the disconnect between Jordanian law as it now stands, and the priorities of the Jordan's people and its institutions. Chapter five will consider this disconnect in more detail; the following chapter sets out the wider legal framework which induced these changes in Jordanian law. Alongside the amendment of laws, Jordan has also reconstructed the enforcement mechanisms for these laws, which has been an on-going process since its accession to the WTO. As we will see in chapter five, there now are multiple agencies with enforcement responsibilities for IPRs, including the MoIT, the NL, the JISM, the Food and Drug Administration, the customs department, and the Public Security Department. As we will see, the kinds of anomalies noted here with respect to the drafting of laws apply also to the institutions charged with enforcing them.

CHAPTER THREE

THE INTERNATIONAL IP LEGAL FRAMEWORK

The previous chapter discussed the main elements of Jordan's legal system with particular reference to the laws governing IP. We now turn to an examination of the treaties and international agreements that, collectively, underpin the Jordanian IP protection system.

We begin by looking the treatment of IPRs under TRIPS. Jordan entered into TRIPS as part of its accession to the WTO in 2000, and, as will be evident, the requirements of TRIPS are clearly present in Jordanian law. The latter part of the chapter moves on from a discussion of TRIPS to look at two regional and bilateral treaties (RBTs) to which Jordan is a party – the JUSFTA and the JEUAA. Both of these RBTs make considerable extra requirements as regards Jordan's treatment of IPRs, extending beyond what is contained in TRIPS. As we will see in chapters four and five, the developed countries have shown a tendency to shift away from the WTO as a forum to negotiate stricter IPRs; in part, this is because the WTO's consensus system gives developing countries an effective veto in such negotiations. The developed countries are – successfully – seeking fora in which they can exert greater coercive power. The evolution of IPRs beyond those set out in TRIPS is known as the shift to "TRIPS-plus" standards. The contents of both the TRIPS and the TRIPS-plus standards are set out in this chapter.

The Agreement on Trade Related Aspects of Intellectual Property Rights (TRIPS)

The TRIPS Agreement, which is annex 1C of the Marrakesh Agreement establishing the WTO, was signed in Morocco on 15 April 1994.[1] The aim

---

[1] TRIPS is one of twenty-eight agreements that make up the Final Act of the Uruguay Round of Multilateral Trade Negotiations. The negotiations began in Punta del Este in 1986 and culminated in 1994 with the signing of the Final Act and the creation of the WTO.

of the agreement was to create a harmonized multilateral system for regulating intellectual property. From its inception, however, it was clear that the agreement would embody a conception of IPR shaped according to the interests of the developed world, with questionable benefits for the rest.

The initial concerns about TRIPS focused on its potential effect on access to medicine in developing countries, especially given the direct involvement of pharmaceutical multinationals in its drafting.[2] The repercussions of the globalization of patent protection, the associated extension of monopolization, and the subsequent developments are global issues that continue to colour any discussion of the economic role of the WTO and TRIPS.[3] Critical voices noted that harmonization of IP standards through TRIPS would have the effect of restricting the space for national IP policy setting.[4] This is a significant departure from the traditional role of having national IP laws reflect levels of economic development. Developing countries, including Jordan, have traditionally made private ownership of knowledge difficult to obtain and had weaker IPRs than developed countries.[5] This was evident in shorter patent terms, as well as in Jordan's refusal to patent pharmaceuticals, setting concurrent requirements for national registration for copyright and trademark protections. This variation in protection and enforcement standards was not uncommon in the pre-TRIPS era; for example, the Paris Convention for the Protection of Industrial Property (the principal international convention on IP for most of the twentieth century) allowed countries a significant degree of flexibility in designing their patent regimes.[6] Under TRIPS, such variation and flexibility are no longer available, as all but the poorest countries are subjected to the same standards for IP management under a one-size-fits-all approach.

---

[2] See Peter Drahos, "Expanding Intellectual Property's Empire: The Role of FTAs," International Centre for Trade and Sustainable Development, April 22, 2010, http://ictsd.org/i/ip/24737/.

[3] See Duncan Matthews, *Globalising Intellectual Property Rights: The TRIPS Agreement* (London: Routledge, 2002). See also Drahos, "Expanding Intellectual Property's Empire."

[4] Kenneth C. Shadlen, "Policy Space for Intellectual Property Management: Contrasting Multilateral and Regional-bilateral Arrangements," *Econômica* 10, no. 2 (2008): 55–81.

[5] Christopher May, *A Global Political Economy of Intellectual Property Rights*, 1st ed. (Routledge, 2000).

[6] Shadlen, "Policy Space."

The historical roots of the TRIPS Agreement can be traced back to the Paris Convention of 1883,[7] which dealt with the protection of industrial property, and the Berne Convention of 1886,[8] which dealt with copyright protection. Several countries did not ratify the Berne Convention until much later, with the United States (which ratified it in 1989) being one example.[9] In the area of trademarks, the framework that governed their international treatment was the Madrid System for the International Registration of Marks.[10]

Article 72 of the TRIPS agreement effectively mandates those principles to be treated as one bundle that must be taken as a whole.[11] The main elements of those principles are as follows.

National treatment

Article 3 of the TRIPS agreement requires member states to "accord to the nationals of other Members treatment no less favourable than that it accords to its own nationals with regard to the protection of IP."[12] The

---

[7] "Paris Convention for the Protection of Industrial Property," April 23, 2010, http://www.wipo.int/treaties/en/ip/paris/trtdocs_wo020.html, originally agreed March 20, 1883. Last amended September 28, 1979.

[8] "Berne Convention for the Protection of Literary and Artistic Works," April 23, 2010, http://www.wipo.int/treaties/en/ip/berne/trtdocs_wo001.html, originally agreed September 9, 1886. Last amended September 28, 1979.

[9] Orrin G. Hatch, "Better Late Than Never: Implementation of the 1886 Berne Convention," *Cornell International Law Journal* 22 (1989): 171.

[10] Established in 1891, it functions under the Madrid Agreement (1891) and the Madrid Protocol (1989). The International Bureau of WIPO located in Geneva, Switzerland administers it.

[11] "Agreement on Trade Related Aspects of Intellectual Property Rights," 1994, art. 72. "Reservations may not be entered in respect of any of the provisions of this Agreement without the consent of the other Members."

[12] See TRIPS, art. 3:

1. Each Member shall accord to the nationals of other Members treatment no less favourable than that it accords to its own nationals with regard to the protection of IP, subject to the exceptions already provided in, respectively, the Paris Convention (1967), the Berne Convention (1971), the Rome Convention or the Treaty on Intellectual Property in Respect of Integrated Circuits. In respect of performers, producers of phonograms and broadcasting organizations, this obligation only applies in respect of the rights provided under this Agreement. Any Member availing itself of the possibilities provided in Article 6 of the Berne Convention (1971) or paragraph 1(b) of Article 16 of the Rome Convention shall make a notification as foreseen in those provisions to the Council for TRIPS.

2. Members may avail themselves of the exceptions permitted under paragraph 1 in

drafters of the TRIPS agreement alluded to this principle with slightly different wording in article 1, stating "Members shall accord the treatment provided for in this Agreement to the nationals of other Members."

Article 3 is intended to mitigate the possibility that the legislation of a member state would not yet be in full compliance with the TRIPS standards, which would make the requirements of article 1 inapplicable. Such inapplicability continues pending the state's compliance with article 3's assurances of a "minimum" standard of equal treatment based on whatever levels of IPRs protections exist at the time. The principle ensures that equal treatment is in place from the date of accession without the customary one-year amnesty period granted to the applicability of other provisions (art. 65).

The application of this principle is restricted by some exceptions applied through treaties approved by the TRIPS agreement; namely, the Paris Convention for the Protection of Industrial Property, the Treaty on Intellectual Property in Respect of Integrated Circuits, the Berne Convention for the Protection of Literary and Artistic Works, and the Treaty of Rome.[13] These restrictions help to give developing countries a certain degree of flexibility in how they implement the National Treatment principle.

Most-favoured-nation treatment

Article 4 of the TRIPS agreement mandates that a member state must immediately and unconditionally confer on citizens of other member states any advantage, favour, privilege, or immunity granted to any other member state. The goal is to assure that varying levels of IPRs protection would not exist within and between individual member states.

---

relation to judicial and administrative procedures, including the designation of an address for service or the appointment of an agent within the jurisdiction of a Member, only where such exceptions are necessary to secure compliance with laws and regulations which are not inconsistent with the provisions of this Agreement and where such practices are not applied in a manner which would constitute a disguised restriction on trade.

[13] See TRIPS Agreement, arts. 1 and 3.

1. Subject to the provisions of paragraphs 2, 3 and 4, no Member shall be obliged to apply the provisions of this Agreement before the expiry of a general period of one year following the date of entry into force of the WTO Agreement.

2. A developing country Member is entitled to delay for a further period of four years the date of application, as defined in paragraph 1, of the provisions of this Agreement other than Articles 3, 4 and 5.

Certain exceptions, derived or accorded under certain international agreements, are applicable to this principle as well, affecting advantages, favours, privileges, or immunities accorded by a member state.[14]

Minimum and maximum levels of protection

Article 1 of the TRIPS agreement mandates a minimum level of intellectual property rights protection equal to that provided by its provisions, thus creating a "floor" for acceptable levels of protection for any of its members. The requirement to meet those minimum standards is the main driver behind the modification of national IPRs legislations. At the same time, while the language of article 1 suggests preference for even stricter and higher levels of IPRs than the required minimums, it is clear that members are not obligated to seek or implement such levels.

Therefore, from a compliance point of view, the obligatory minimum and maximum levels of protection under the TRIPS agreement are one and the same. Unlike the one-size-fits-all approach applied under the circumstances of the WTO accession talks, this allows the member states, primarily those with developing economies, the benefit of tailored approaches based on an actual cost-benefit analysis when considering any extra IPRs protection (art. 72).

Effective dates

Article 65 of the TRIPS agreement discusses effective dates and outlines the transitional arrangements for the application of the TRIPS provisions. Member states must apply the provisions "before the expiry of a general

---

[14] Art. 4: Exempted from this obligation are any advantage, favor, privilege or immunity accorded by a Member:
(a) deriving from international agreements on judicial assistance or law enforcement of a general nature and not particularly confined to the protection of IP;
(b) granted in accordance with the provisions of the Berne Convention (1971) or the Rome Convention authorizing that the treatment accorded be a function not of national treatment but of the treatment accorded in another country;
(c) in respect of the rights of performers, producers of phonograms and broadcasting organizations not provided under this Agreement;
(d) deriving from international agreements related to the protection of intellectual property which entered into force prior to the entry into force of the WTO Agreement, provided that such agreements are notified to the Council for TRIPS and do not constitute an arbitrary or unjustifiable discrimination against nationals of other Members.

period of one year following the date of entry into force of the WTO agreement" (art. 65(1)). Thus, the agreement grouped the countries into three areas, with each group having a legal standard commensurate with its economic status and its level of development (i.e., developed, developing, or least developed). The TRIPS agreement provided further consideration for countries moving from centralized to free-market economies (art. 65(3)).

Those transitional arrangements, which were the biggest concessions accorded by the developed countries to the developing and least developed ones, represent one of the major negotiating successes for both parties. They allowed the developing countries more time to meet the IPRs standards under the agreement. Accordingly, "grace periods" were created, throughout which the terms of the agreement are suspended, except for the national treatment and the most-favoured-nation principles.[15]

Under the first grace period (outlined in article 65(1) of the TRIPS agreement), member states, in general, have up to one year from the date of entry into the WTO agreement to apply its provisions. The WTO agreement came into force on January 1, 1995, at which time member states were expected to be in full compliance with TRIPS provisions no later than January 1, 1996.[16] Developing countries, on the other hand, were permitted to delay the application of TRIPS provisions for a period of five years, also commencing from January 1, 1995, and set to expire on January 1, 2000 (art. 65(2)). The same grace period was granted to countries transitioning from a centrally planned economy to a market-based economy, undertaking structural reform of their IP system, and facing special problems in the preparation and implementation of IP laws (art. 65(3)).

Under article 65(4) of the TRIPS agreement, developing countries are provided with the option of delaying the application of the provisions on product patents of section 5, part II, of the TRIPS agreement for an additional period of five years, if product patents were not protected in their territory on the general date of application of the agreement for the member state.[17] The most common candidates for this exception were

---

[15] See L. Peter Farakas, "Trade-Related Aspects of Intellectual Property," in *The World Trade Organization: Multilateral Trade Framework for the 21st Century and U.S. Implementing Legislation* (American Bar Association, 1996).

[16] H. El-Said and M. El-Said, "TRIPS-Plus Implications for Access to Medicines in Developing Countries: Lessons from Jordan–United States Free Trade Agreement," *The Journal of World Intellectual Property* 10, no. 6 (2007): 438–475.

[17] Product patents refer to the chemical structure defining a chemical compound, or

patents covering pharmaceuticals and chemicals, and developing countries had to fulfil certain administrative requirements for patent filing and were subject to certain marketing concessions in their territory (art. 70(9)).

Article 65(5) provides that any country availing itself of a transitional period under paragraphs 1, 2, 3, or 4 has an obligation to ensure that any changes in its laws and regulations during that period do not result in a lesser degree of consistency with the provisions of the TRIPS agreement, than the degree of consistency when they first entered the agreement. This can be described as "a standstill clause" because it requires that IP protection may not deteriorate beyond the levels present.[18]

Since Jordan was not a member of the WTO prior to January 1, 1995, it did not benefit from the grace provisions under the TRIPS agreement; accordingly, it had to adjust its legal and legislative framework governing IPRs prior to joining the WTO. Therefore, all current Jordanian IP laws had to be *a priori* compliant with the requirements of TRIPS.

Intellectual property coverage under TRIPS

The TRIPS agreement provided protection for eight types of IP in addition to emphasizing the continued validity of several previous international treaties. Below is a brief description of the eight types. This summary is not meant to be exhaustive, but simply to provide a road map to the various areas of protection under the agreement.

Copyright and authors' rights

Copyright and authors' rights are discussed in articles 4 through 19 of section II of the TRIPS agreement, which also emphasizes the need for member states to abide by articles 1 through 21 of the 1971 Berne Convention. This seems to be the TRIPS agreement's attempt to create a common denominator and a starting point for its treatment of the subject (art. 9). The protection period for copyright and author's rights is set to no less than fifty years from the end of the calendar year of authorized publication (art. 12). The term of protection granted for broadcasts was set to at least twenty years from the end of the calendar year in which the broadcast took place.

---

composition, which is the product consumed by consumers, whereas process patents are directed at protecting the means or the method of obtaining an end result.

[18] Farakas, "Trade-Related Aspects."

An important distinction between the TRIPS agreement and the Berne Convention is the introduction of copyright protection for computer programs and databases, two types of work that emerged after the 1971 update of the Berne Convention (art. 10). Under the TRIPS agreement, both types were granted international protection, which they had not previously enjoyed. The consideration of computer programs and the associated code as literary works did not create an obvious implementation problem. As for databases, which are selections or arrangements of existing works, more specificity was needed to clarify that the protection granted to the database does not affect the copyright protections, or lack thereof, of the works arranged or selected in the database. To be accorded protection, therefore, a database should provide added value by bringing the selection or the arrangement together in a way that "constitutes [an] intellectual creation"[19] (i.e., the originality of the structure and comprehensiveness of the selection or arrangement were accorded protection but not the data or material itself).

Additionally, the TRIPS agreement creates rental rights for at least two types of works: computer programs and cinematographic works.[20] For the latter, such an obligation arises only if there is widespread copying of the cinematographic works that is "materially impairing the exclusive right of reproduction" of the right-holder (art. 11). The rental right for computer programs, on the other hand, does not apply if the programs are not the subjects of the rental. From the perspective of developed countries, the language of article 11 is a minimum standard that most of them have surpassed in their national legislations by creating broader rental rights (e.g., the European Union's Council Directive 92/100/EEC).[21]

---

[19] Art. 10(2) reads: Compilations of data or other material, whether in machine readable or other form, which by reason of the selection or arrangement of their contents constitute intellectual creations shall be protected as such. Such protection, which shall not extend to the data or material itself, shall be without prejudice to any copyright subsisting in the data or material itself.

[20] Art. 11 reads: In respect of at least computer programs and cinematographic works, a Member shall provide authors and their successors in title the right to authorize or to prohibit the commercial rental to the public of originals or copies of their copyright works. A Member shall be excepted from this obligation in respect of cinematographic works unless such rental has led to widespread copying of such works which is materially impairing the exclusive right of reproduction conferred in that Member on authors and their successors in title. In respect of computer programs, this obligation does not apply to rentals where the program itself is not the essential object of the rental.

[21] The Council of the European Communities, Council Directive 92/100/EEC, 1992, on rental right and lending right and on certain rights related to copyright in

Trademarks

The TRIPS agreement's treatment of trademarks also encompasses service marks, and it uses the terms "well-known trademarks" and "collective trademarks," which are also used in the current Jordanian trademark law. The protection period for such marks was set to a minimum of seven years (art. 18) and the TRIPS agreement embraced the notion of the trademark as a contractual object (art. 21). While copyright protections under the TRIPS agreement built on the Berne Convention, the sections related to trademarks relied on the Paris Convention of 1967 as their foundation.

Unlike the Paris Convention, the TRIPS agreement did define what makes a mark a protectable subject matter;[22] in article 15(1), it lists two requirements needed for a trademark to meet the standard for registration: a sign or combination of signs (names, letters, numerals, figurative elements, and/or combination of colours), and a distinctiveness that can be acquired through use of the goods or services.

Article 16 of the TRIPS agreement outlines the rights conferred through the registration of a trademark.[23] Under those rights, the right-

---

the field of intellectual property, amended by the Council of the European Communities, Council Directive 2001/29/EC, n.d.

[22] Art. 15(1) reads: Any sign, or any combination of signs, capable of distinguishing the goods or services of one undertaking from those of other undertakings, shall be capable of constituting a trademark. Such signs, in particular words including personal names, letters, numerals, figurative elements and combinations of colors as well as any combination of such signs, shall be eligible for registration as trademarks. Where signs are not inherently capable of distinguishing the relevant goods or services, Members may make registrability depend on distinctiveness acquired through use. Members may require, as a condition of registration, that signs be visually perceptible.

[23] Art. 16, reads: 1. The owner of a registered trademark shall have the exclusive right to prevent all third parties not having the owner's consent from using in the course of trade identical or similar signs for goods or services which are identical or similar to those in respect of which the trademark is registered where such use would result in a likelihood of confusion. In case of the use of an identical sign for identical goods or services, a likelihood of confusion shall be presumed. The rights described above shall not prejudice any existing prior rights, nor shall they affect the possibility of Members making rights available on the basis of use.

2. "Paris Convention for the Protection of Industrial Property," art. 6bis. shall apply, *mutatis mutandis*, to services. In determining whether a trademark is well-known, Members shall take account of the knowledge of the trademark in the relevant sector of the public, including knowledge in the Member concerned which has been obtained as a result of the promotion of the trademark.

3. Article 6*bis* of the Paris Convention shall apply, *mutatis mutandis*, to goods or

holder is given exclusive right to *exclude* others from using the mark if that usage involves (1) the use of similar or identical signs, (2) in the course of trade, (3) for goods identical or similar to those used with the registered sign, and (4) that will likely result in confusion in the mind of the consumer. This very broad definition raises more questions than it answers; for example, what is meant by "similar," and under what standard is such a concept of similarity to be judged, with the understanding that the boundaries of such a definition will determine if the right-holder's exclusionary rights can be exercised? Further, there is considerable confusion as to the meaning of "likelihood of confusion" and whether it should be defined from the perspective of the government employee, the consumer, or some other criterion.

It is also not clear whether the concept of confusion, as intended by that language, also encompasses the notion of dilution of the mark or whether it is simply restricted to confusion as to the mark's origin. Since joining the WTO, the Jordanian trademark jurisprudence has yet to settle these issues, and it remains to be seen how it will interpret the language discussed above.

Two issues that arise in the international use of trademarks, involving mark termination and cross-border exploitation of foreign marks, were also covered under the TRIPS agreement. Article 19 mandates a minimum term of three years before a registered trademark can be cancelled for non-use, and even such cancellation can be challenged if the right-holder shows a good reason for the non-use.

The unhindered exploitation of foreign trademarks in the global market was ensured by article 20 of the TRIPS agreement, which abolished statutory requirements to associate the foreign trademark with local trademarks or limit its use to a special form or manner before it can be marketed locally. However, the TRIPS agreement still allowed for such restrictions if they were made in a contractual form when licensing or assigning the trademark. That unhindered exploitation was further complemented with article 21, which restricted compulsory licensing of trademarks. Marks, therefore, were considered a transferable commodity that can be contractually arranged independent of the business with which they are associated.

---

services which are not similar to those in respect of which a trademark is registered, provided that use of that trademark in relation to those goods or services would indicate a connection between those goods or services and the owner of the registered trademark and provided that the interests of the owner of the registered trademark are likely to be damaged by such use.

Geographical indications

Articles 22 through 24 of the TRIPS agreement covered the rights arising from the association of a product with a certain geographical area in one of the member states. The protections and exceptions provided under the TRIPS agreement are reflected in the Jordanian law protecting geographical indications (Geographical Indications Law No. 8 – which did not exist prior to WTO membership).

The TRIPS agreement provides a minimum standard for the protection of geographic indications, which it defines as "indications which identify a good as originating in the territory of a Member, or a region or locality in that territory, where a given quality, reputation or other characteristic of the good is essentially attributable to its geographical origin" (art. 22). The basic standard of protection is presented in a negative form, requesting that member states prevent "the use of any means in the designation or presentation of a good that indicates or suggests that the good in question originates in a geographical area other than the true place of origin in a manner which misleads the public as to the geographical origin of the good," as well as "any use which constitutes an act of unfair competition within the meaning of the Paris Convention (1967)" (arts. 22(2)(a)–(b)). The reference to unfair competition under the Paris Convention effectively extends the notions of confusion, false allegations, and the misleading of the public to goods whose use of a geographical indicator that, while "literally true as to a territory, region or locality in which goods originate, falsely represents to the public that the goods originate in another territory" (art. 22(4)).

Article 23 is devoted exclusively to geographical indications for wines and spirits, indicating the significance of IP for that industry. The article grants protection to each indication in the case of homonymous geographical indications for wines and establishes a multilateral system of notification and registration of geographical indications for wines eligible for protection in participating member states. Member states are requested to enter into negotiations aimed at increasing the protection of individual geographic indications under article 23, while they are prohibited from diminishing their protection of geographical indications that existed immediately prior to joining the WTO. In other words, if a member state's standard of protection is less than that required by the TRIPS agreement provisions, it must be raised to meet the TRIPS standards, but if its standard already exceeded the TRIPS agreement protections before joining the WTO, that standard must not regress to a lower one.

There remain certain questions as to the value of providing protection for geographical indications. It has been suggested that geographical indications bring certain economic benefits, such as the enhancement of geographical reputation, increased publicity for the localities, and more effective competition through enhanced capability to sell directly to end customers.[24] Other evidence, however, suggests geographical indications have adverse effects on competition and market entry and that their overall economic benefits are suspect at best.[25] Several competition law cases from the European Union, for example, found that geographical indications were used to create barriers to market entry, control total supply through the imposition of production quotas, and impose price controls through various anti-competitive measures.[26]

Industrial designs

The terms and provisions of the Jordanian law protecting industrial designs (Designs & Industrial Models Law No. 14, 2000) reflect the provisions of articles 25 and 26 of the TRIPS agreement, which cover this specific type of IP. Jordanian law also reflects the TRIPS agreement's approach to industrial designs as having a dual IP rights nature. First, there is the utilitarian aspect of the industrial design, which is protected under the notions of industrial design law, and second, there is the aesthetic aspect, which the TRIPS agreement explicitly places under copyright protection.[27]

Protection is provided for "independently created industrial designs that are *new* or *original*"; thus, the patent concept of novelty is used. Such novelty is determined if the new designs "significantly differ from known designs or combinations of known designs," thus introducing the patent concept of non-obviousness (TRIPS art. 25(1)). The concepts of copyright law demanding "independent creation" and "originality" are also part of the analysis to determine the eligibility for protection.[28] As to the duration

---

[24] See W. Moran, "Rural Space as Intellectual Property," *Political Geography* 12, no. 3 (1993): 263–277.

[25] See F. Addor and A. Grazioli, "Geographical Indications beyond Wines and Spirits," *Journal of World Intellectual Property* 5, no. 6 (2002): 865–897.

[26] Meir Perez Pugatch, *The Intellectual Property Debate* (Edward Elgar, 2006).

[27] TRIPS, art. 25(2) states: Each Member shall ensure that requirements for securing protection for textile designs, in particular in regard to any cost, examination or publication, do not unreasonably impair the opportunity to seek and obtain such protection. *Members shall be free to meet this obligation through industrial design law or through copyright law* [emphasis added].

[28] See Nuno Pires de Carvalho, *The TRIPS Regime of Trademarks and Designs* (Kluwer Law International, 2006).

of protection, the length granted to industrial designs seems more in line with the shorter periods granted to patents than the much longer durations granted to copyrighted material.[29]

Patentable subject matter

The Paris Convention, which is the pre-TRIPS international convention on patents, suffered from a problem similar to the Berne Convention's regarding trademarks: it did not provide patentability requirements or a definition of what constitutes a patentable invention. The lack of a specific definition beyond simply meeting the granting criteria allows for flexibility but at the same time results in a very broad range of potential subject matter for inventions. The TRIPS agreement addressed this issue in article 27, which provides both patentability requirements (newness/novelty, an inventive step, and industrial applicability)[30] and a description of those inventions that can be excluded from patentability by member states.[31]

---

[29] TRIPS art. 26(3) states: The duration of protection available shall amount to at least 10 years.

[30] TRIPS art. 27(1) states in part: "Subject to the provisions of paragraphs 2 and 3, patents shall be available for any inventions, whether products or processes, in all fields of technology, provided that they are new, involve an inventive step and are capable of industrial application." The article proceeds to add in a footnote, in acknowledgment of the terminology used in the US patent system, that "the terms 'inventive step' and 'capable of industrial application' may be deemed by a Member to be synonymous with the terms 'non-obvious' and 'useful' respectively."

[31] TRIPS arts. 2 and 3 state:

2. Members may exclude from patentability inventions, the prevention within their territory of the commercial exploitation of which is necessary to protect *ordre public* or morality, including to protect human, animal or plant life or health or to avoid serious prejudice to the environment, provided that such exclusion is not made merely because the exploitation is prohibited by their law.

3. Members may also exclude from patentability:

(a) diagnostic, therapeutic and surgical methods for the treatment of humans or animals;

(b) plants and animals other than micro-organisms, and essentially biological processes for the production of plants or animals other than non-biological and microbiological processes. However, Members shall provide for the protection of plant varieties either by patents or by an effective *sui generis* system or by any combination thereof. The provisions of this subparagraph shall be reviewed four years after the date of entry into force of the WTO Agreement.

The newness/novelty requirement is intended to ensure that the information pertaining to the invention is not already in the public domain.[32] The requirement of inventiveness or non-obviousness is aimed at assuring that the invention makes a contribution to the field of knowledge, which is to be judged by someone trained in the art.[33] The industrial applicability, or usefulness, requirement should eliminate one-hit wonders (i.e., inventions that cannot be duplicated or replicated at an industrial scale). Of equal importance is the requirement that patent rights should be available for any invention, which effectively expanded the field of patentability and removed patentability barriers that existed primarily in developing countries (e.g., the distinction between process and product patents, which led to the exclusion from patentability of inventions in fields like pharmaceuticals).[34]

The TRIPS agreement acknowledges exclusions to patentability for inventions that disturb the *ordre public* and morality (art. 27(2)). However, the fact that this optional exception comes after the demand that "patents shall be available for any inventions" (art. 27(1)) indicates that it is not automatic and that a case-by-case review of each is warranted.

The rights conferred upon a patent holder can vary based on whether the type of patent granted is a product or a process patent (art. 28). The right-holder's full disclosure of the patent to the public is the requirement for complete disclosure of the invention in a manner "sufficiently clear and complete for the invention to be carried out by a person skilled in the art, and may require the applicant to indicate the best mode for carrying out the invention known to the inventor," in return for the patent right (art. 29). For a product patent, the right-holder can prevent others from making, using, offering for sale, selling, or importing that product for these purposes (art. 28(1)(a)). For a process patent, the right-holder can prevent unauthorized parties from using, offering for sale, selling, or importing for these purposes the product obtained directly by that process. Those conferred rights also have some exceptions that can be applied by member states, provided that "such exceptions do not unreasonably conflict with a normal exploitation of the patent and do not unreasonably prejudice the legitimate interests of the patent owner, taking account of the legitimate interests of third parties" (art. 30).

---

[32] J. A. Ordover, "A Patent System for Both Diffusion and Exclusion," *The Journal of Economic Perspectives* 5, no. 1 (1991): 43–60; S. Scotchmer and J. Green, "Novelty and Disclosure in Patent Law," *The RAND Journal of Economics* (1990): 131–146.

[33] Scotchmer and Green, "Novelty and Disclosure."

[34] Ordover, "A Patent System"; Scotchmer and Green, "Novelty and Disclosure."

The Jordanian law allows for a research and development exception (Patent Law No. 32 art. 31), which falls under compulsory licensing (defined by TRIPS as the "use without authorization of the right holder"), an area that developed countries must have been keen to place under tight regulation. The main elements used by TRIPS to regulate compulsory licensing are as follows:

1. Case-by-case consideration
2. "Prior efforts" requirement to obtain authorization from the right-holder
3. Limited scope and duration
4. Non-exclusiveness and non-assignability of the issued license
5. "Domestic market" requirement
6. Automatic termination upon the change of circumstances causing the licensing
7. Fair and equitable compensation to right-holder
8. Judicial review of the licensing decision, as well as the amount of compensation offered in return, is permitted.

Exceptions to some of the requirements were allowed in the case of a domestic emergency, public non-commercial use, and the need to correct anti-competitive practices.

The TRIPS agreement guarantees the right-holder a judicial review if the patent was revoked or forfeited (art. 32) and set a minimum patent term of twenty years from the date of filing (art. 33). In the case of infringements of process patents, the TRIPS agreement shifts the burden of proof to the alleged infringer by requiring the infringer to prove, if the two products are identical, that the process used was different from the patented one. Thus, TRIPS makes the initial assumption that the identical product was produced using the patented process, unless the alleged infringer proves otherwise (art. 34).

Topographies and integrated circuits

The TRIPS agreement references the protections presented in the Treaty on Intellectual Property in Respect of Integrated Circuits (IPIC).[35]

[35] "Treaty on Intellectual Property in Respect of Integrated Circuits," 1989. Also known as the Washington Treaty, this was adopted by the conference held in Washington DC in 1989. The Treaty is open to member states of the WIPO or the United Nations and to intergovernmental organizations meeting certain criteria.

However, the IPIC's incorporation by reference into the TRIPS was subject to some modifications, which included the following changes:

1. The term of protection was set for at least ten years (rather than eight years under IPIC) from the date of filing an application, or of the first commercial exploitation, but Members may provide a term of protection of fifteen years from the creation of the layout design (TRIPS, art. 38).
2. The right-holder's exclusive rights are extended to articles incorporating integrated circuits in which a protected layout-design is incorporated, insofar as it continues to contain an unlawfully reproduced layout-design without the prior authorization of the right-holder.[36]
3. The circumstances in which layout-designs may be used without the consent of right-holders is more restricted subject to the same conditions set forth earlier for patents. That restriction was also reflected in the Jordanian Integrated Circuits Law No. 10 (2000).
4. Certain acts, when committed unknowingly, would not constitute infringement.[37]

[36] TRIPS art. 36 outlines the scope of protection and states: "Subject to the provisions of paragraph 1 of Article 37, Members shall consider unlawful the following acts if performed without the authorization of the right holder: importing, selling, or otherwise distributing for commercial purposes a protected layout-design, an integrated circuit in which a protected layout-design is incorporated, or an article incorporating such an integrated circuit only in so far as it continues to contain an unlawfully reproduced layout-design."

[37] TRIPS art. 37(1) states: "Notwithstanding Article 36, no Member shall consider unlawful the performance of any of the acts referred to in that Article in respect of an integrated circuit incorporating an unlawfully reproduced layout-design or any article incorporating such an integrated circuit where the person performing or ordering such acts did not know and had no reasonable ground to know, when acquiring the integrated circuit or article incorporating such an integrated circuit, that it incorporated an unlawfully reproduced layout-design. Members shall provide that, after the time that such person has received sufficient notice that the layout-design was unlawfully reproduced, that person may perform any of the acts with respect to the stock on hand or ordered before such time, but shall be liable to pay to the right holder a sum equivalent to a reasonable royalty such as would be payable under a freely negotiated license in respect of such a layout-design."

Protection of undisclosed information

TRIPS characterized trade secrets as information considered valuable as a result of its non-disclosure (art. 39). The context for providing such protection was within the provision of trade secrets to governmental agencies during the course of product licensing.

TRIPS incorporated the Paris Convention's treatment of unfair competition[38] and added criteria to determine whether information would qualify for protection, including (art. 39(2)):

1. The information is a secret in the sense that it is not, as a body or in the precise configuration and assembly of its components, generally known among or readily accessible to persons within the circles that normally deal with the kind of information in question
2. The information has commercial value because it is secret
3. The information has been subject to reasonable measures under the circumstances, by the person lawfully in control of the information, to keep it secret.

Article 39(3) focuses on the non-disclosure requirement for protected information exclusively from the perspective of pharmaceutical and agricultural chemical products. The drafting of article 39(3) is a direct result of the lobbying by the major pharmaceutical and agricultural corporations to secure more precise language for the protection of their trade secrets,[39] which they must share with governmental agencies in the course of regulatory or other government-related dealings.[40] The Jordanian statute of Unfair Competition and Trade Secrets Law No. 15 (2000) picked up on those issues and mandated that governmental agencies

---

[38] Ibid. art. 39(1) states: "In the course of ensuring effective protection against unfair competition as provided in Article 10*bis* of the Paris Convention (1967), Members shall protect undisclosed information in accordance with paragraph 2 and data submitted to governments or governmental agencies in accordance with paragraph 3."

[39] See Matthews, *Globalising Intellectual Property Rights*.

[40] TRIPS art. 39(3) states: "Members, when requiring, as a condition of approving the marketing of pharmaceutical or of agricultural chemical products which utilize new chemical entities, the submission of undisclosed test or other data, the origination of which involves a considerable effort, shall protect such data against unfair commercial use. In addition, Members shall protect such data against disclosure, except where necessary to protect the public, or unless steps are taken to ensure that the data are protected against unfair commercial use."

requesting confidential information for the purpose of approving pharmaceutical or agricultural products must (art. 8):

1. Agree to protect the trade secret from use by others for up to five years from the date the approval of the pharmaceutical or agricultural product is granted
2. Not divulge the information unless necessary for protecting the public and, if necessary, prevent others from commercially exploiting the trade secret.

Thus, member states are mandated to protect undisclosed information provided to them in the course of regular governmental work.

Control of anti-competitive practices in contractual licenses

The TRIPS agreement (art. 40) outlines an approach to the control of anti-competitive practices in IP licenses. This is supported in article 7, which states that the "protection and enforcement of IPRs should contribute to the promotion of technological innovation and to the transfer and dissemination of technology."

Similarly, article 8(1) authorizes member states to "adopt measures necessary … to promote the public interest in sectors of vital importance to their socio-economic and technological development." Article 8(1)'s broad language is tempered by the requirement that such measures be "consistent with the provisions" of the TRIPS agreement (art. 8(2)).

While TRIPS recognizes the general right to "conclude licensing agreements" as part of the patent grant (art. 28(2)), it nonetheless moves to limit certain uncompetitive practices that might arise under licensing and would "have adverse effects on trade and may impede the transfer and dissemination of technology" (art. 40(1)). The explicit right of member states to legislate against such practices is explicitly mentioned, and each country is further allowed to explicitly legislate certain practices that constitute "in particular cases an abuse of IPRs having an adverse effect on competition in the relevant market."[41]

---

[41] The "relevant market" in the realm of intellectual property could mean a physically defined market, or one that is marked by non-physical boundaries. Examples of the later include the Technology Markets, where saleable goods are the ownership and/or licensing of intellectual property, and Innovation Markets, where nothing is sold or bought, but preparations are made to sell innovation at a later time. The TRIPS agreement's lack of a specific definition has spawned controversy.

Article 40(2) lists three examples of licensing practices that member states may move to limit:

1. Exclusive grant-back conditions
2. Conditions preventing challenge to validity
3. Coercive package licensing.

The Jordanian Unfair Competition and Trade Secrets Law No. 15 (2000) explicitly prohibits all three (art. 9). Those examples seem to have been the result of a compromise, as the drafting history had a much longer and more detailed list of practices that might be subject to regulation.[42] The collective language on this issue seems to be more of a policy statement without actual substantive impact, leaving the trans-national dispute-resolution mechanisms of the WTO to settle any ambiguous points and practices. The remaining provisions of article 40 deal with such a mechanism.

The Doha Declaration

The Doha Declaration on the TRIPS Agreement and Public Health (2001) presented a significant development regarding the clarification of the ambiguities surrounding the implications of the TRIPS agreement on developing countries, particularly the concerns about possible restrictions on access to affordable medicines in developing countries. The Declaration affirmed that "the TRIPS Agreement does not and should not prevent Members from taking measures to protect public health." It emphasized, with certain conditions, the right of member states to grant compulsory licenses. The declaration also granted the member states the freedom to determine the grounds upon which these licenses can be granted (paras. 5/b and 5/c).

Article 31 of TRIPS sets forth a number of conditions for granting a compulsory license, including a case-by-case review of applications and the payment of equitable remuneration to the patent holder. The Declaration allowed, however, in the case of national emergency or other circumstances of extreme emergency, the waiver of certain requirements, such as the need for prior negotiations to obtain a voluntary license from the patent holder, a need that was already provided for under article 31 of TRIPS. Parallel importing and the principle of exhaustion can be

---

[42] See Herbert Hovenkamp et al., *IP and Antitrust: An Analysis of Antitrust Principles Applied to Intellectual Property Law* (Aspen Publishers, 2001).

important tools enabling access to affordable medicines that are sold at different prices in different markets, because there can be substantial differences in cost for a pharmaceutical product in different markets.[43] Article 6 of the TRIPS Agreement explicitly states that practices related to parallel importation cannot be challenged under the WTO dispute-settlement system. The Doha Declaration reaffirmed that member states are free to establish their own regimes for such exhaustion without challenge. The Doha Declaration also adopted decisions clarifying the obligations of developing member governments with respect to issues including agriculture, subsidies, textiles, and clothing; technical barriers to trade; trade-related investment measures; and rules of origin.[44]

These were important developments for Jordan, because by the time the Doha declaration was announced, Jordan was already a member state of the WTO. Its pharmaceutical sector, which is the most developed and vibrant in the Middle East and North Africa, particularly stood to gain from the easement of restrictions on the exhaustion principle.[45] However, around the same time, Jordan was about to conclude a separate Free Trade Agreement with the United States, which imposed further restrictions on compulsory licensing. The Jordan–European Union Free Trade Agreement contained similar restrictions as well.

---

[43] The principle of exhaustion states that once patent holders, or any party authorized by them, have sold a patented product, they cannot prohibit the subsequent resale of that product since their rights in respect of that market have been exhausted by the act of selling the product.

[44] The Doha Declaration on the TRIPS Agreement and Public Health further extended the transition period for least-developed countries until January 1, 2016 with respect to the TRIPS obligations concerning pharmaceutical product patent protection and the protection of undisclosed pharmaceutical test data against unfair commercial use (Sects. 5 and 7 of Part II of the TRIPS Agreement). In 2002, the WTO's Council for Trade-Related Aspects of Intellectual Property Rights (TRIPS Council) agreed to grant a waiver to least-developed countries concerning the obligation to provide exclusive marketing rights for pharmaceutical products (TRIPS art. 70(9)) until January 1, 2016. This waiver is subject to approval by the WTO's General Council. There is no waiver of the obligation to adopt "mail box" provisions (TRIPS article 70(8)) for pharmaceutical product patent applications.

[45] Abdel-Aziz Ahmad Sharabati, Shawqi Naji Jawad, and Nick Bontis, "Intellectual Capital and Business Performance in the Pharmaceutical Sector of Jordan," *Management Decision* 48, no. 1 (September 2, 2010): 105–131.

Enforcement of IPRs under the TRIPS agreement

The TRIPS agreement outlines the general commitments that must be provided for in order to assure that all the procedures within the agreement's framework are equitable and fair and provide for a deterring effect against the infringement of IPRs (art. 41). The member states should ensure that enforcement procedures are available under their laws so as to permit effective action against infringement of IPRs, and that such procedures are designed so as "to avoid the creation of barriers to legitimate trade and to provide for safeguards against their abuse" (art. 41(1)).

How invasive such affirmative requirements can be to national sovereignty is not yet clear.[46] Meeting the affirmative requirements presents a challenge for many developing countries, which are hoping to reduce their technological gap.[47] Some of the approaches proposed include integrating IP laws into the national development goals, using competition law to curb monopolistic abuse, designing an IP regime aimed at supporting local innovation, resisting the drive towards stronger international IPRs, and strengthening the national infrastructure for knowledge dissemination and acquisition.[48]

Jordan has not been effective in using the right, guaranteed under article 8 of the TRIPS agreement, to adopt certain measures consistent with the TRIPS agreement in order to protect public health and nutrition and to promote the public interest in sectors of vital importance to their socio-economic and technological development. Developed countries have benefited from Jordan's non-affirmative approach to IP laws by placing their own favourable interpretation on the terms of the TRIPS agreement, allowing them to focus their assistance quite narrowly.[49] Such assistance is requested by TRIPS (art. 67) to provide technical and financial

---

[46] Tuan Samahon, "TRIPS Copyright Dispute Settlement after the Transition and Moratorium: Nonviolation and Situation Complaints against Developing Countries," *Law and Policy in International Business*, Spring 2000.

[47] See "TRIPS: Background, Principles and General Provisions," in Carlos Correa and Abdulqawi Yusuf, *Intellectual Property and International Trade* (Kluwer Law International, 2008).

[48] Jerome H. Reichman, "From Free Riders to Fair Followers: Global Competition Under the TRIPS Agreement," *New York University Journal of International Law and Politics* 29 (January 1, 1996): 11–93.

[49] I am grateful to my interviewees for advising me on this point and others in this paragraph. See appendix one for more information on the interviews which guided this study.

cooperation in favour of developing countries in implementing the provisions of the agreement.

TRIPS (art. 42) requires member states to make civil judicial procedures available to right-holders concerning the enforcement of any IP right covered by the TRIPS agreement. These procedural rights guarantee an international minimum standard for nationals of other member states within the meaning of article 1(3) of the TRIPS agreement.[50]

The TRIPS agreement also reemphasizes (art. 43) the need for the protection of confidential information obtained in the course of evidence-gathering and requests that courts have the authority to order the reproduction of evidence, given that there must be in place measures to assure the protection of confidential information.

The right of national courts to issue injunctions is granted in cases where such an injunction is necessary to "desist from an infringement," such as for the prevention of the entry of imported goods that involve the infringement of an IP right. But such authority is not required if the protected subject matter is ordered by a person who does not know that "dealing in such subject matter would entail the infringement of an IP right" (art. 44). Courts must also have the authority to dispose of infringing goods without compensation and to order "that materials and implements the predominant use of which has been in the creation of the infringing goods be, without compensation of any sort, disposed of outside the channels of commerce in such a manner as to minimize the risks of further infringements, but proportionality between the seriousness of the infringement and the remedies ordered as well as the interests of third parties shall be taken into account" (art. 46).

The judicial authorities in a member state will have the authority to order the knowing infringer to compensate the right-holder for the injury incurred as a result of the infringement of the right-holder's IPRs (art. 45). Additionally, the courts must have the authority to order the infringer to pay the right-holder's expenses, which may include appropriate attorney's fees. In appropriate cases, members may authorize the judicial authorities to order recovery of profits and/or payment of pre-established damages even where the infringer did not knowingly, or with reasonable grounds to know, engage in infringing activity" (art. 45(2)).

The TRIPS agreement, however, does not discuss the basis for estimating damages, which is a key missing detail. That issue was addressed in the JUSFTA, which stated that damages will be calculated on the retail value of the legitimate product that is infringed rather than the

[50] John T. Masterson, *International Trademarks and Copyrights* (ABA Web Store, 2004).

street value of the pirated or counterfeit products,[51] resulting in the maximization of the value of the infringed goods and the damages incurred.

Indemnification for wrongfully enjoined or restrained parties is provided for through compensation for the injury suffered, including appropriate attorney's fees (art. 48). The civil and administrative procedures and the remedies presented in TRIPS are reflected in the Jordanian IP laws.

Dispute settlement under TRIPS

The Dispute Settlement Understanding (DSU) under TRIPS is not limited to issues related to IP disputes; rather, it governs the whole multilateral trading system that is governed by the WTO. With clearly defined rules and timetables for completing a case, the WTO's procedure presents a binding, objective, and legitimate conflict-resolution mechanism, complete with an appeal process. The whole process is not dissimilar to the legal rules and procedures in a domestic judicial process, and while a precedent system is not written into the DSU itself, the appeal panels have been careful to consider past decisions. It is therefore important to understand such a mechanism as it impacts the interpretation and application of the TRIPS provisions. The de facto precedents set by the DSU are key to clarifying ambiguous procedures, concepts, duties, and rights that TRIPS did not expounded upon with sufficient detail and specificity.

The Dispute Settlement Body (DSB), which is composed of representatives of member states, administers the DSU's rules and procedures. The DSB establishes panels, adopts reports by those panels and by the appellate bodies, maintains surveillance of implementation of rulings and recommendations, and authorizes suspension of concessions and other obligations under the covered agreements. Only member states that are signatories to a specific plurilateral trade agreement can present a complaint before the DSB, which makes its decisions by consensus (i.e., no member state shall officially object to the proposed decision).

[51] Jordan–US Free Trade Agreement (2000) art. 4(24): "Injury to the right holder shall be based upon the value of the infringed-upon item, according to the suggested retail price of the legitimate product, or other equivalent measures established by the right holder for valuing authorized goods."

Table 3-1. Approximate time for a dispute settlement procedure under TRIPS[52]

60 days	Consultations, mediation, etc.
45 days	Panel set up and panellists appointed
6 months	Final panel report to parties
3 weeks	Final panel report to WTO members
60 days	Dispute Settlement Body adopts report (if no appeal)
Total = 1 year	*(without appeal)*
60–90 days	Appeal Report
30 days	Dispute Settlement Body adopts appeals report
Total = 1 year and 2–3 months	*(with appeal)*

Jordan would do well to give closer attention to the Dispute Settlement mechanism in order to understand its rights and obligations and tools offered to it under the WTO agreement.[53] But perhaps one should not be harsh on Jordan on this issue, as current evidence suggests that this is a problem common to most developing countries, since the majority of cases before the WTO dispute panels come from a handful of developed countries who are therefore presumably controlling the interpretation of the terms of the WTO agreement.[54] Another dimension to the interpretation of the WTO agreement comes from some members granting their national courts the right to interpret WTO law, as is the case with the United States, which might create "an international law with an American accent."[55]

[52] Source http://www.wto.org/english/thewto_e/whatis_e/tif_e/disp1_e.htm (last visited April 25, 2010). The periods are approximate and the countries can settle their dispute themselves at any stage.

[53] A point emphasized by the interviewees with whom the author spoke while preparing this study. See appendix one.

[54] The United States and the European Union seem to be the heaviest users of the system. The United States also pursues parallel tracks to achieve the same end result of guarding the intellectual property rights of international corporations. Among such tracks was the creation of the Special 301 program, which enables the US Trade Representatives to make a watch-list of countries that are not protecting American intellectual property rights, which might result in trade sanctions against them. Additionally, the United States is pursuing international agreements that should be binding and contain enforcement provisions.

[55] Jeffrey Dunoff, "Free Trade or Fair? The Softwood Lumber Dispute and Beyond," *Alberta Law Review* 45 (2007): 319–356.

A better understanding of the DSU would be a key factor in helping developing countries impact the implementation of the TRIPS agreement.[56] The DSU offers developing countries a new venue for solving some of their difficulties in trade issues, including IPRs. Furthermore, because the DSU brings disputes under a multilateral mechanism, thus assuring that developing countries will not be threatened by unilateral actions by developed countries, it should provide a valuable venue for disputing unfavourable conditions or even for testing ambiguous legal positions, especially since precedents set through the DSU can be as binding as the TRIPS agreement itself.[57]

In this connection, however, it is important to note that RBTs provide for alternative dispute mechanisms other than the DSU, thus impacting its global effectiveness.[58] As we will now see, they also introduce higher levels of IP protections (TRIPS-plus), thus countering the harmonizing role of the TRIPS agreement.[59] Thus, the intended cohesive impact of the WTO agreement on international trade law is undermined by regional and bilateral agreements that splinter the interpretation of international law.[60] Dispute-settlement mechanisms outside the DSU create the potential for forum shopping, and the creation of "separate islands" of legal rules, interpretation, and institutions that further contribute to the splintering of international trade law, leading to the weakening of the global dispute settlement forum envisioned by the DSU and thus of the WTO itself.[61] This also creates a "back door" to challenge a verdict by the DSU (if that point is even reached), whereby the losing party could choose to go to the bilateral dispute settlement forum to reargue it case; there is no double jeopardy doctrine here.

---

[56] David Gantz, "Dispute Settlement Under the NAFTA and the WTO: Choice of Forum Opportunities and Risks for the NAFTA Parties," *American University International Law Review* 14 (1999): 1025.

[57] Carvalho, *The TRIPS Regime*.

[58] Both the JUSFTA and the JEUAA have such clauses.

[59] Mohammed El-Said, "From TRIPS-minus to TRIPS to TRIPS-plus: Implications of IPRs for the Arab World," *The Journal of World Intellectual Property* 8, no. 1 (2005): 53–65.

[60] Kenneth Shadlen, "Globalisation, Power and Integration: The Political Economy of Regional and Bilateral Trade Agreements in the Americas," *Journal of Development Studies* 44, no. 1 (January 2008): 1–20.

[61] Drahos, "Expanding Intellectual Property's Empire."

The Jordan–United States Free Trade Agreement (JUSFTA)

As we have already noted, Jordan's commitments under TRIPS have been significantly enhanced by its participation in regional and bilateral treaties with the United States and the European Union. The developing countries have shifted the forum of negotiations of IPR away from the WTO, and into arenas where they can exert greater coercion. The following sections discuss the impacts of these RBTs as regards IP law in Jordan.

The Free Trade Agreement (FTA) between Jordan and the United States was signed on October 24, 2000, and entered into force on December 17, 2001. It marks a milestone in the economic relationship and history of bilateral trade agreements for both countries, because it was only the second such bilateral agreement between the United States and any other country (the first being with Israel). Previously, the United States had entered into the North American Free Trade Agreement (NAFTA), which is technically a multilateral agreement, as it included three countries: Canada, Mexico, and the United States. The JUSFTA was designed to achieve significant and extensive liberalization across a wide spectrum of trade issues. Its major provisions include:

1. Tariffs: The JUSFTA eliminates duties and commercial barriers to bilateral trade in goods and services originating in the United States and Jordan
2. IPRs: The JUSFTA includes the most up-to-date international standards for copyright, patent, and trademark-related commitments
3. Electronic Commerce: The JUSFTA promotes a liberalized trade environment for electronic commerce (e-commerce)
4. Trade-Related Environment: The JUSFTA includes provisions to implement environmental protection laws
5. Labour Provisions: The JUSFTA includes provisions to protect worker's rights
6. Services: The JUSFTA provides liberalization in certain sectors of trade
7. Consultation and Dispute Settlements: The JUSFTA provides for a dispute-settlement panel that will issue legal interpretations of the JUSFTA after consultation of both countries.

In order to limit access to the benefits of the agreement, Rules of Origin were specifically applied to the JUSFTA in order to determine from what country a product is imported, especially when two or more countries contribute to its production. Since the United States already has a bilateral investment treaty with Jordan, the JUSFTA does not include an investment chapter.

Since signing this treaty, the United States has made similar agreements with other countries in the Middle East and North Africa (MENA) region, such as Bahrain and Morocco, as well as countries outside the MENA regions like Singapore, Australia, and Vietnam. The JUSFTA's inclusion of terms on labour and the environment became standard language for all future FTAs signed by the United States. However, despite its ground-breaking nature, there since has been a growing concern that the JUSFTA carries imbalances in the area of IPRs, resulting from the Jordanian policy makers' lack of familiarity with that subject and a lack of internal consultation when Jordan acceded to the WTO and negotiated the JUSFTA.[62]

The JUSFTA's inclusion of international standards higher than those under TRIPS ushered Jordan into an era of what is now known as the TRIPS-plus standard; that is, a standard of protection for IPRs higher than that demanded or contemplated by the TRIPS agreement itself.[63] Additionally, the JUSFTA grants evidentiary presumption for the owners of copyright and related rights for the purpose of ownership of the copyright-related rights, in both civil and criminal cases.[64] That presumption is not contemplated under the TRIPS agreement, which nonetheless grants member states considerable latitude in designing their evidentiary systems and the presumptions that flow from them.

The JUSFTA requires that all tariff barriers shall be lifted for the majority of goods traded between Jordan and the United States within ten years of the JUSFTA's entry into force (art. 2). Strict rules of origin apply to the goods benefiting from that tariff elimination. The JUSFTA provides for an elaborate and detailed schedule to assign a large number of goods

---

[62] ICG, "The Challenge of Political Reform: Jordanian Democratisation and Regional Instability" (International Crisis Group, 2003), p. 7.

[63] M. El-Said, "From TRIPS-minus to TRIPS to TRIPS-plus."

[64] JUSFTA art. 4(27) states: "In civil cases involving copyright or related rights, each Party shall provide that the natural person or legal entity whose name is indicated as the author, producer, performer or publisher of the work, performance or phonogram in the usual manner shall, in the absence of proof to the contrary, be presumed to be the designated right holder in such work, performance or phonogram. It shall be presumed, in the absence of proof to the contrary, that the copyright related right subsists in such subject matter. Such presumptions shall pertain in criminal cases until the defendant comes forward with credible evidence putting in issue the ownership or subsistence of the copyright or related right."

into varying categories, with duties removed for each category according to a separate timeline (Annex 2).

The JUSFTA emphasizes the inappropriateness of encouraging "trade by relaxing domestic environmental laws" (art. 5). As such, both countries are asked to strive to ensure that they do not "derogate from, or offer to waive or otherwise derogate from, such laws as an encouragement for trade with" one another. Interestingly enough, however, there is no demand for higher environmental standards for both parties similar to those demanded for IPRs. Instead the JUSFTA recognizes the right of each party to "establish its own levels of domestic environmental protection and environmental development policies and priorities, and to adopt or modify accordingly its environmental laws" (art. 5). Actions of either party are in compliance if they reflect a "reasonable exercise of such discretion," as self-regulation and monitoring were considered satisfactory (art. 5).

Customs administration was also addressed by the JUSFTA in very broad terms, along with the rules regarding the eligibility for the preferential tariff treatment provided under the JUSFTA, including the list included in Annex 2.2 of the JUSFTA (art. 14). But the main dispute for customs and borders issues was related to IPRs and article 4(26), which stipulates that "[e]ach Party shall provide, at least in cases of copyright piracy or trademark counterfeiting, that its authorities may initiate criminal actions and border measure actions *ex officio*, without the need for a formal complaint by a private party or right holder" (art. 4(26)). The current Jordanian Customs Law only grants the authority to prevent the entry of counterfeit goods, leaving the initiation of legal action to the right-holder. This issue continues to threaten that Jordan might be included on the list maintained by US Trade Representatives (USTR) of trading partners not fulfilling their trade obligations. Because the USTR list is linked to the level of aid given by the US Government to the respective countries, it is a major concern for developing countries like Jordan.

The dispute-resolution mechanism under the JUSFTA is separate and distinct from the WTO's DSU; while the JUSFTA procedure comprises the same steps used under the DSU (i.e., consultation followed by panel adjudication), they have little else in common. The JUSFTA envisions the creation of a three-member Joint Committee to "supervise the proper implementation of the JUSFTA and to review the trade relationship between" the United States and Jordan (art. 15).

Section 4, which covers the issues related to IP in the JUSFTA, is its longest and most detailed section. The section's goal of establishing a high standard of IP rights protection is evident from its first sentence, which declares that the protection levels provided under the JUSFTA are a "minimum." It addresses several areas ranging from copyright, patents, trademarks, and geographical indications to enforcement of IP and transition periods. It also sets standards for IPRs protection that exceed the limits demanded by the TRIPS, thus setting in motion a TRIPS-plus standard. The subsections below will address some of these elements.

Initial provisions

In addition to the IPRs protections, the JUSFTA (art. 4(1)) also calls on both parties to adopt the following provisions from other international IPRs treaties:

1. Articles 1 through 6 of the Joint Recommendation Concerning Provisions on the Protection of Well-Known Marks (1999) adopted by the Assembly of the Paris Union for the protection of industrial property and the General Assembly of WIPO, which deals with the definition of well-known marks.
2. Articles 1 through 22 of the International Convention of the Protection of New Varieties of Plants (UPOV Convention, 1991), which provides recognition of the rights of plant breeders.
3. Articles 1 through 14 of the WIPO Copyright Treaty (WCT, 1996),[65] with the exception of Articles 1(4) and 6(2) of the treaty, provided that this exception should not prejudice the obligations to the WCT treaty itself.
4. Articles 1 through 23 of the WIPO Performance and Phonograms Treaty (WPPT, 1996),[66] with the exception of Articles 5, 8(2), 12(2) and 15 of the WPPT treaty, without prejudice to each party's rights and duties under the WPPT, the Berne Convention and TRIPS.

Additionally, each party is required to use its best efforts to ratify the PCT (1984) and the Madrid Protocol Concerning the International Registration of Marks (1989). Jordan is not yet a member of either.

---

[65] WIPO Copyright Treaty, 1996. Jordan acceded to this treaty on January 27, 2004 and it came into force on March 27, 2004.

[66] WIPO Performances and Phonograms Treaty, 1996. Jordan acceded to this treaty on February 24, 2004 and it came into force on May 24, 2004.

Trademarks and geographical indications

The JUSFTA expands the definition of trademarks by encompassing geographical indications, even though under the TRIPS trademarks and geographical indications are treated separately. Furthermore, the JUSFTA introduced several new obligations in this area, including:

1. The commitment to join the Protocol Relating to the Madrid Agreement Concerning International Registration of Marks.
2. The requirement to give effect to articles 1 through 6 of the Joint Recommendation Concerning Provisions on the Protection of Well-Known Marks (1999) adopted by the Assembly of the Paris Union for the protection of industrial property and the General Assembly of WIPO.
3. The requirement not to require recording of trademark licenses to establish the validity of the license or to assert any rights in a trademark.
4. The requirement to raise the maximum criminal fine to JD 6,000, which was included in paragraph 3 of the Memorandum of Understanding between Jordan and the United States.[67]

In response to requirements (2) through (4), the Jordanian government presented several amendments to its Trademark Law, which were approved by the Parliament in 2008 to bring the law into compliance.

Copyright and related rights

The JUSFTA added significant requirements to this area, including:

1. Giving performers and producers of phonograms the right to prohibit unauthorized broadcasting of their works.
2. Giving right-holders control over allowing or denying the importation of the protected work(s), whether the work is pirated or an authorized version.[68]

---

[67] Memorandum of Understanding on Issues Related to the Protection of Intellectual Property Rights Under the Agreement Between the United States and Jordan on the Establishment of a Free Trade Area, 2000, www.jordanusfta.com/documents/memo_property.pdf.

[68] JUSFTA art. 4(11) states: "Each Party shall provide to authors and their successors in interest, to performers and to producers of phonograms the exclusive right to authorize or prohibit the importation into each Party's territory of copies of

3. Asking the signatories to combat technology that is intended to circumvent the effective technological measures that are used by performers or producers in connection with the exercise of their rights in accordance with article 11 of the WCT[69] and article 18 of the WPPT (art. 4(13)).[70]
4. Asking governmental agencies to only use authorized computer software. Both parties must actively regulate the acquisition and management of software for government use (art. 4(15)).
5. Requiring "that statutory maximum fines are sufficiently high to deter future acts of infringement with a policy of removing the monetary incentive to the infringer" (art. 4(25)).[71]

The Jordanian Copyright law was amended first in 1999 to comply with the TRIPS agreement requirements and then again in 2001, 2003, and 2005 to bring it into closer compliance with the JUSFTA requirements. The criminal fines were increased to a maximum of JD 6,000 (art. 51), and provisions were added to protect performers (arts. 53 and 56(d)). Further, technologies used to circumvent anti-coping measures were prohibited (art. (55)).

Patents

A new Patent Law was enacted in 1999 to comply with the TRIPS agreement obligations. In 2001, new patent regulations were introduced to help facilitate the process of filing for a patent. While the 1999 law is in compliance with the TRIPS agreement obligations, the JUSFTA (art. 4)

---

works and phonograms, even where such copies were made with the authorization of the author, performer or producer of the phonogram or a successor in interest."

[69] "Contracting Parties shall provide adequate legal protection and effective legal remedies against the circumvention of effective technological measures that are used by authors in connection with the exercise of their rights under this Treaty or the Berne Convention and that restrict acts, in respect of their works, which are not authorized by the authors concerned or permitted by law."

[70] "Contracting Parties shall provide adequate legal protection and effective legal remedies against the circumvention of effective technological measures that are used by performers or producers of phonograms in connection with the exercise of their rights under this Treaty and that restrict acts, in respect of their performances or phonograms, which are not authorized by the performers or the producers of phonograms concerned or permitted by law." The Jordanian Prime Minister issued an executive order to that effect.

[71] Jordan increased the criminal fines to JD 6,000.

introduced several new requirements in the filing of patents and regulated products, including:

1. Making available an extension of the patent term to compensate the patent holder for unreasonable curtailment of the patent term as a result of the marketing approval process (art. 4(23)). Jordan has yet to meet this requirement.
2. Committing to joining the PCT. Jordan has yet to meet this requirement.
3. Clarifying that the exclusion from patent protection of "mathematical methods" in article 4(b) of Jordan's Patent Law does not include such "methods" as business methods or computer-related inventions.[72] The Jordan Patent Office is now accepting business methods patent applications in light of this commitment.

The Jordan–European Association Agreement (JEUAA)

The JUSFTA is not the only RBT to which Jordan is a partner. The European Union signed an Association Agreement with Jordan on November 24, 1997, which was ratified by the Jordanian Parliament in September 1999 and came into effect on May 1, 2002, after being ratified by European Union countries. In November 2010, after its accession to the WTO and the signing of the FTA with the United States, which highlighted the country's commitment towards trade liberalization, Jordan was accorded advanced status with the European Union. The JEUAA gave Jordan preferential treatment in terms of the entrance of goods to the European Union.

The political and security issues within the JEUAA focused on the creation of a common ground for future cooperation, including areas of human rights, personal and public liberties, and rule of law. It emphasized dialogue and the movement towards peace, security, democracy, human rights, and regional development as an engine for change.

---

[72] Memorandum of Understanding on Issues Related to the Protection of Intellectual Property Rights Under the Agreement Between the United States and Jordan on the Establishment of a Free Trade Area, para. 5.

IPRs under the Jordan–EU Association Agreement

While the IP component of the JEUAA is not as sweeping as that of TRIPS or article 4 of the JUSFTA, it does nonetheless require Jordan to fulfil the following IPRs requirements (annex VII):

1. The Berne Convention for the protection of literary and artistic works (Paris Act, 1971)
2. The Convention for the Protection of Performers, Producers of Phonograms and Broadcasting Organizations (Rome, 1961)
3. The Nice Agreement concerning the International Classification of Goods and Services for the purposes of the Registration of Marks (Geneva Act, 1977, amended 1979)
4. The Madrid Agreement concerning the International Registration of Marks (Stockholm Act, 1967, amended 1979)
5. The Protocol relating to the Madrid Agreement concerning the International Registration of Marks (Madrid, 1989)
6. The Budapest Treaty on the International Recognition of the Deposit of Microorganisms for the purposes of Patent Procedure (1977, modified 1980)
7. The International Convention for Protection of New Varieties of Plants (UPOV, Geneva Act, 1991).

Furthermore, the JEUAA also requires Jordan to join the PCT within seven years of the ratification of the association agreement.[73] Within the JEUAA itself, article 56 and Annex VII are the provisions related to IP. Article 56 states:

[73] A PCT patent application is called an international application or PCT application. The PCT operates by allowing a single filing of an international application with a Receiving Office (RO) in one language. A search is then performed by an authorized International Searching Authority (ISA), accompanied with an International Search Report (ISR) and a written opinion regarding the patentability of the subject of the application. The International Preliminary Examining Authority (IPEA) can do an optional preliminary examination for certain states, called Elected or Designated Offices. The international search report can help the applicant to decide whether it would be worth going ahead and seeking national protection, what is called "entering the national phase" and if so, in how many countries. The PCT does not lead to the grant of an "international patent," which does not exist. The PCT member states, i.e., the Contracting States, constitute the International Patent Cooperation Union.

1. Pursuant to the provisions of this Article and of Annex VII, the Parties shall grant and ensure adequate and effective protection of intellectual, industrial and commercial property rights in accordance with the highest international standards, including effective means of enforcing such rights.
2. The implementation of this Article and of Annex VII shall be regularly reviewed by the Parties. If problems in the area of intellectual, industrial and commercial property affecting trading conditions were to occur, urgent consultation shall be undertaken, at the request of either Party, with a view to reaching mutually satisfactory solutions.

The term "highest international standards" effectively requires Jordan to adopt the highest standards available regardless of their suitability to its needs or circumstances. This could also have a direct impact on Jordan's ability to exercise its sovereignty in deciding which international treaties it will or will not join, as it is debatable whether this language obligates Jordan to ratify new treaties (e.g., the Anti-Counterfeiting Trade Agreement, ACTA) as soon as they are introduced.

Annex VII of the JEUAA stipulates the need to accede to the seven treaties listed earlier, as well as the PCT. It also requires Jordan to provide "adequate and effective protection of patents for chemicals and pharmaceuticals in line with Articles 27 to 34 of the WTO Agreement on Trade Related Aspects of IPRs, by the end of the third year from the entry into force of this Agreement or from its accession to the WTO, whichever is the earliest."

The Annex VII language is broad enough to include language that might bind Jordan to the provisions of "other multilateral conventions" in the field of intellectual, industrial and commercial property. That broad language is in line with the JEUAA's earlier reference to the term "highest international standards" of article 56. It assures that the JEUAA's language does not need to be constantly amended to reflect changes in IPRs standards. By virtue of the current Annex VII language, the Association Council may decide that the need to accede to IPRs treaties and provide effective protection of patents for chemicals and pharmaceuticals shall apply to other multilateral conventions in the IPRs field.[74]

[74] The Association Council, established under Title VIII of the JEUAA, shall consist of the members of the Council of the European Union and members of the Commission of the European Communities, on the one hand, and members of the Government of Jordan, on the other. See "Jordan–European Union Association Agreement" (1999), Title VIII, Institutional, General and Final Provisions, article

Jordan in the TRIPS-plus era

As we have seen, as Jordan moved away from an IP system that was non-compliant with international standards, it became engaged at two levels: first, through its involvement in multilateral treaties such as the WTO and the associated TRIPS agreement; second, through its involvement in the bilateral framework as represented by the JUSFTA and the JEUAA. The end result was an underestimation of the burdens and requirements of enforcement, even as those burdens ballooned with the shift to TRIPS-plus standards under the bilateral treaties framework.

There is no evidence in its legislative history to suggest that Jordan adopted TRIPS with an adequate understanding of its suitability to the local social and economic environment.[75] That conclusion is supported by the very short time it took to negotiate, sign, and ratify the JUSFTA (less than one year) as well as by the lack of public debate and input. And yet despite the implementation and enforcement issues Jordan now faced in the move from a TRIPS-minus standard to TRIPS, it then found itself engaged in a speedy transition to the even more stringent TRIPS-plus standards.

While there is no standard definition of what constitutes a TRIPS-plus system, it is generally agreed that it encompasses any obligations above and beyond the requirements set forth in the TRIPS agreement itself.[76] The components of a TRIPS-plus system, therefore, while common in demanding standards higher than TRIPS, differ in what exactly constitutes those higher standards. Under the JUSFTA, for example, Jordan committed to providing protection to plant patents, even though TRIPS allows member states to exclude those types of patents. Additionally, Jordan is required under the JEUAA to implement shorter transition periods than those demanded by TRIPS.[77] Both the JUSFTA and JEUAA demanded that Jordan join specific international agreements covering specific areas of IP, such as the WIPO's Internet Treaties,[78] the International Convention for the Protection of New Varieties of Plants

---

90(1).

[75] This point was underscored by interviewees. See appendix one.

[76] El-Said and El-Said, "TRIPS-Plus Implications for Access to Medicines."

[77] JEUAA Annex VII, para. 3, states: "Jordan undertakes to provide for adequate and effective protection of patents for chemicals and pharmaceuticals in line with Articles 27 to 34 of the WTO Agreement on Trade-Related Aspects of Intellectual Property Rights, by the end of the third year from the entry into force of this Agreement or from its accession to the WTO, whichever is the earliest."

[78] These include the WCT and the JEUAA, art. 97.

(UPOV Convention), the PCT, and the Joint Recommendation Concerning Provisions on the Protection of Well-Known Marks.

As additional examples of the added enforcement requirements, the JUSFTA stipulated that the level of IPRs penalties be adjusted, which obliged Jordan to raise the criminal penalty for copyright and trademark counterfeiting and piracy to JD 6,000.[79] It also demanded that the customs authorities initiate criminal charges in the case of copyright piracy and trademark counterfeiting, without the need for either a formal complaint by the right-holder or a court order.[80] Additionally, the JUSFTA (art. 4(6)) obliges Jordan to treat geographical indications as trademarks for the purposes of protection, registration, and implementation, even though they are distinctly treated as separate from trademarks under TRIPS.

Stronger protections for famous and well-known trademarks were expanded to include goods not similar to but identified by the famous and well-known trademarks (art. 4(7)). Stronger protection also applied to new uses for old chemicals, such that protection for "new chemical entities" shall also include protection for new uses for old chemical entities for a period of three years (art. 22). The meaning of "new uses" is not clear; it is not explicitly stated whether it refers to the use of the chemical entity alone or in combination with others, nor whether "use" refers only to a means to produce something or whether the new use of the material can be the desired end in itself. The Supreme Administrative Court had held in one of its earliest patent decisions that the use of a known material (the Arabic word for "material" also encompasses "chemical entities") to produce a known product was not considered patentable subject matter, unless the production involved an inventive step.[81]

---

[79] Memorandum of Understanding on Issues Related to the Protection of Intellectual Property Rights Under the Agreement Between the United States and Jordan on the Establishment of a Free Trade Area, art. 3, states: "with respect to article 4(25) of the Agreement, Jordan shall raise its criminal penalties to JDs 6000, so as to meet its obligation to ensure that statutory maximum fines are sufficiently high to deter future acts of infringement."

[80] JUSFTA, art. 4(26) states: "each party shall provide, at least in cases of copyright or trademark counterfeiting, that its authorities may initiate criminal sanctions amid border measure actions *ex officio*, without the need for a formal complaint by a private party or right holder."

[81] Opinion No. 3/1954 (n.d.). The court's holding is limited to the use of a known material to produce a known commodity, and does not touch on other scenarios such as the use of the known material in a new way either to produce something new, or to create a new use for the material itself.

Dispute resolution under TRIPS-plus

The JUSFTA and the JEUAA introduced dispute-resolution mechanisms that were separate from those proposed by the WTO.[82] Article 17 of the JUSFTA, which is devoted to dispute settlement, presents an elaborate scheme for handling disputes, from consultation to referral to a dispute-settlement panel. Under the JEUAA, each party is given the option to refer "to the Association Council any dispute relating to the application or interpretation of this Agreement." The arbitrators' decisions, which are taken by a majority vote, are binding on all parties, and steps must be taken by Jordan and the European Union to implement them (art. 97(4)).

The dispute-settlement mechanisms under the JUSFTA and the JEUAA are more restrictive in the venues they propose and the appeal options they provide, and, because the mechanism is collaborative and essentially unique to the needs and requirements of each dispute, there is no clear timeline as to how long a dispute can take to be resolved, unlike the much clearer DSU process. There is also little chance that the body of DSU decisions, which carries some precedential weight under the DSU process, will carry any weight under the bilateral dispute-settlement mechanism. This adds a considerable dimension of unpredictability to the dispute-resolution process and places an added premium on superior legal and dispute-settlement expertise, which usually is lacking for developing countries like Jordan. The DSU process creates a more coherent and standardized interpretation of the TRIPS agreement provisions, which are undermined by the bilateral dispute settlement panels created under the bilateral trade treaties.

Both of these dispute-resolution mechanisms bypass the WTO's dispute-resolution mechanism, and this arguably weakens the multilateral framework of the WTO.[83] This fragmentation and splintering of international trade law is a worrisome development. Developing countries, with their limited legal expertise, stand to lose the most from engaging in a bilateral dispute-resolution mechanism that has its own rules and regulations outside the scope of the WTO.

---

[82] Such as the International Center for Settlement of Investment Disputes (ICSID), the International Chamber of Commerce, and the UN Commission on International Trade Law (UNCITRAL).

[83] Drahos, "Expanding Intellectual Property's Empire."

Ever-higher standards

The term "highest international standards," as used in the JEUAA, carries with it an intrinsic and continued threat of ever-evolving requirements that can make IP standards compliance a moving target, especially since the JEUAA does not define what is meant by "highest international standards." Most likely, this ambiguity will affect not only IPRs but also related areas such as FDI and foreign aid because the inflow of aid can potentially be linked to meeting such "highest international standards."

The inclusion of the "highest international standard" language further restricts the negotiation options of developing countries because it creates a base in trade negotiations with other countries, thus ensuring that the "highest international standard" perpetuates itself.[84] This has major consequences not only to the country's own ability to determine the levels of IPRs that it deems necessary and suitable, but also potentially to other countries with whom a bilateral trade agreement is contemplated. The high standards of protection can lead neighbouring countries to compete in applying those high levels of IP protections to enhance their perceived chances in attracting foreign investments.[85]

It is not uncommon, therefore, for group of countries to urge a neighbouring country not to join an FTA that imposes higher IPRs because it might hinder regional cooperation among them. The Gulf Cooperation Council (GCC), for example, called on Bahrain to denounce or drop its FTA with the United States because of its negative effect on future cooperation within the GCC countries.[86] As such, higher international

[84] For example, the JUSFTA was the first trade agreement to incorporate provisions related to labour and environment, making it a template for future FTAs. See M. El-Said, "From TRIPS-minus to TRIPS to TRIPS-plus."

[85] I say "perceived" because economic gains from bilateral agreements are not certain at best, and overestimated at worst. A simulation study in a World Bank Report estimates that a broad global trade agreement, *à la* WTO, could increase world income by US$ 263 billion by 2015, of which US$ 109 billion would go to poor countries. If developing countries all had bilateral agreements with major trading partners (the European Union, the United States, Canada, and Japan), global income would rise by much less: US$ 112 billion. The rich countries would will scoop all this up and more: US$ 133 billion. Although a handful of developing countries, such as Brazil and China, would gain something, poor nations as a group would be worse off than they are today. World Bank, *Global Economic Prospects 2005: Trade, Regionalism, and Development* (World Bank, 2004), 149.

[86] "Bahrain Defends Right to Sign FTA with US," *Khaleej Times OnLine*, November 29, 2004. See also David Price, "The U.S.–Bahrain Free Trade Agreement and Intellectual Property Protection," *Journal of World Intellectual*

standards within an FTA with a willing country in a particular region could turn out to be a force multiplier for the whole region, because higher standards applied by a neighbouring country will set the standard for all. An FTA thus becomes an economic and political tool – both a building block and a forceful negotiating and pressuring tool.[87] Thus, the real effect of an FTA's higher IP standards has yet to be fully recognized and realized.

Conclusion

The adoption and enforcement of TRIPS-plus standards can backfire if it becomes associated with economic and technological repression and control. The potentially damaging effects of the TRIPS-plus standard and its circumvention of the WTO's DSU mechanism is thrown into even sharper relief when it is considered that one of the main features of the TRIPS agreement is its relative flexibility in providing opportunities for creative and individualistic interpretation.

The evolution of IP laws and standards that culminated in TRIPS is widely viewed as a shift in the direction of maximizing private rights over public interests. Sell and May view TRIPS as the latest episode in a long process of expansion of IP protection,[88] arguing that TRIPS has resulted in the shifting of IPRs towards monopolies of the right-holders at the expense of the public interest.

May takes this argument further, arguing that developed countries and multinational companies are pushing for the *reification* of IPRs in order to depoliticise the IP discourse, and to emphasize a technocratic policy-making approach to IPRs.[89] By "reification," May means the process of transforming an abstract idea or concept (in this case IP standards) into a

---

Property 7, no. 6 (2004): 829–850.

[87] A clear example of this is the United States' suspension of negotiations of an FTA with Egypt in response to Egypt's decision not to join the United States in a WTO complaint against the EU ban on genetically modified food. Cited by Mohammed El-Said, "From TRIPS-minus to TRIPS to TRIPS-plus."

[88] Susan Sell and Christopher May, "Moments in Law: Contestation and Settlement in the History of Intellectual Property," *Review of International Political Economy* 8, no. 3 (September 2001): 467–500.

[89] Christopher May, "The Denial of History: Reification, Intellectual Property Rights and the Lessons of the Past," *Capital & Class* 30, no. 1 (Spring 2006): 33–56. Another consequence of reification is the cementing of the "natural" status quo, such that criticism of the "natural state" becomes unnatural, which can be portrayed by MNC's and developed countries as destabilizing and even dangerous.

concrete concept that is not subject to debate in terms of the reduction of its scope or limits. Reification leads to any discussion of decreasing the limits of protection of IPRs to be considered socially unorthodox, because it contradicts entrenched expectations of ever-increasing protection for IPRs. He emphasizes that IPRs are not natural, but the result of a historical process of political-legal developments, noting that reification aims to remove the harmonization of IPRs from their proper historical context.[90]

Developing countries that adhere to the bilateral trade agreements find their coping mechanisms severely restricted, since significant legal and international experience is necessary to ensure that the interpretation is in line with the accepted norms. To reduce the monopolistic tendencies that can be fuelled by higher IPRs, Jordan would do well to use the tools it has available to combat economic concentration, including governmental controls on the prices of commodities and products (as contained in the Competition Law No. 49). Current laws allow for such controls if a commodity or product is considered a basic material as per the directions of the MoIT (art. 4(a)), or in the case of exceptional circumstances or an emergency (art. 4(b)). Such provisions would not be in contravention of either TRIPS or the JUSFTA, as both of them allow for compulsory licensing as a remedy for uncompetitive activities (art. 4(20)(a)).

The Jordanian government should also endeavour to estimate and clarify the costs associated with higher IP standards. This would be an important starting point towards the development of a national IP policy, which must be incorporated into the country's development goals. For that to happen, the debate on IP must move beyond the cliché that IP is indispensable to spur innovation and instead examine its socio-economic role. Without such understanding, Jordan will not be able to ascertain the proper levels of IP protection that actually are suitable for Jordan, and will continue to be beholden to the one-size-fits-all approach espoused under TRIPS and RBTs.

The reasons why Jordan fails to make use of the flexibilities which are provided for under TRIPS, and why it has allowed itself to move into the TRIPS-plus era, are partly to be found in a consideration of the pressures that were exerted on Jordan to join the relevant legal frameworks. These pressures, which comprise a mixture of promises, ideological framing, and economic coercion, are the subject of the following chapter.

---

[90] May, "Denial of History"; "The Hypocrisy of Forgetfulness: The Contemporary Significance of Early Innovations in Intellectual Property," *Review of International Political Economy* 14, no. 1 (2007): 1–25.

CHAPTER FOUR

PERSUASION AND COERCION

Jordan now has thirteen laws that deal directly or indirectly with IP. Some of these, such as the patent and trademark laws, contain drafting mistakes. Given the speed of its transition from a TRIPS-minus to a TRIPS framework, one might wonder whether Jordan calculated that the reputational rewards and economic benefits of passing this legislation outweighed any need for reflection on the feasibility of enforcing them.

Developing countries, particularly in the Middle East, fully understand the importance of window-dressing and lip service to donors in the areas of so-called sustainable economic development, democratization, and human rights.[1] However, it would be highly misleading to view Jordan's revision of its IPR laws as a cost-free cosmetic exercise designed to ingratiate itself with the world's major economic powers. Rather, it is important to understand the complex domestic politics of the enforcement agencies and their relationships with foreign agencies, as well as the wider socio-economic factors impacting compliance. An analytical approach based on empirical data is necessary for piecing together the network of factors which are at work here. In particular, it is crucial to understand the role of the various IP enforcement agencies and how they interact, both with each other and with donor countries. Governmental sectors such as the JISM, the JFDA, and the Patent Office clearly view the heightened enforcement of IPRs in Jordan as important to their capacity-building and their ability to continue to attract funding and support from the United States and the European Union.[2] Meanwhile, the private sector feels it is left without any benefits from this rush to heightened enforcement and additional IP standards, particularly since there is no public research and development expenditure, and the ability to imitate to help innovate is

---

[1] Emilie M. Hafner-Burton and Kiyoteru Tsutsui, "Human Rights in a Globalizing World: The Paradox of Empty Promises," *American Journal of Sociology* 110, no. 5 (March 1, 2005): 1373–1411.

[2] A point emphasized in the interviews conducted in the course of this study. See appendix one.

restricted by the very IPRs that are supposed to spur innovation. There is thus an apparent dichotomy between the attitudes of the public and private sectors. The unifying explanatory factor which underpins this dichotomy is that unless there is value to be exerted from the use of national resources for enforcement efforts, there is no national incentive to make such an effort. It is not the case that Jordan entered into the TRIPS agreement in bad faith; rather, it was largely compelled to enter, and, having done so, lacks both capacity and incentive to enforce the new legal framework.

The sources of pressure on Jordan to accede to TRIPS and TRIPS-plus standards can be loosely grouped into three. First, there are the largely ideational factors rooted in the framing of multilateral trade issues, and the shaping of discourses through development and capacity-building funding in the area of legal and economic policy. Second, there are political pressures connected to the operation of international diplomatic machinery. Third, there are the more overt economic pressures rooted in the various treaties to which Jordan is, or would wish to be, a party. This division is not entirely robust – donor aid, for instance, is certainly political, and can function both to shape mindsets and, through the threat of suspension, enforce compliance – but is useful as a way framing the discussion in the present chapter.

Ideational factors and other incentives

The influence exerted through technical assistance and capacity-building for developing countries is no less significant than the influence of economic pressures. Ideational factors such as technical assistance are important in explaining compliance and enforcement patterns. They impact and alter the terms of the debate by framing it according to the views of one side. Shadlen, Schrank, and Kurtz have shown that framing, socialization, and selective use of capacity development and trade dependency all have statistically significant effects on shaping the level of protection provided through IPRs.[3] Specifically, those ideational factors play a significant role in how developing countries understand and interpret their obligations under TRIPS or RBTs, mainly because those factors play a role by supporting a certain type of expertise to the exclusion of other types, resulting in enforcement, executive, and even legislative officials accepting the notion of stronger IP as a given.[4] Below,

---

[3] Kenneth C. Shadlen, Andrew Schrank, and Marcus J Kurtz, "The Political Economy of Intellectual Property Protection: The Case of Software," *International Studies Quarterly* 49, no. 1 (2005): 45–71.

[4] Peter Drahos, *A Philosophy of Intellectual Property* (Dartmouth Publishing Co.

we will discuss some specific factors influencing the entrenchment of higher IP standards within the Jordanian context.

Framing

The way an issue is framed determines the meanings that will be attached to it. Framing thus builds understandings and subsequently produces specific actions and solutions to be adopted later as policy.[5] This is done through the creation of focussed advocacy groups whose goal is to constantly promote and perpetuate the designation of meanings, the building of understandings, and the subsequent adoption into policy of the solutions produced as a result. Such groups gain their legitimacy by claiming that they are knowledge or expertise communities, or communities of activists such as experts, journalists, academics, and public officials, and would therefore present their views disinterestedly and objectively. Socialization by external inducements, mentioned above, is an important step in such a process. Of course, those calling for a more balanced IP system can use this approach as well.

The usual constituents of such knowledge centres are patent attorneys and lawyers, patent administrators, and other specialists who collectively play a key part in the exploitation, administration, and enforcement of the patent system. These knowledge centres are also populated with regular users of the patent system, such as pharmaceutical companies.[6] Within this system, the alignment of economic power around "objective" expertise works to frame the positions held by such experts as the conventional wisdom within regulatory agencies and throughout society.[7] This is especially true in developing countries such as Jordan, where the Patent Bar is almost non-existent and the governmental trade and industry facilities are starved of know-how and training.

The pro-IP teams' efforts in Jordan in that regard extend into the private sector through Chambers of Commerce and the funding of papers, research, and similar products that advocate their point of view,[8]

Ltd., 1996); R. Mayne, "The Global Campaign on Patents and Access to Medicines," in *Global IPRs: Knowledge, Access and Development* (Palgrave Macmillan, 2003), 244–259.

[5] Drahos, *A Philosophy of Intellectual Property*.

[6] Peter Drahos, "Biotechnology Patents, Markets and Morality," *European Intellectual Property Review* 21, no. 9 (1999): 441–449.

[7] Graham Dutfield, *IPRs, Trade and Biodiversity* (Earthscan Publications Ltd., 2002).

[8] See, for example, A. Attaran and L. Gillespie-White, "Do Patents for

sometimes even relying on donor dollars to accomplish such goals. Overall, such positions intend to link higher IP standards with innovation, economic development, integration into the world economy, and economic stability, essentially selling the idea that competitive advantage can be engineered through regulation. Even if governmental IP administrators privately hold doubts about this, the industry is always there to remind them of the argument.[9]

In parallel with this national-level approach, the United States applies considerable diplomatic pressure to ensure that any negative view of the effect of TRIPS-plus standards on development is not granted the imprimatur of any international body or organization. Examples include the pressure exerted on the World Bank in 2005 to retract and revise an analytical note examining the impact on development caused by TRIPS-plus provisions in US RBTs. Similarly, the United States called on the WHO to withdraw its sponsorship of two WHO papers, one published jointly with the South Centre addressing TRIPS flexibilities and the other published jointly with ICTSD addressing guidelines for the grant of pharmaceutical patents.[10]

WIPO, as an international organization with a vested interest in the more aggressive adoption of IP standards, played a similar role by exerting soft power through technical assistance that emphasized stronger IP protections and linked IPRs with development. All of WIPO's technical assistance, support, and publications are geared toward that goal. A perfect example is the 2003 WIPO publication titled "IP – A Power Tool for Economic Growth," which advocated the position that IP is a force for good that is not yet being used to optimal effect, particularly in the developing world.[11] The 2002 WIPO-drafted patent law for Cambodia did not even take into account any TRIPS flexibilities in its mandate for the issuing of pharmaceutical patents, even though, as a least-developed country, Cambodia was not expected to meet that requirement until 2016. The role WIPO plays by emphasizing stronger IP protections is hardly surprising, as WIPO and similar organizations have no economic incentive

---

Antiretroviral Drugs Constrain Access to AIDS Treatment in Africa?" *JAMA: The Journal of the American Medical Association* 286, no. 15 (October 17, 2001): 1886–1892.

[9] Drahos, "Biotechnology Patents."

[10] Deere, *The Implementation Game: The TRIPS Agreement and the Global Politics of Intellectual Property Reform in Developing Countries* (Oxford: Oxford University Press, 2008).

[11] Kamil Idris, *Intellectual Property – A Power Tool for Economic Growth* (World Intellectual Property Organization, 2003).

to hold a different position; similar to a patent office, they are unlikely to move in ways that diminish the size of their organizational domain (as measured by number of members and fees paid).[12]

Given this pattern of ideational reinforcement, one can have a better understanding of why developing countries in general, and Jordan in particular, leapt from pre-TRIPS to TRIPS and then to TRIPS-plus IP standards. Jordan strove, and continues to strive, almost with abandon, to promote itself as an avant-garde country on the economic front, actively embracing the new economic world order with its good governance, economic modernization, and legal reforms. This is an important reality that must be taken into account when viewing its IP legislation and enforcement efforts. The positions held by its government officials clearly point to the diffusion of pro-IP ideas through the successful framing of the issues. Statements from Jordanian officials frequently demonstrate the diffusion of pro-IP ideas within official Jordanian policy through framing – a recent example is an op-ed piece by a former MoIT minister calling for stronger enforcement of existing IP laws and linking piracy, without much explanation or proof, to the violation of Arabic cultural values.[13] The piece also pointedly mentions the risk of being listed on "watch lists" if IPRs are not adequately protected.

The effects of framing are visible in the academic literature as well. Nawafleh, for example, has called for even stronger IPRs,[14] arguing that this will increase foreign direct investment (FDI) into Jordan as well as investment in the information technology (IT) sector. He bases his views on foreign reports and reviews by agencies like USAID, and does not provide any local analysis to support his conclusions. Al-Dajani also claims that there is a link between increased FDI inflows into Jordan and Jordan's upgrading of its IP laws to TRIPS standards, over a certain period of time, but fails to substantiate it.[15] In two separate works, Sirhan and Al Sharari follow Nawafleh's trend by recommending stronger IPRs

---

[12] James Boyle, "Manifesto on WIPO and the Future of Intellectual Property," *Duke Law and Technology Review*, no. 9 (2004); Christopher May, "The World Intellectual Property Organization," *New Political Economy* 11, no. 3 (September 2006): 435–445.

[13] Jawad Anani, "IPRs," *Alghad Daily Newspaper*, November 1, 2009.

[14] A. Nawafleh, "Development of Intellectual Property Laws and Foreign Direct Investment in Jordan," *Journal of International Commercial Law and Technology* 5, no. 3 (2010): 142–153.

[15] E. M. Al-Dajani, "Post-Saddam Restructuring of Intellectual Property Rights in Iraq Through a Case Study of Current Intellectual Property Practices in Lebanon, Egypt, and Jordan," *J. Marshall Rev. Intell. Prop. L.* 6 (2006): i.

enforcement in Jordan and the allocation of more human resources to such enforcement.[16] They both see weaker IPRs leading to fewer jobs, less research and development, and increased costs in all sectors.[17] Their work, however, does not provide any basis for such a conclusion other than citing foreign scholars who have written generally about the benefits of IPRs. Such circular patterns of citation bear the marks of framing, whereby accepted wisdom is allowed to trump the lack of real evidence.

Other general, non-specific, and unsubstantiated statements about the effect of IP on investments abound, such as the declaration by the director of the National Library that "IPRs are one of the main pillars for attracting investments."[18] This position was echoed by the MoIT Undersecretary, who declared that "IP is a key requirement for attracting foreign investments."[19] Local officials and foreign donors like the United States also linked IPRs to not only economic but also social development and described it as key factor for helping society progress.[20] Observing that stronger IP had become one of the most vital issues in the modern world, the head of the largest economic free zone in Jordan, the Aqaba Special Economic Zone Authority (ASEZA), proclaimed that IP is the cornerstone of the new economic world order.[21] He stressed that IP laws were "attracting investments into Aqaba," despite the fact that at the time of his remarks, there wasn't a single IP-related investment project at ASEZA, as the vast majority of such investments were related to the real estate and tourism infrastructure.

Anti-piracy campaigns were also a major component of the pro-IP framing efforts, with the launching of periodic high-profile campaigns to

---

[16] A. A. Sirhan, "Intellectual Property and Copyright Laws and Their Impact on Digital Resources in Jordan" (n.d.); S. Al Sharari, "Intellectual Property Rights Legislation and Computer Software Piracy in Jordan," *Journal of Social Sciences* 2, no. 1 (2006): 7–13.

[17] Sirhan, "Intellectual Property and Copyright Laws and Their Impact on Digital Resources in Jordan," MS; Al Sharari, "Intellectual Property Rights Legislation and Computer Software Piracy in Jordan," *Journal of Social Sciences* 2, no. 1 (2006): 7–13.

[18] "Head of NL: IP Key for Investments," *Alghad Daily Newspaper*, April 10, 2006.

[19] Tareq Deajah, "Abiding by Intellectual Property Conditions Is Key for Attracting Foreign Investments," *Alghad Daily Newspaper*, July 15, 2009.

[20] "Joint Jordanian USAID Media Campaign Promoting IP," *Alghad Daily Newspaper*, October 2, 2005.

[21] Ahmad Rawashdeh, "IP Cornerstone of New Economic World Order," *Alghad Daily Newspaper*, June 17, 2009.

promote awareness of IPRs,[22] protect the public from the dangers of pirated products,[23] safeguard the national economy and assure its integration into the global market,[24] and pressure the government to do more to enforce IPRs.[25]

Opponents who advocate a more flexible approach to IPRs by Jordan have also engaged in their own framing efforts. They have attempted to re-frame the debate to emphasize the need for less restrictive IP standards or, at a minimum, to establish a more accommodating timeline for enforcement and compliance with registration and licensing requirements.[26] Similarly, they have pushed, with minimal success, for offering original products at reduced prices to reflect the disparity in income between the intended customer in the developed countries and the intended customer in the developing countries, specifically Jordan.[27] Such activities were sometimes undertaken in spite of a governmental decision to the contrary, as when the members of the Engineering Offices syndicate refused to abide by a decision of the Engineers Union to open their offices for inspection to ensure that software programs used by those offices were original.[28]

Overall, however, the popular efforts in Jordan to reframe the debate towards a more flexible approach to IPRs have not been as successful as those in other parts of the world, such as Africa, South America, and Southeast Asia. Similarly, not much effort is being made to reframe the debate from an intellectual point of view. The philosophical and logical basis held by the pro-IP camp is not deconstructed or seriously challenged by the Jordanian intelligentsia. Many reasons can account for such a weak effect, including the difficulty of presenting an opposing point of view in light of the government agencies' control of the mainstream media, especially if such a viewpoint runs against the national trade policies advocated by the government and the Monarch himself. This also explains the minimal coverage of IPRs issues except from the pro-IP point of view.

---

[22] "Launching of the IP Arab Day," *Alghad Daily Newspaper*, December 6, 2009.

[23] "NL Warns Public from Buying Pirated Products," *Alghad Daily Newspaper*, November 9, 2005.

[24] Rawashdeh, "IP Cornerstone."

[25] Omar Obeidat, "Jordan Should Do More to Combat Piracy," *The Jordan Times*, February 14, 2010.

[26] "Engineering Offices Demand IP Law Postponement," *Alghad Daily Newspaper*, January 23, 2007.

[27] "Agreement to Supply Software Programs at Discount," *Alghad Daily Newspaper*, April 25, 2007.

[28] "Engineering Offices Protest Union's Decision," *Alghad Daily Newspaper*, September 12, 2007.

Another significant factor in the weakness of the counter-currents is that one of the main areas of global convergence for popular opposition to stricter IP standards has been agricultural liberalization and traditional knowledge. This is not a prominent issue in Jordan, as it imports the majority of its grains and does not have any significant traditional knowledge. Thus, neither the agricultural sector nor notions of Jordanian tradition were available to act as a foundation for the development of critical voices. In addition, a general lack of understanding of IP issues on the behalf of the legislators helped push several changes to IP laws through the legislature without much analysis or discussion, and has contributed to the lack of a point of view counter to the pro-IP camp. Further, the laws for the WTO accession and the JUSFTA were passed under the executive authority of the King while parliament was dissolved, without much public debate or involvement. Finally, the technical and financial support that the donor countries and multi-national companies provide for pro-intellectual-property Jordanian NGOs (e.g., JIPA) and Jordanian professional organizations (e.g., the JPMA) helps such entities to promote the pro-IP point of view to a credulous public.

The very obvious involvement of foreign donor organizations and state-sponsored aid agencies (e.g., USAID) in the efforts to promote and publicize the importance of meeting IPRs signals the use of agreements such as the JUSFTA as tools of foreign policy.[29] As Weintraub puts it, an RBT is seen not necessarily as "an agreement in which all parties benefit from trade expansion, but rather a favour to be bestowed based on support of US foreign policy."[30] In that context, for a small country like Jordan, stringent IP laws are simply part of the price to be paid for good foreign relations with the world's most powerful countries.

Monitoring and capacity building

Monitoring and capacity building present a mutually supportive approach for influencing enforcement of IP standards. They allow for the pressuring of individual countries on TRIPS implementation through monitoring, while at the same time influencing that implementation through the ideational and economic power of capacity building.

---

[29] On the relationship between RBTs and political security, see Lloyd Gruber, *Ruling the World: Power Politics and the Rise of Supranational Institutions.* (Princeton University Press, 2000).

[30] Sidney Weintraub, "The Politics of US Trade Policy," http://news.bbc.co.uk/2/hi/business/3169649.stm, accessed February 16, 2010.

In the case of Jordan, the broad spectrum of capacity development tools included legislative and policy advice (as when the patent and trademark laws were amended after the JUSFTA accession to incorporate references to the PCT and the Madrid protocol), training and technical development, and support for enforcement at the institutional level. Such programs, however, support a one-size-fits-all solution and do not take into account Jordan's stage of development as an indicator of the appropriate forms of IPRs protection.[31] Overall, those programs focus on "best practices" and aim to reorient Jordan's legal and enforcement regime in line with TRIPS, although Jordan has no expertise or tradition in the IP field commensurate with the level of TRIPS sophistication. The best-practices approach, which aims to reorient Jordan's legal and enforcement regime, reflects a global model in the use of capacity development as a tool for political and ideological re-orientation, as the capacity development programmes emphasize standard solutions for enforcement and compliance, with countries' specific circumstances accorded weight only where this does not conflict with "best practice."[32]

The US Special 301 Report process, discussed in detail later in this chapter, represents one of the most important examples of the use of monitoring to influence enforcement, and its approach is mirrored by the European Union's "IP Enforcement" surveys. Those surveys build on the EU Commission's "Strategy for the Enforcement of IPRs in Third Countries,"[33] with the goal of setting out a list of priority countries in which the counterfeiting and piracy of IPRs remains a serious problem that should be the focus for future EU work. This strategy, the EU Commission states, is not meant to "impose unilateral solutions" or to propose a "one-size-fits-all approach to promoting IPRs enforcement"; rather, it is intended to identify "a limited number of countries on which the efforts of the Commission in the framework of the present strategy should be concentrated." Another stated goal is to assure the meeting of the "very high standard of protection of IP (including the enforcement thereof)" included in the numerous bilateral agreements established by the European Commission. The EU Commission then states, in a clear coupling of monitoring and capacity building, that, since most such agreements also

---

[31] This point was emphasized in several of the interviews conducted for this study. See appendix one.

[32] May, "The World Intellectual Property Organization."

[33] Directorate General of Trade, *Strategy for the Enforcement of IPRs in Third Countries*, Commission Communication (Brussels: European Commission (EC), 2004).

include a clause allowing for technical cooperation in the area of IP, "those clauses must be carefully monitored and effectively implemented."

In addition to the formal governmental monitoring discussed above, industry lobbyists and groups conduct and publish their own lists of rankings and reports, according to their sector-specific goals, which cover, for example, the pharmaceutical industry through PhRMA, the software industry through the BSA, and general IP protection through the IIPI.[34] Their findings are widely publicized and often find their way into the Special 301 Report.

The WTO has its own monitoring approach through the Trade Policy Review Mechanism (TPRM), which is intended to monitor the "adherence by all Members to rules, disciplines and commitments made under the Multilateral Trade Agreements and, where applicable, the Plurilateral Trade Agreements."[35] Such monitoring is intended to occur through a Trade Policy Review Body, which "will subject the trade policies and practices of all Members to periodic review."

For a TPRM meeting, the WTO member under review should provide written answers, by the beginning of the review meeting, to questions submitted at least two weeks before the meeting. Questions posed subsequently should be answered, to the extent possible, before the start of the second session of the meeting. For Jordan's first TPRM, held November 10–12, 2008, the following delegations submitted questions in writing: Brazil, Taiwan, Penghu, Kinmen and Matsu (Chinese Taipei), Colombia, Argentina, Japan, the Republic of Korea, the United States, and China. Written questions by Canada, the European Community, and India were submitted after the two-week deadline.[36]

Effectively, this review process increases the oversight of TRIPS implementation, placing further pressures on Jordan to implement stronger enforcement measures. Collectively, this process places an emphasis on compliance by giving other WTO members the opportunity to voice concerns on issues that they perceive as still lacking proper implementation or clarification, including the status of IP laws. A significant portion of the questions in Jordan's TPRM came from developing countries, such as Brazil, Colombia, Argentina, Korea, and India, but the most detailed questions came from the United States, Canada, and the European Community. For example, the United States

---

[34] Annual reports by those organizations are available on their websites.

[35] Agreement Establishing the World Trade Organization, Annex 3: Trade Policy Review Mechanism, 1994.

[36] *Trade Policy Review, 10 and 12 November 2008 – Jordan*, Minutes of Meeting (World Trade Organization, December 19, 2008).

posed questions about the creation of an "IPRs entity" for enforcement with regards Jordan's progress in increasing its courts' specialization (especially their ability to try IP cases), and about the status of amendments to the Copyright, JISM, and Trademark Laws.[37] Questions posed by Canada included a request for more information on exclusions from patentability under Jordanian law, the compulsory licensing amendments of Jordanian Patent Law, and the Jordanian courts' handling of cases covering "famous trademarks."

Overall, therefore, the TPRM serves as an additional tool for scrutiny, which the developed countries seem to be using adroitly, thus making it harder for Jordan to conceal weaknesses in enforcement and compliance and forcing it to confront those issues in a global forum on a regular basis. This process plays a role in shaping Jordan's enforcement and compliance by keeping such issues at the forefront of Jordan's review process.

Donor funding

Jordan's excessive dependence on donor support affords a clear opportunity for donors to exert undue influence on policy decisions. Jordan uses donor funds to maintain not only discretionary spending on projects supported by those donors, but also to support the national budget and thus the overall national debt levels.[38] Thus, donor funding has steadily grown to become a fixture in the annual budget preparation process in Jordan.[39] Of course, this dependence makes Jordan susceptible to the agendas presented by donors in return for their largesse. It also lends an inflexibility to national policy making and political alliance building which can cause considerable harm.[40]

---

[37] WTO Press Release, "Trade Policy Review: Jordan – Continued Reform would Help an Already Strong Economic Performance," November 10, 2008.

[38] Overall foreign aid to Jordan in the period 1999–2008 was $9.1 billion, with the United States providing 47% of that amount, followed by the EU, Japan, and Germany at 9%, 5%, and 4.3% respectively. Of the total foreign aid, 64% comes in the form of grants and the remainder in the form of long-term loans. See Mohammed Khresat, "More Foreign Aid Expected," *Alghad Daily Newspaper*, May 16, 2009.

[39] The United States provides Jordan with regular annual economic foreign aid of $370 million and military aid of $150 million. See "Jordan to Receive $150 million more in Military Aid," *Alghad Daily Newspaper*, February 15, 2010.

[40] Deborah Bräutigam, "Foreign Aid and the Politics of Participation in Economic Policy Reform," *Public Administration and Development* 20, no. 3 (August 1, 2000): 253–264.

While resource-poor MENA countries' dependence on donor support is common, for many years Jordan has been skilful in masking this behind figures of economic growth, such as the rise in GDP and national economic growth figures, which it claimed to show that it was not dependent on donor aid. This concealment came to an abrupt end with the onset of the global economic crisis in 2008–2010. The collapse of donor funding over the 2009–2010 period was expected to cause the budget deficit in 2010 to go up to JD 1.105 billion ($1.6 billion), or 8% of the GDP (up from 5.5% the previous year),[41] and the national debt level to rise by 12.9% by the end of 2010, to JD 9.66 billion (compared to JD 8.55 billion in 2008), or 62% of the GDP.[42] The collapse of donor funding clarified the relationship between the levels of donor funding and the national fiscal policy in Jordan, as 50% of foreign grants in 2010 were used to support budgetary items.[43] The high level of donor funding also provided support to the claims that such funding has been playing an important role in shaping national policies and strategies, including the enforcement and implementation of IP laws.

Using donor aid to influence IPRs, however, is not a recent or accidental development, and the WTO itself called on developed countries to assist developing countries in their implementation of TRIPS (TRIPS, Chap. 3). In Jordan's case, the United States, through its Patent and Trademark Office and USAID, was heavily involved in the provision of technical assistance in the area of IPRs. The majority of the training courses in the field of IP for 2008 occurred in the United States.[44] Overall, 150 trainees from Jordan attended courses in the United States, compared to thirty trainees who attended courses in the rest of the world. This is in line with the US Government's efforts to design its financed technical assistance to help put TRIPS-plus standards in place across a range of developing countries, including Jordan. It is also in line with comments made by officials in Jordan, which clearly pointed to a training agenda focused by the United States and the European Union on the provision of technical assistance in the areas of "best practices" and enforcement with little or no focus on flexibilities.[45] A new US foreign aid agency was

---

[41] "Gov't Issues JD160m Budget Supplement," *Jordan Times*, March 3, 2010.

[42] Omar Obeidat, "Income Tax Revenues to Drop in 2010," *Jordan Times*, March 1, 2010.

[43] Khalid Neimat, "Half of Foreign Grants to Support Budget," *Jordan Times*, February 23, 2010.

[44] Jordanian Judicial Council, *Annual Courts Report – 2008* (Jordanian Judicial Council, 2008).

[45] A point emphasized in interviews. See appendix one.

created in February 2004 to administer the Millennium Challenge Account (MCA) initiative. The MCA is intended to concentrate significantly higher amounts of US resources in a few low and low-middle income countries, including Jordan, that have demonstrated a strong commitment to political, economic, and social reforms.

The agendas behind the technical assistance provided by developed countries, international organizations, and multi-national corporations have not gone unnoticed. Such agendas were branded as biased towards compliance-oriented policies, which encourage the broadening of IPRs protections regardless of specific needs and circumstances.[46] Critics have questioned the neutrality of international organizations like WIPO and UPOV.[47]

With IP technical expertise within the Jordanian governmental entities strongly influenced by the technical assistance, training, support, and other services provided by international donors, its positions on implementation of IP standards are vulnerable to the donors' points of view. The bulk of donor resources to Jordan in the IP area are channelled towards public campaigns or training to further enforcement activities rather than towards commercializing technology or inventions. This shows that the donors are more interested in protecting their own IP interests than in introducing IPRs to promote innovation. Further, the actual drafting of IP laws, which was influenced by the above dynamic, is not consistent with the economic and technological levels within Jordan, and the IP laws do not meet local economic interests. All of the above perpetuates ignorance towards them and makes the process of enforcement exceedingly difficult.

For Jordan, the adage applies that whoever takes the King's shilling must do the King's bidding. Its dependency on foreign aid is forcing it to move in the same direction as its donors, toward tighter IP standards and an ever-expanding enforcement role for the governmental agencies. Given that the national economic model is heavily dependent on foreign aid, one cannot seriously expect an objective governmental review of the realities of IP legislation and obligations in Jordan.

---

[46] UNCTAD, *UNCTAD Least Developed Countries Report 2007. Chapter 3 – Intellectual Property Rights and Other Incentive Mechanisms for Learning and Innovation*, n.d.

[47] UPOV Secretary-General Barry Greengrass, for example, was criticized over UPOV's aggressive approach to promoting plant variety protection and for the way it recruited new members to the Convention, which Jordan joined on September 24, 2004. See Deere, *The Implementation Game*.

Political pressures

Before moving on to examine overt financial pressures, it is worth looking in more detail at two other modes in which the developed world has operated in order to induce compliance from developing countries as regards IPRs. Falling between "soft" pressures such as framing and donor funding, and the openly financial, these can best be classed as political pressures. They concern the ways in which developed countries have been able to shift the forum of negotiation of IP issues so as to gain a coercive advantage, and the way issues of IPRs have become enmeshed in a wider – and perhaps unexpected – range of issues.

Forum shifting

We have already noted that developed countries, aware of the developing countries' growing attempts to counter the strengthening of TRIPS through the WTO, shifted the debate to where the developing countries' ability for collective, and therefore, effective action was weakest. This "forum-shifting" occurred as the developed countries pushed their expansive agenda across multilateral organizations that were less resistant to it. For patents, that agenda has three components: (i) ratification of the Patent Law Treaty, (ii) amendment of the PCT, and (iii) a new Substantive Patent Law Treaty (SPLT) to supplement the substantive obligations contained in TRIPS.[48] All three components would place considerable compliance requirements on Jordan, forcing it to more readily accept foreign patents and give them equal protection under Jordanian law, without having the necessary infrastructure to properly examine them, as Jordan currently relies on WIPO to review patent applications.

The developed countries' frustration with the level of progress on those issues prompted them to intensify their efforts towards substantive patent harmonization by bypassing more experienced representatives in Geneva and going directly to the capitals of developing countries,[49] as well as by seeking former developing country officials to participate in the advancement of that agenda.[50] For Jordan, the top political leadership

[48] C. Correa and S. Musungu, "The WIPO Patent Agenda: The Risks for Developing Countries" (South Center, November 2002).

[49] "Clash Continues on U.S.–Central America Trade Deal," *Intellectual Property Watch*, March 1, 2005.

[50] "India Joins Opposition To Casablanca Patent Meeting Outcome," *Intellectual Property Watch*, April 10, 2005, http://www.ip-watch.org/weblog/2005/04/10/india-joins-opposition-to-casablanca-patent-meeting-outcome/.

often met with the USTR during its visits to Jordan, and the USTR often pays annual visits to Jordan during which it tours various facilities and meets high-ranking officials.[51] Jordan has been under intense pressure by the USTR to amend its Customs Law to give border agents the capacity to initiate legal action *sue sponte* even if the right-holder does not.[52]

The proliferation of international organizations and forums that deal with, and aim to impact, the level of IP standards regulation has resulted in the growing complexity, and therefore the weakening, of the global IP system. This is because the ability of international organizations to extend harmonized IP standards has been decreased, and therefore the likelihood of their global adoption has been weakened.[53] Even when such adoption took place, the added complexity made the enforcement and compliance process at the national level more difficult.

As a result, the developing countries have sought assistance from international donors and NGOs to meet their compliance requirements, creating a major conflict of interest; most of those international donors and some of the NGOs had vested interests in promoting the rights-holder's positions and therefore influenced the developing countries' policies to that effect. Jordan is one of the examples where such conflicts existed for both international donors and local NGOs, such as the Jordan IP Association (JIPA), which is funded or sponsored by rights-holders. In contrast, NGO work on IPRs in developed countries has advocated a more cautious approach to IP standard-setting and often called for a full review of TRIPS to address its impact on development.[54] Questioning the claimed economic benefits of the increased IP standards is one of the glaring omissions of the economic and legal discussion in Jordan over the past decade.

---

[51] Office of the United States Trade Representative, "USTR Team Holds Meetings in Jordan," September 30, 2009, http://www.ustr.gov/about-us/press-office/press-releases/2009/september/ustr-team-holds-meetings-jordan-discuss-labor-ri.

[52] Tawfiq Tabbaa, *Update on Compliance with IPRs in Jordan*, Improved Economic Opportunities For Jordanians (USAID – Sustainable Achievement for Business Expansion and Quality (SABEQ), February 14, 2007).

[53] Carolyn Deere-Birkbeck, "Reforming Governance to Advance the WIPO Development Agenda," in *Implementing the World Intellectual Property Organization's Development Agenda*, ed. J. de Beer (Waterloo, ON: Wilfred Laurier University Press, 2009).

[54] An example of that trend is the work done by the South Center and the Center for International Environmental Law (CIEL).

IP's expanding connectedness

The branching out of the IP standard-setting battles ultimately led to making IP a component in areas traditionally beyond the realm of the classic IP laws, including patent, copyright, and trademarks. This has made the definition of IP more expansive, made the negotiations in those newer areas more complex, and added enforcement requirements where previously there were none. For example, IP debates arose during the efforts to finalize a treaty for the management of plant genetic resources at the UN Food and Agriculture Organization (FAO).[55] Similarly, the United States tried and failed to derail a UNESCO document on cultural diversity that the United States alleged "could be used by other countries to construct trade barriers to US exports of film, music or other cultural products."[56] Along the way, the United States sought to include in the UNESCO document more than a dozen references to IPRs but was prevented from doing so by developing countries.

This intermingling of IP standards within areas that would usually not have been associated with them is a tool that, in the case of Jordan, was used to influence changes in policy on several fronts. Whereas the enforcement of the JUSFTA's IP standards is a mainstay of the discussions between the United States and the Jordanian governments, the JUSFTA also included articles on labour and environmental policy – the first of their kind in any RBT signed by the US Government.[57] Over the past decade since the signing of the JUSFTA, not only have IP issues arisen between the two countries, but disputes on the issues of rights of workers and the quality of environmental standards have also surfaced. In an example of strategic manipulation, the United States has shifted pressure for compliance and enforcement from one area to another (labour to environment to IP); as a result, an enforcement dispute in one area is swiftly linked to enforcement issues in other areas. For example, the issue of better working circumstances for workers within Jordanian industrial areas allowed to export to the US market, known as QIZ (Qualified Industrial Zones), was linked to the enforcement of a prohibition on the sale of knock-off products in the local market by the same QIZ entities.[58]

---

[55] Geoff Tansey and Tasmin Rajotte, *The Future Control of Food* (Earthscan, 2008).

[56] "US 'Pulls Out All Stops' as UNESCO Backs Culture Treaty," *Intellectual Property Watch*, October 17, 2005.

[57] JUSFTA art. 5 deals with the environment and art. 6 deals with labour issues.

[58] International Labour Organization, "Forced Labour and Trafficking in Jordan – A Pilot Programme on the Qualified Industrial Zones," Project, March 1, 2009,

Similarly, the push for the enforcement of environmental standards is often coupled with calls to regulate low-cost factories that also produce what are considered infringing goods.[59]

The relationship between IP and human rights, similar to the QIZ situation discussed above, has also been steadily growing globally. In 1998, to commemorate the fiftieth anniversary of the proclamation of the Universal Declaration of Human Rights, WIPO, in collaboration with the United Nations Office of the High Commissioner for Human Rights (OHCHR) Mary Robinson, organized a Panel Discussion that linked IP and human rights. The OHCHR remarks linked the concepts of "non-discrimination" and "national treatment" to concepts of human rights, thus asking that indigenous peoples and local communities are consulted and notified by companies and researchers, and their consent sought.[60] That ushered in the increased interest of the international human rights community in IP issues, and several NGOs subsequently highlighted areas of conflict between TRIPS and human rights as part of their examination of the human rights implications of the different facets of economic globalization.[61] In 2001, the OHCHR issued a report on the impact of TRIPS on human rights, with special attention to access to medicine. Other UN bodies, like the United Nation's Committee on the Rights of the Child, also followed suit and issued recommendations regarding the impact of FTAs and TRIPS on public health, emphasizing the need to assure that implementation does not impact the health of the poor or their access to medication.[62]

The growing prominence of the social and economic effects of IP standards turned the question of controlling the international IP organizations into a major issue in its own right and further influenced the

---

http://www.ilo.org/sapfl/Projects/lang--en/WCMS_104023/index.htm.

[59] "Ministry of Environment Signs MoU with U.S. Embassy," *Alghad Daily Newspaper*, October 23, 2008.

[60] Mary Robinson, "Opening address by Mr. Brian Burdekin on Behalf of Mrs. Mary Robinson, United Nations High Commissioner for Human Rights," *WIPO*, 1998.

[61] The report was titled "Globalization and Human Rights" and the NGOs were the Lutheran World Federation, Habitat International Coalition, and the International Commission of Jurists.

[62] See, for example, "Access to Affordable Drugs: Victims of HIV/AIDS Should Not Suffer From Trade Rules, Press Release," October 2004, and "Access to Affordable Drugs: A Right no FTA Can Ignore," Press Release, May 2004. For a more comprehensive list of these and other publications, see http://www.3dthree.org/en/page.php?IDpage=26&IDcat=5 and http://www.3dthree.org/en/page.php?IDpage=13&IDcat=5.

developed countries' push for forum shifting to avoid places where their ideas were strongly challenged. One of the first victims of this approach was WIPO, which was increasingly attacked by developing countries and civil-society activists who accused WIPO of not providing sufficient technical assistance on the issue of flexibilities within TRIPS and called upon WIPO to abandon its current culture of expanding monopoly privileges without regard to social cost.[63] WIPO was criticized for its "faith-based" approach for ever-stronger IP protection driven by special interests and right-holders.[64] The implication was that WIPO was no longer regarded as a neutral arbiter but rather as an institution with its own agenda,[65] which further intensified the call by developing countries for a new WIPO Development Agenda, first advocated in 2004 by Argentina and Brazil, who were later joined by thirteen other Friends of Development developing countries.

At the centre of that Development Agenda was the call to decelerate the continued push for ever-stronger IP standards and to address the Development Agenda's co-sponsors' needs.[66] The Development Agenda sought to re-orient WIPO towards a more development-focused set of concerns, and set out the argument that the effort to protect and enforce IPRs cannot be seen as an end in itself.[67] The Development Agenda also detailed a list of complaints that were supported by NGOs and other civil-society institutions, including poor recruitment practices of IP technical cooperation providers, conflicts of interest, low-quality seminars, and biased content training programs.[68] The Development Agenda eventually bore some fruit for its advocates in 2007, when WIPO adopted a series of recommendations related to it and suspended the new SPLT.[69] But it

---

[63] Lawrence Kogan, "Brazil Challenges the Established Global IPR Framework," 2006, http://findarticles.com/p/articles/mi_qa5479/is_1-2_8/ai_n29431940/pg_26/.
[64] Boyle, "Manifesto on WIPO."
[65] May, "The World Intellectual Property Organization."
[66] WIPO (2004), proposal by Argentina and Brazil for the Establishment of a Development Agenda for WIPO.
[67] May, "The World Intellectual Property Organization."
[68] See for example Medecins Sans Frontieres, "MSF: Doha Derailed: Technical 'Assistance' – A Case of Malpractice?" (2004); Sisule Musungu, *Designing Development-oriented Intellectual Property Technical Assistance Programmes* (ICTSD-UNCTAD Dialogue, 2nd Bellagio Series on Development and Intellectual Property, 2003), http://ictsd.org/i/ip/24504/.
[69] William New, "WIPO Launches New Agenda on IP And Development," *Intellectual Property Watch*, 2007.

seems that much of the implementation of the Development Agenda will require reforming WIPO's governance.[70]

Economic pressures

The discussion so far has centred on the role of ideational and persuasive factors in influencing Jordan to adopt TRIPS and TRIPS-plus standards, even in the face of evidence that such standards would afford little benefit. We turn now to more overt economic pressures. Throughout the process of acceding to TRIPS, economic incentives were applied both on a multilateral (i.e., WTO) and bilateral level. As we have noted in previous chapters, the most important development in IP standard-setting since the adoption of TRIPS has been the advance of the RBT system. Though this system pre-dates TRIPS in its conception, it has taken on a different role in the post-TRIPS era. The rise of RBTs has led to the imposition of even stricter IP laws on developing countries while at the same time being emblematic of a transformation of the global political and economic system.

Pre-TRIPS unilateral enforcement: Special 301 Reports

From the mid-1970s to the early 1980s, both the United States and the European Union made efforts to strengthen their trade laws, which included stronger IP protection. As their trade relations with developing countries expanded, it was only natural that stronger protections were pushed on those developing countries as well. The 1974 amendment of section 337 of the US Trade Law allowed the US Government to take unilateral action against foreign products in ways that violated the IPRs held under US laws.[71] This unilateral approach had its drawbacks, not least of which were the conflicts that arose between the language of section 337 and the requirements under the GATT. Reports were issued finding that certain aspects of section 337 violated the national treatment provision contained in article III of GATT, thus prompting subsequent amendments.[72]

---

[70] Deere-Birkbeck, "Reforming Governance."

[71] Section 337 of the Tariff Act of 1930 is a unique provision in US trade law permitting the US International Trade Commission (ITC) to investigate complaints brought by private parties in order to determine whether imported articles should be barred from entering the United States.

[72] Bryan Schwartz, "The Fate of Section 337 Litigation after the Uruguay Round Agreements Act," *Law and Policy in International Business* 27 (1995); Lisa Barons, "Amending Section 337 to Obtain GATT Consistency and Retain Border

In 1984, the US Congress authorized the US administration, through Sections 301 and 305 of the US Trade and Tariff Act, to link the benefits it offered its trading partners to their performance in the area of IP protection, and to link US trade negotiations objectives with its IP interests.

Section 301 and its so-called Special Provisions specifically authorized the USTR to specify priority countries that failed to make sufficient progress in negotiations with it and to initiate investigations that could lead to remedial action, which ranged from the use of monitoring to the threat of actual imposition of trade sanctions. The USTR's Special 301 Report reflects the annual review of the IP practices of the US trade partners, identifying countries that, in the USTR's opinion, failed to provide adequate IP protection or fair and equitable access to markets for US nationals relying on IP.

Given the broad scope of authority assumed by the Special 301 Report provisions, as well as their explicit extraterritoriality, it should come as little surprise that their legality has been debated by trade scholars. Such extraterritoriality, scholars argue, is "highlighted by the fact that it does not refer to any sense of norm or principles in order to define adequate IP protection among US trade partners – the implicit assumption being that any level of protection inferior to that provided by US law is unfair trade practice."[73] The absence of any set of standards according to which IP protection is defined has drawn criticism because it implies that standards can be assigned according to the wishes of the reviewer (i.e., the USTR) and quite possibly can be judged against the levels of protection provided under US law. The resulting outcry does not seem to have caused the USTR to revise its approach in preparing the Special 301 Report. In effect, this means that there is no set definition of applicable standards for the Report except those under the Report itself. The end result is that "non-compliant" countries continue to be threatened with retaliatory action, including aid reduction.

For Jordan, this has meant that IP compliance has become a moving target that gets shifted and refocused based on the requirements of the Special 301 Report, as Jordan annually attempts to avoid being listed as non-compliant. The absence of objective standards in the Special 301 Report and the resulting ad hoc governmental reaction to its pronouncements have also had the negative effect of draining the energy

---

Protection," *Law and Policy in International Business* 22 (1991).

[73] M. J. Trebilcock and Robert Howse, *The Regulation of International Trade* (Routledge, 2005).

out of the calls for a national IP strategy.[74] Because the goal of avoiding getting listed on the Special 301 Report has become the main drive for shaping the national policy on IP, Jordan has had little policy incentive to think about the long-term implications of IP on its economic and developmental goals.

The Special 301 reports are not the only tool used to secure compliance from the United States' trading partners. There have been instances when private investors were successful in obtaining concessions from their joint venture partners that the US Government, Section 301 notwithstanding, had been unable to secure.[75] At the same time, research has shown that the substance and timing of the US policies that induced changes to improve IP protection in targeted countries can be explained as the product of a strategy of coercion, including the use of Special 301 Report powers.[76] This strategy, which exemplifies the asymmetry in economic power between developed and developing countries, uses Special 301 Report powers to draw targeted countries to the negotiations table, while at the same time requiring that stronger IP standards be agreed to in exchange for greater market access. This strategy goes hand in hand with the use of RBTs. A country targeted for a bilateral trade agreement is often pre-listed on the Priority Watch List, as was the case with Jordan, thus placing it at risk of trade sanctions or the withdrawal of unilateral trade preferences. The carrot side of the strategy consists of being removed from the Priority Watch List or, at a minimum, being downgraded from the Priority Watch List to the Watch List. Jordan is a classic example of that strategy; it was listed on the Watch List of the Special 301 Report but was removed in 2000, when it agreed to TRIPS-plus standards incorporated within the JUSFTA.

RBTs as the continuation of the Special 301 Report by other means

RBTs such as the JUSFTA and the JEUAA are among the most potent tools for encouraging developing countries to adopt TRIPS-plus

---

[74] A point noted in the interviews conducted for this study. See appendix one.

[75] Susan K. Sell, *Power and Ideas: North–South Politics of Intellectual Property and Antitrust* (SUNY Press, 1998), citing the example of Texas, IBM, and Microsoft's use of licensing agreements with local Taiwan industries for the production of computer hardware, software, and chip production.

[76] Alan O. Sykes, "Constructive Unilateral threats in International Commercial Relations: The Limit Case for Section 301," *Law & Policy in International Business* 23, no. 2 (1992): 263–330.

standards.[77] Both are model agreements in this regard, as their terms include obligations to accede to specific international agreements, decrease copyright requirements, expand patent coverage to new subject matter, and (under the ultimate catch-all requirement used in the JEUAA) adopt the "highest international standards." One example of these TRIPS-plus standards for IP is the JEUAA's requirement, in addition to the "highest international standards" requirement, that Jordan provide patent protection for chemicals and pharmaceuticals two years earlier than required under TRIPS.[78]

The expansive approach of the Special 301 Report regulations is further augmented by the United States' approach of incorporating IP standards and provisions in its RBTs. The European Union has followed the same route, but it thus far lacks a platform similar to the USTR's Special 301 Report that allows it to bring to the fore, on an annual basis, countries that are not in compliance with those provisions. In the European Union's RBTs, IP provisions are less prominently featured than those typically used by the United States, which tend to be much more detailed. Yet the language used by the European Union is equally effective.

Section 4 of the JUSFTA, which covers IP, is the longest section of the agreement and touches upon several areas of IPRs, as well as enforcement measures and transition periods. The JEUAA, on the other hand, devotes less space to IP provisions but states that Jordan and the European Union shall abide by the "highest international standards" to ensure the adequate and effective protection of IPRs. The JEUAA's IP provisions, therefore, are more subtly inserted but no less significant in scope, and actually are more open-ended by virtue of the use of the term "highest international standards," creating an open ceiling for enforcement and implementation efforts. The European Union has ridden the coattails of aggressive IP provisions introduced by the United States, "sometimes sending in negotiators to conclude a bilateral agreement on IP with a developing

[77] In certain cases such as China, the United States signed a series of bilateral agreements prior to China's accession to the WTO, undoubtedly influenced by the size of the Chinese market. The first such agreement was the 1992 Sino–American Memorandum of Understanding on the Protection of Intellectual Property. See also Andrew Mertha and Robert Pahre, "Patently Misleading: Partial Implementation and Bargaining Leverage in Sino-American Negotiations on IPRs," *International Organization* 59, no. 3 (2005): 695–729.

[78] Article 3 of Annex VII of the JEUAA called for such protection either within three years of the JEUAA coming into force or Jordan's accession to the WTO, whichever came earliest.

country after US negotiators had brought that country to the negotiating table using the 301 process."[79]

The overall result of the United States and European Union's bilateral trade agreements with Jordan is to make IPRs standards more stringent and to move Jordan firmly into the TRIPS-plus era. The progression from pre-TRIPS to TRIPS to TRIPS-plus standards exemplifies a "take and demand" approach by the developed countries. On the one hand, TRIPS was supposed to represent the universe of IPRs regulation. On the other, developing countries are asked to sign RBTs containing TRIPS-plus provisions even though most of them have yet to fully implement the TRIPS standards in the first place.

The consequences of this assault on TRIPS provisions from an enforcement point of view could not be more distorting and confusing, as TRIPS-plus encroaches even on the modest flexibilities allowed under TRIPS. An additional consequence of the expanding universe of the RBT's IP provisions is the limiting of the developing countries' ability to tailor their IP laws to national priorities at a reduced cost.[80] The adoption of country-specific IP regulations and enforcement models became markedly more difficult as a result of Jordan's speedy move from TRIPS to TRIPS-plus. By signing an RBT with the United States and the European Union shortly after adopting TRIPS, Jordan was robbed of the opportunity to obtain a sound understanding of the economic and social effects of the somewhat flexible TRIPS provisions before embarking on the more rigid TRIPS-plus provisions.

RBTs negotiated by the United States and the European Union indicate that they both view the "minimum standards" of TRIPS as the beginning, rather than the end, of the road towards higher standards.[81] The United States, it seems, has altogether abandoned the WTO forum as a venue for accomplishing a more stringent IP standards goal and instead shifted to the forum provided through the bilateral and multilateral RBTs.[82] The direct

[79] Peter Drahos and R. Mayne, eds., "Negotiating IPRs: Between Coercion and Dialogue," in *Global IPRs: Knowledge Access and Development* (Basingstoke: Palgrave Macmillan, 2002), 161–182.

[80] Susan K. Sell, *Private Power, Public Law: The Globalization of Intellectual Property Rights* (Cambridge University Press, 2003).

[81] Ken Shadlen, "Globalisation, Power and Integration: The Political Economy of Regional and Bilateral Trade Agreements in the Americas," *Journal of Development Studies* 44, no. 1 (January 2008): 1–20.

[82] The US signed two FTAs before 2000 (Israel and NAFTA), and nine FTAs as of that year (Jordan 2001, Australia 2004, Chile 2004, Singapore 2004, Bahrain 2006, Morocco 2006, Oman 2006, Peru 2007, Dominican Rep.–Central America Free Trade Agreement 2005).

consequence from an economic perspective is the ability of MNCs to further cement the "original" status of their products in foreign markets by using the local legal system to pursue infringers. Furthermore, TRIPS-plus brought added protections above and beyond those under TRIPS, which would otherwise have been impossible to negotiate into TRIPS through the WTO. From an enforcement perspective, the end goal of meeting the compliance requirements for TRIPS is made into a moving target by virtue of TRIPS-plus standards. The developing economic status of the majority of countries that have entered into RBTs with the United States since 2000 (Jordan 2001, Singapore 2003, Australia 2004, Chile 2004, Bahrain 2006, Morocco 2006, Oman 2006, Peru 2007, Dominican Republic–Central America Free Trade Agreement 2005), calls into question the value of higher IP standards given that these countries have yet to identify the value gained from the TRIPS standards.

The trend of including TRIPS-plus standards in trade agreements is also used by smaller trade groups like the European Free Trade Area (EFTA) countries (Iceland, Lichtenstein, Norway, and Switzerland), who include TRIPS-plus standards, such as joining intellectual-property-related treaties and providing stronger patents and data protections, in their negotiations with developing countries. The EFTA–Jordan Free Trade Agreement reflects such measures and TRIPS-plus standards and calls for the provision of enforcement mechanisms under national laws at the same level as that provided for in the TRIPS agreement.[83]

These agreements have had a significant impact on a regional basis, and on trade agreements between developing countries, by acting as a force multiplier for TRIPS-plus standards between developing countries. In general, RBTs between developing countries have not included provisions addressing IP. Where one developing country has already implemented TRIPS-plus standards, they will most likely be reflected in trade agreements with other developing countries to maintain consistency and equal treatment requirements.

Enforcement by coercion

The signing of the RBT and the acceptance of TRIPS-plus standards are only the beginning of the enforcement road, as the added commitments under the RBT are used to provide more ammunition for future threats of

[83] Jordan–EFTA Free Trade Agreement, signed June 21, 2001, entered into force 1 September 2002. Protections for IPRs are addressed under Annex VI of the Agreement. EFTA states have similar agreements with Turkey, Israel, and Singapore.

placement on the Special 301 Report Watch List. The Special 301 Report powers are continuously threatened to nudge the targeted country towards complete compliance, and developing countries are familiar with this strategy. Any remaining illusions of lackadaisical monitoring on the part developed countries are quickly displaced as the various corporate lobbyists in Washington start requesting that the targeted country meet its full obligations under the RBT. Even a disagreement on the interpretation of certain clauses is a basis for threatening the targeted country with the Special 301 Report powers.

Again, Jordan represents the classic example of that scenario. Within four years of signing the JUSFTA, in its 2005 Special 301 Report Submission, the Pharmaceutical Manufacturers Association (PhRMA) called for Jordan to be placed on the 2006 Priority Watch List, claiming that the health authorities were not effectively implementing the JUSFTA and that "unsupportable adverse interpretations" were being applied to the protection of data.[84] In addition, the report claimed that PhRMA members were facing some market-access barriers, particularly through pricing directives and regulatory requirements. PhRMA also requested that Jordan be listed on the Watch List in 2007 due to recent weaknesses in IP protection and alleged barriers to market access for US firms in Jordan; however, Jordan was not actually placed on the watch list that year. Similar calls were made in 2009, when again Jordan was ultimately not included on the Watch List, but only after a letter to the USTR by local industry representatives detailing commitments to push for stronger implementation of IP standards.[85] This method of avoiding being listed on the Special 301 Report Watch List is worth reflection upon, because it essentially consisted of accepting all the positions advocated by the US Government and acknowledging that they had not yet been met.

---

[84] PhRMA, "PhRMA 'Special 301 Report' Submission," 2005, www.cptech.org/ip/health/trade/2005phrma301.pdf.

[85] "USAID Supports AmCham Paper on Jordan's IP Laws," *Alghad Daily Newspaper*, February 21, 2009. The letter was drafted by the American Chamber of Commerce in Jordan (AmCham) and the Jordan Intellectual Property Association (JIPA), and it called on the USTR not to list Jordan in the Special 301 Report because it would hamper the kingdom's image and ability to attract investments. They said that they were prompted into action in light of pressure by representatives from the US private sector to include Jordan on the list due to what they said were cases of IPRs violations manifested in selling pirated software, DVDs, and CDs in the kingdom. The letter called for stringent actions against piracy, particularly audiovisual and optical piracy, against known locations and traders in Jordan. They also called for specialized courts to deal with issues of IPRs violations.

Even though the 2009 letter to the USTR was issued by private organizations rather than by the Jordanian government, it is highly unlikely that it had not been authorized by governmental agencies, especially since it involved the dreaded Special 301 Report Watch List. References within the letter to helping Jordan avoid the negative impact of being listed on the Watch List hint at behind-the-scenes governmental drafting. The quasi-official sanctioning of the 2009 letter to the USTR, therefore, is one that will likely come back to haunt Jordan if future questions arise regarding whether or not the letter's self-imposed enforcement benchmarks were met. The letter further limits Jordan's ability to interpret the JUSFTA clauses by accepting the United States' position on the contested issues.

Contrary voices and counter-currents

The success of external inducements and coercive factors in silencing critical voices within developing countries is thrown into even greater relief when set in comparison with the relative diversity of views expressed the developed world. TRIPS-plus and the reduction in TRIPS flexibilities under RBTs have not escaped the attention of regulators within developed countries, even when their counterparts in the developing countries, such as Jordan, have been conspicuously silent. For example, the legitimacy of imposing TRIPS-plus standards on bilateral partners and restricting the Doha Declaration flexibilities was challenged within the US Government; twelve members of the US Congress argued in a letter that the insertion in RBTs of IP provisions that restrict access to generic drugs "violate[s] the requirement in section 2101 (b)(4)(C) of the Trade Promotion Authority Act 2002 to uphold the 2001 WTO Declaration on Public Health."[86] That letter also attacked the USTR's inclusion of the allowance for such flexibilities in appending letters instead of in the body of the RBT itself. This led in 2007 to a compromise known as the New Trade Policy Template, which calls for enhanced provisions in all future US bilateral and regional FTAs on IP protection.

---

[86] Hilda Solis et al., "Letter from 12 Members of Congress to President Bush on Intellectual Property Provisions in CAFTA," 2004, http://www.cptech.org/ip/health /trade/cafta/congress09302004.html. The Trade Act of 2002, also known as the US Trade Promotion Authority Act, grants the President of the United States the authority to negotiate trade deals with other countries and gives Congress the authority only to vote up or down on the agreement, not to amend it. This authority is sometimes called fast-track authority. Agreements negotiated under this authority include FTAs.

This compromise aims at striking a balance between the rights of drug companies to protect their patents and the need of developing countries for life-saving drugs. As a direct result, the United States' RBTs with Colombia, Peru, and Panama now do not reach beyond TRIPS, unlike the RBTs signed previously (including the JUSFTA). This is evident in the relaxing of several patent-related rules in those later agreements, including rules on data exclusivity, patent linkage, and patent extension. An unprecedented explicit reference to the Doha Declaration and the need for each country to be able to protect the public health of its citizens was also added in the body of these agreements rather than as an appended letter. Similarly, the importance of "respecting and preserving traditional knowledge and practices of indigenous and other communities" was recognized. Overall, these results seem to indicate that the criticisms related to some aspects of the agreements, particularly those concerning the reduction of TRIPS flexibilities, have produced concrete results.[87]

Conclusion

In examining the reaction of Jordan's private and public sectors to the enforcement demands and coercion of the United States, both sectors can be characterized as being influenced by "socialization by external inducements," in which socialization plays an important role both in establishing an international order and in facilitating the functioning of that order.[88] Such socialization, which in Jordan's case originates from the institutionalized cooperation formalized in bilateral agreements, leads the political and economic elite to believe that US norms are in their best interest. This change in belief can result from technical assistance, capacity-building programs, or the frequent contacts with foreign authorities that usually follow the signing of an RBT.[89] The importance of socializing policy makers through training and education can produce advocates in domestic policy elites for the new protections of IPRs, thus helping to overcome and silence the local objections.[90]

---

[87] *A Shift in Intellectual Property Policy in US FTAs?* (International Centre for Trade and Sustainable Development, August 2007), http://ictsd.org/i/news/bridges/4128/.

[88] G. John Ikenberry and Charles A. Kupchan, "Socialization and Hegemonic Power," *International Organization* 44, no. 3 (1990): 283–315.

[89] J-F. Morin, "Multilateralizing TRIPs-plus Agreements: Is the US Strategy a Failure?" *The Journal of World Intellectual Property* 12, no. 3 (2009): 175–197.

[90] May, "The World Intellectual Property Organization."

However, as a result of Jordan's failure to show tangible economic benefits that have materialized from applying stricter IP standards (as discussed in the following chapter), the efforts to convince the Jordanian public of the value of enforcement efforts will suffer a setback over the short to medium term. The Special 301 Report's political arm-twisting, which leads to coercion-based enforcement, will add to the sense of resentment and subjugation felt by developing countries, and the aggressive attempts to induce compliance by such means are likely to backfire and produce little in the way of long-term results. Developed countries must understand that there will be little to gain from the continuous drive to ratchet up the levels of IP standards, when the economic promises made to justify the enforcement of those standards ring hollow. Describing this as a process of "commodification" of IPRs, May argues that it will ultimately be self-defeating, because increased commodification will cause rational people to reject the role of IPRs. He argues that such a rejection will occur because such stringent IPR laws construct a scarcity model that is neither natural nor self-evidently beneficial to all, thus creating a non-efficient model of supply and demand focused on the protection of rights for the express purpose of raising prices.[91] In an open society, the influence of, and support for, ideational hopes will diminish if that society realizes the lack of progress being made on the economic and development promises. The following chapter evaluates precisely these promises.

---

[91] Christopher May, "Between Commodification and 'Openness': The Information Society and the Ownership of Knowledge," *The Journal of Information, Law, and Technology* 2005, no. 2–3 (2005).

CHAPTER FIVE

THE IMPACTS OF TRIPS LEGISLATION IN JORDAN

Although Jordan had an IPR framework prior to the turn of the century, its current IP legislation owes all of its major developments to the WTO, the JUSFTA, and the JEUAA. The rapid legal transformation from the post-Ottoman period was impelled, in part, by promises of the economic benefits that would follow the adoption of modern IP laws. The first part of this chapter investigates whether those promises were fulfilled. A second question concerns whether the legislation thus put in place is actually functioning. A country may possess a body of legislation covering IPRs but lack the capacity or expertise to put the laws consistently into effect. Jordanian culture did not view IPRs seriously before Jordan joined the WTO in 1999 and the IP laws were overhauled; as a result, the new legal system is characterized by a paucity of judicial opinions pertaining to IP (with a notable exception in the area of trademarks), and a lack of personnel with training in this area. As we will see, this has contributed to the dysfunctionality of the legal system in Jordan. Finally, we look at the deleterious effects of the RBT system, used to enforce TRIPS-plus standards in Jordan, on the multilateral legal system.

The impact of the new IP standards on economic development

The direct overall effect for foreign corporations from the introduction of uniform IP systems/standards has been the expansion of the number of foreign territories in which Western corporations can consider doing business. The introduction of uniform IPRs, therefore, made large exporting companies the clear winners in the early phase of introduction of the TRIPS agreement.[1] The question, however, is whether there has also

[1] Evelyn Su, "The Winners and the Losers: The Agreement on the Trade-Related

been a concomitant benefit for Jordan as a result of the greater freedom of movement for MNCs, and whether the higher standards of regulation have also been advantageous for Jordanian business.

Foreign Direct Investment

The discourse on the link between IPRs and major economic indicators is marked by certain noteworthy anomalies. When it comes to measuring the economic effects of higher IPRs and the level of compliance with them, it is easy to be side-lined by a generalized discussion of the levels of FDI which does not consider whether such an increase actually had any impact on the level of welfare. Another point often missed concerns what percentage of the FDI increase was actually contributed by intellectual-property-sensitive products, goods, or services. In a similar manner, general FDI numbers do not tell us much about the impact of IPRs on increasing FDI flows into any country or region; this means that while useful inferences can be extracted from comparative or multi-country studies, any actionable conclusions based on the economic impact of IP standards must be country-specific. For Jordan, the discourse about the effect of IPRs on economic development suffered from all these shortcomings; general figures for FDI, for example, are commonly cited as an indication of the impact of IPRs on attracting investment into the country without providing a breakdown for those numbers. This is, indeed, characteristic of the difficulty of obtaining reliable and disaggregated economic statistics for Jordan.

The literature generally holds that there is a positive relationship between stronger IPRs, and higher levels of FDI and imports. The results cited vary according to factors such as degree of industrialization (the more industrialized the nation, the more positive the response to strong IPRs), the sector (the more technically advanced the sector, the more sensitive it will be to IPRs), and even the level of existing FDI (the more FDI a country has, the more likely it is that it will get more).[2] Some studies, however, point to a picture that is too complex to assume a simple and direct correlation between increased trade and higher IP standards.[3]

Aspects of Intellectual Property Rights and Its Effects on Developing Countries," *Houston Journal of International Law* 23 (2003): 169.

[2] See W. Lesser, "The Effects of TRIPS-Mandated Intellectual Property Rights on Economic Activities in Developing Countires" (WIPO, 2001), www.wipo.int.

[3] See the Commission on Intellectual Property Rights (UK), *Integrating Intellectual Property Rights and Development Policy* (London, 2002).

Nevertheless, trends in both exports and imports should provide an insight into whether increased IPRs have benefitted Jordanian business.

Jordan's top exports are garments, vegetables, phosphate, pharmaceuticals, potash (fertilizers), and transportation equipment.[4] Of these items, only pharmaceuticals fall within a major area of IPRs. If economic development is judged based on the increase in levels of FDI, then imports should present an equally important insight into the benefits of stronger IPRs. Data released by Jordan's Central Bank reveal that 40% of Jordan's imports for 2009 were transportation equipment, crude oil, iron and steel, electrical machinery, raw materials for the garment industry, and heavy equipment for industry and agriculture.[5] Closer examination of those items further reveals that the raw material imported for the garment industry is used almost exclusively by the garment industry for re-exportation to the United Stated in accordance with the Qualified Industrial Zones Agreement (QIZA) and the JUSFTA. Such imports, therefore, present very little added value to the national economy.[6] Two-thirds of the employees in the garment industry are foreign workers, and the garment industry, valued at $1 billion in 2008, has secured an exemption from Jordan's monthly minimum wage requirement of JD 150 ($210); it is allowed to pay its workers JD 120 ($170) – meanwhile, Jordan's official unemployment rate for the past decade has been around 12–14%.[7]

[4] Source: Jordan Central Bank, 2009. Jordan's gross domestic product (GDP) in 2008 was estimated at $30.8 billion (purchasing power parity, PPP) and per capita GDP is estimated at $5,000 (PPP). Jordan's official unemployment rate for 2008 was estimated to be 12.9 percent, although unofficial estimates range up to 30 percent. While about 86.3 percent of Jordan's GDP is from the services sector, such as tourism, 3.6 percent is from agriculture, and about 10.1 percent is from other industries including garment and clothing, phosphate mining, fertilizers, and pharmaceuticals.

[5] Figures provided by the Jordanian Central Bank and the Department of Statistics, as reported in "CBJ Issues Import Export Numbers," *Al Arab Alyawm Daily Newspaper*, October 25, 2009.

[6] Even when it comes to employment of local work force, the benefits are not clear in the garment sector, as only 10,000 Jordanians number among the 45,000 employed by the garment exporting industry. The author's discussions with factory owners revealed that local workers require up to twelve months' training, and therefore it makes more economic sense for the factories to import skilled labour from Bangladesh and elsewhere. The garment industry also suffers from discrimination against married female local employees, because the industry prefers unmarried female workers who will work the various shifts, and not be constrained by the demands of their families.

[7] The extensive use of foreign labour, along with the fact that many FDI funds are not targeting production or job-generating projects, helps explain why despite the

Similarly, exported transportation equipment represents the use of Jordan as a transit zone for re-exporting transportation vehicles to surrounding countries, especially Iraq.[8] There is no IP component to either of these segments of the Jordanian economy.

Jordanian companies fall in the bottom 20% (ranked 108 out of 133) in spending on research and development according to the Global Competitiveness Report (GCR).[9] This is an indication that they have little incentive to abide by or push for the enforcement of IPRs, as they have little at stake and little to gain from such enforcement. Yet Jordan's low ranking is rather at odds with its 26th position out of 133 on the GCR's ranking for the availability of scientists and engineers, the so-called innovation enablers, which is measured based on the number of academic degrees awarded. This lopsided result is even more puzzling when one considers the case of Vietnam, which the GCR ranks as 27th in company spending and 62nd on availability of scientists and engineers. The GCR also gives Jordan a low ranking (68th out of 133) on the cooperation between industries and universities in research and development. Contrasting the lack of Jordanian innovation against the large supply of Jordanian engineering and science graduates indicates that most university studies are theoretical in nature. The low number of Jordanian patents filed on a yearly basis substantiates this conclusion.

This situation cannot be blamed on a lack of funds: Vietnam, for example, which is ranked lower than Jordan in the number of engineering graduates, is ranked higher than Jordan on company R&D spending, even though it has a per capita GDP of $1,040 compared to Jordan's $5,421.[10] The problem, rather, seems to lie with the institutional and cultural response to the need for innovation, which apparently is lacking and/or

---

steady increase in FDI for over nine years the overall "official" rate of unemployment has remained unchanged, hovering around 14%. Of course, unemployment rates within certain age groups are much higher, as for example the age group 20–24 with an unemployment rate of 28%; and for women in general it is around 27%.

[8] Such mediocre labour standards are in fact common wherever the United States advocates its transnational labour protections, which are characterized by legal weaknesses – in particular, their failure to institutionalize the minimal rudiments of modern formal legality. See, for example, William E. Scheuerman, "False Humanitarianism? US Advocacy of Transnational Labour Protections," *Review of International Political Economy* 8, no. 3 (2001): 359–388.

[9] World Economic Forum, *Global Competitiveness Report 2009–2010* (World Economic Forum, 2010).

[10] World Economic Forum, *Global Competitiveness Report 2009–2010*.

deeply misunderstood by the Jordanian official planners and their counterparts in the private sector.

Jordan has not historically had a concerted strategy to attract FDI based on a strategic placement of IP standards; it did not matter where the money came from, as long as a significant portion was channelled into the kingdom's economy. Data supports this contention. In 2002, FDI totalled only $186 million, whereas in 2006 it totalled $1.5 billion, with more than 90% from Arab sources[11] and with the United States, Canada, and Europe investing a shockingly low combined total of $42.9 million in new projects.[12] These figures shed light on the minuscule role IPRs played in attracting FDI to Jordan. Since more than 90% of the 2006 FDI came from Arab countries, which do not have much of an IP base to speak of, it is safe to assume that the majority of those funds neither had an IP component nor were influenced by IP standards in Jordan. In fact, this increase in the inflow of FDI probably reflects the excess of petro-dollars that needed to be invested and did not reflect any intrinsic advantage for the Jordanian economy. This is clear from the collapse in FDI inflows to Jordan at the start of the global economic crisis, which plummeted by more than 80% and then started to rise again as oil prices moved upwards in 2010.[13]

The 2006 FDI data shows that 80% of the FDI was poured into the industrial sector, with 14% earmarked for the country's growing tourism industry.[14] Yet when it comes to measuring the impact of IPRs on FDI levels, there is little evidence that any relationship exists between the two. Thus, for Jordan, it is not in general plausible to claim that IPRs have a significant effect on FDI.[15]

---

[11] See US Government Accountability Office, *International Trade: Four Free Trade Agreements GAO Reviewed Have Resulted in Commercial Benefits, but Challenges on Labor and Environment Remain*, 2009. This states that "while Jordan does not maintain official detailed statistics of FDI, aggregate inflows of registered capital tracked by the Central Bank indicate that the main source countries for foreign investment are Middle Eastern (Iraq, Kuwait, United Arab Emirates, Saudi Arabia, Egypt, and Bahrain) or European (Denmark, Belgium, and the United Kingdom)."

[12] November 2006, figures reported by AMEinfo at http://www.ameinfo.com/103831.html.

[13] Mohammad Ghazal, "Investments Benefiting from Incentives Hit Record High in First Two Months," *Jordan Times*, February 28, 2010.

[14] November 2006 figures reported by AMEinfo.

[15] This analysis supports the opinion, voiced by Paul Heald, that the "evidence that maximum enforcement of all sorts of IP law – especially patent law – will stimulate investment should not remain unchallenged." What is equally important

The pharmaceutical sector

The pharmaceutical sector, which for Jordan is economically the most significant IP-sensitive sector, might present an exception to this picture. This sector was characterized by minimal technology transfer until 2003.[16] Evidence further points to a heavy dependence on generics, with no discernible effect of joint ventures on the growth of the assets, capital profit, sales, weighted assets, weighted capital, weighted profit, and weighted sales of the pharmaceutical industry. This minimal level of technology transfer is still being maintained, despite the fact that surveyed pharmaceutical companies agreed that joint ventures are the most important method of technology transfer. Another review that covers the period until early 2007 indicates that there are only three companies out of the seventeen in the pharmaceutical sector with strategic alliances, licensing agreements, or production facilities outside Jordan.[17]

The recent global recession had the growth projections for the Jordanian pharmaceutical industry showing a 19% decline in the 2009 export volume compared to the 20% increase originally projected, representing a 39% gap. Further, the Jordanian pharmaceutical industry remains fundamentally without a research and development base and is a prime candidate for acquisition by larger foreign pharmaceutical companies. There is little evidence of well-defined benefits that would not have materialized for the pharmaceutical sector had Jordan not acceded to the WTO or signed the JUSFTA.[18]

It is important to point out, however, that there is no evidence, either in the literature or in the data reviewed, of a concerted effort to prevent the Jordanian pharmaceutical sector from achieving those goals. In the areas of licensing and technology transfer, for example, analysis indicates that the Jordanian pharmaceutical failure is a result of misguided assumptions that Western pharmaceuticals would overlook economies of production in favour of Jordanian companies. As for exporting to the Western markets,

---

for developing countries is "to take into account the costs and benefits of protection in the context of their unique economic situation" and even to consider minimal compliance. Paul J. Heald, "Misreading a Canonical Work: An Analysis of Mansfield's 1994 Study," *Journal of Intellectual Property Law* 10 (2003).

[16] Rasha Laswi, "Effect of Technology Transfer Contracts on the Growth of the Pharmaceutical Sector (Jordan-Case Study)" (Master's Diss., Jordan Institute of Diplomacy, 2002).

[17] Dana Baradei, "The Right Prescription," *Jordan Business*, January 10, 2007.

[18] The points made in this paragraph were underscored in several of the interviews conducted for this study. See appendix one.

Jordanian pharmaceuticals were slow to understand the importance of acquiring and implementing the regulatory and quality standards of the American Food and Drug Administration (FDA) and its EU counterpart.

Data exclusivity

The public debate about the value of the JUSFTA among the pharmaceutical industrialists and their lobbying group in Jordan – the Jordanian Association of Manufacturers of Pharmaceuticals and Medical Appliances (JAPM) – has cited unequivocally positive results; but it seems their conversations with US government officials carried a different slant.[19] A report by the US Government Accountability Office (GAO) noted that for generic medicine producers there was some frustration with IPRs related to data exclusivity, concerning a lack of transparency in rights and obligations. The GAO report cites a 2007 study by Oxfam on Jordan's pharmaceutical industry, stating that as a result of the TRIPS provisions of the WTO and the TRIPS-plus provisions of the JUSFTA, many Jordanian generic pharmaceuticals are precluded from the market through the acceptance procedure of "data exclusivity." Data exclusivity means that, for market approval of a generic drug that had already been shown to be equivalent to the original one, drug regulatory agencies are prevented for a period of five years from using the clinical trial data developed by the originator company to establish the safety and efficacy of the medicine. These delays, according to Oxfam, impede or prevent generic competition and can lead to higher prices than would otherwise be the case.[20]

Rebuttals to the Oxfam report, including the one cited by the GAO, cite exceptions to Oxfam's assertions concerning the lack of a Jordanian pharmaceutical research and development (R&D) base, but they are so few (two companies specializing in drug delivery systems) that they end up proving Oxfam's point. Rebuttals to the statement that there is a dearth of pharmaceutical production facilities and agreements are aspirational in

---

[19] US Government Accountability Office, *International Trade: Four Free Trade Agreements*. "As far as IPR (intellectual property rights), the majority of Jordanian pharmaceutical businesses manufacture generic medicines, and there are concerns that the IPR provisions of the FTA are hurting the generic industry." The report, issued July 2009, can be found via the website of the US Government Accountability Office, http://www.gao.gov.

[20] Oxfam, *All Costs, No Benefits: How TRIPS-plus Intellectual Property Rules in the US–Jordan FTA Affect Access to Medicines*, Briefing Paper (Oxfam, March 2007).

nature (using language like "Multinational managers expect that manufacturing deals will be struck as Jordanian companies come into compliance"), and lack sufficient numbers to show a trend.

Public health and medical tourism

Some of the more outrageous claims of purported positive effect of increased IPRs included linking IPRs to improvements in public health and to medical tourism. In fact, the share of medical tourism as a percentage of the total tourism sector has been more or less constant throughout the past decade and focuses mainly on the expertise of the medical professionals rather on the availability of medical drugs. Jordan relies on medical tourism that is supported by hospitals and trained medical staff, and not because it has any reputation as a centre for pharmaceutical research. If anything, medical trials have negative connotations in the minds of Jordanians, as they associate them with abuse of third-world citizens by pharmaceutical companies that use them to conduct experiments that are otherwise prohibited in the Western world.

IPRs cannot take any credit for continued improvements in public health statistics either, as those mainly result from improvements in general hygiene and the use of vaccination and other affordable and accessible medications, which are not related to high-end pharmaceutical research or patented drugs. This is especially the case in Jordan and other MENA countries since HIV-AIDS does not register as a national health issue, and thus the patented drugs required for its treatment are not a priority as is the case in sub-Saharan African countries or in South America.[21]

Pricing of brand-name drugs

For Jordan, the most immediate effect of the adoption of TRIPS on access to medicine has been a tightening of access to counterfeit brand-name drugs; however, the more lasting effect has been the on-going struggle to fix the prices of brand-name drugs, which experiences a constant tug between affordability and availability. Jordan, not being a major regional drug importer or having a significant regional market population, has never had the necessary leverage or bargaining power to counter the

---

[21] At 0.2% the Middle East and North African Region (MENA) region has the lowest HIV/AIDS adult prevalence percentage globally. See World Bank, *Preventing HIV/AIDS in the Middle East and North Africa: A Window of Opportunity to Act* (World Bank, 2005).

effects of escalating drug prices as a result of the implementation of TRIPS. As a result, to lessen the impact of price increases by pharmaceutical brand-name producers, Jordan must rely on a complicated mechanism that ties the prices of brand-name pharmaceuticals to various benchmarks.

The JFDA regulates the pricing of drugs in Jordan using the Provisional Drugs and Pharmaceuticals Law[22] and the relevant pricing standards.[23] If the product is only registered and priced in its country of origin, then it will be priced based on the price of other drugs with similar chemical compositions or treatment effects (sec. 4(e)). The prices of imported products with generic equivalents registered and priced in Jordan are determined by the following pricing mechanisms (sec. 5):

1. If purchased on a Cost, Insurance and Freight (CIF) basis, the factory price plus customs duties, insurance, clearing, inland transport, local client's margin (for products purchased on a Free on Board (FOB) basis, shipping costs must be added); or
2. The public selling price in the country of origin (after deducting the said country's wholesaler's and retailer's margin), plus freight costs, insurance, custom duties, inland transport and local client's margin; or
3. The export price from Saudi Arabia. In the event the product was not registered in Saudi Arabia, the price shall be reviewed upon its registration in Saudi Arabia (where the agent importing the product must inform the FDA of the requested price within four months of its registration in Saudi Arabia). Saudi Arabia is chosen because it is the largest in market population and in spending per capita in the region.

Advocates of equitable access to medicine want to bring the World Health Organization (WHO) into the battle for control of IP policy within international organizations. In recent years, the WHO has become one of the main arenas for debate between NGOs and the pharmaceutical industry.[24] At the forefront of this debate have been issues such as access to medicine, extended patent rights, and the industry's lack of focus on research and development on some drugs that disproportionately afflict the developing world, because the markets cannot meet the costs of drug development. The WHO itself concedes that the implications of trade agreements on public health have been among the most controversial

[22] Drugs and Pharmaceuticals Law No. 80.

[23] Drug Pricing, Price Revision and Price Objection Standards, 2007.

[24] William New and Mara, Kaitlin, "WHO Session on IP and Health Clashes on Vision, Practicalities," *Intellectual Property Watch*, 2007.

topics in recent years, particularly the impact of the TRIPS Agreement on access to essential medicines.[25] In 2004, WHO member states were further encouraged to ensure that RBTs take into account the flexibilities contained in the TRIPS Agreement on Public Health. However, there is little evidence either that Jordan is availing itself of the potential flexibilities under TRIPS, or that the IPR legislation it has enacted is bringing any benefits, either in terms of the trade in pharmaceuticals or in broader public health issues. In both these respects, then, the promises associated with the adoption of TRIPS standards have not materialized, and a similar negative result holds as regards FDI flows considered in the round. The case of Jordan provides no evidence that a stronger IP regime attracts FDI, and Jordan does not have an export profile that was apt to benefit from greater IP protection. Nor is the strengthened regime likely to engender one.

IPR enforcement in Jordan

Although Jordan possesses a legal framework which provides for strong IPRs protection, it falls short in its efforts to enforce that framework. Many of the enforcement and regulatory agencies that exist today, such as the Food and Drug Administration, did not exist at the turn of the century, nor did the current setup of the registrars for the various IPRs, and they have yet to fully mature into capable regulators.[26] The same can be said of the court system, which has yet to develop a level of sophistication that signals the maturing of the IP legal practice. As a result, Jordan is dependent on external expertise, particularly WIPO. At the same time, there is external pressure on Jordan to take on even greater responsibilities for the enforcement of IPR. These questions of administrative capacity are the subject of the present section.

In order to discuss the administrative enforcement system in more detail, it is important to recognize the numerous different administrative agencies that handle different types of IP. These are listed below, first by IP sector and then by agency:

[25] WHO, "Trade, IPRs and Access to Medicines," January 12, 2010, http://www.who.int/medicines/areas/policy/globtrade/en/index.html.

[26] An observation made in one of the interviews conducted for this study. See appendix one.

By IP sector

Patents: Regulated by the Industrial Property Protection Directorate (IPPD) within the Ministry of Industry and Trade (MoIT), which is responsible for supervising the registration and classification of trademarks, designs, and layout designs of integrated circuits and patents.
Trademarks: Regulated by the IPPD, which is in charge of trademark registration; however, the JISM is in charge of the actual implementation of enforcement against counterfeit trademarks.
Copyright: Regulated by the Author's Right Protection Office (ARPO) at the National Library (NL), which is responsible for protecting copyright rights.
Customs: Regulated by the Customs Department, which established a special section to deal with copyright and trademarks.
Product-specific agencies: In addition to the state agencies and departments listed above, several other agencies play a role in IP enforcement. The Jordanian Food and Drug Administration (JFDA), for example, deals with IPRs related to pharmaceuticals.

Table 5-1 shows the number of court cases dealing with IPRs enforcement in 2008. The number of pharmaceutical enforcement cases in this table reflects the cases specifically associated with IP violations, for which enforcement falls to the JFDA. The majority of the cases are for copyright infringement, which reflects the increased importance authors are giving to asserting their copyright. The total number of cases (i.e., both IP and non-IP related) referred to the courts by the JFDA in 2008 was in fact 66, marking a dramatic drop on previous years (see table 5-2). The main catalyst for that change seems to be the Public Health Law, which criminalized, with up to five and no less than three years' imprisonment, the sale, importation, or smuggling of counterfeit drugs.[27]

[27] See Public Health Law No. 47, 2008, sec. 65.

Table 5-1. Number of cases dealing with IPRs enforcement in 2008[28]

Copyright enforcement	Pharmaceutical enforcement	Trademark enforcement	Custom enforcement	Cases filed by private entities[29]
345	14	5	109	216

Table 5-2. Number of cases referred by JFDA (2004–2008)

Year	2004	2005	2006	2007	2008
Total no. cases	11	75	100	144	66
IP cases	NA	NA		61	14

By agency

Ministry of Industry and Trade (MoIT)

The MoIT[30] dates back to the 1950s. According to its law (*MoIT Law*, 1998), it is in charge of regulating industrial activity in Jordan and preparing the programs aimed at improving its competitiveness. It also takes on responsibility for the regulation of internal and external trade through monitoring and the preparation of the studies and agreements that serve those purposes.

The scope of the MoIT's role in IP administration and enforcement revolves around the JISM and the IPPD. The JISM works through the border points to inspect and validate goods bearing a specific trademark to assure their authenticity; controversially, nonconforming goods with counterfeit trademarks are confiscated and destroyed. The IPPD is responsible for supervising the registration and classification of trademarks, designs, and layout designs of integrated circuits and patents.

---

[28] Jordanian Judicial Council, *Annual Courts Report – 2008* (Jordanian Judicial Council, 2008).

[29] Because the number of cases filed reflects the total number of cases filed through administrative and private entities, the number of judicial enforcement cases comes from subtracting the number of all cases referred to Jordanian courts by the administrative agencies from the total number of cases filed.

[30] In April 2013 the MoIT was renamed the Ministry of Industry and Trade and Supply.

Jordan Institute of Standards and Metrology (JISM)

The JISM, which was created pursuant to the Institute of Standards and Metrology Law No. 22, has four stated objectives:[31]

1. Adopting a national system for standardization and metrology based on accepted international practices.
2. Keeping pace with scientific and technical developments in the fields of standards, metrology, conformity assessment, and laboratory accreditation.
3. Ensuring the health and safety of the kingdom's citizenry and protection of the environment by making sure that products approved are in compliance with the technical regulations adopted by the institution for that purpose.
4. Raising the quality of local products through the adoption of appropriate Jordanian Standards in order to enhance their competitiveness in the local and international markets and thus support the national economy.

Administratively, the JISM has four divisions: Border Control, Factories Surveillance, Market Surveillance, and the Inspection Division. The main tasks and duties of the four divisions are:[32]

1. Controlling all imported materials (except for pharmaceuticals, veterinary medicines, and vaccines) to assess their conformity to Jordanian Standards and Technical Regulations and labelling requirements.
2. Controlling local products and assessing their conformity with Jordanian Standards, technical regulations, and labelling requirements.
3. Inspecting electrical elevators prior to usage to ensure that they meet the JESS safety requirements.
4. Participating in preparing and modifying Jordanian Standards.
5. Following up with customer complaints regarding non-conforming products.
6. Issuing export conformity certificates.
7. Issuing tender conformity certificates for governmental institutions upon request.

[31] See JISM website at http://www.jism.gov.jo/ (last visited August 2, 2009).
[32] See JISM website.

None of these duties contains any specific reference to enforcement of IPRs. The JISM's mandate explicitly excludes pharmaceuticals and medicines – they fall under the purview of the Jordan Food and Drug Administration. However, the JISM has exercised enforcement authority over trademarks, including the confiscation and destruction of fake and forged products and goods.[33] For example, in association with customs, the JISM systematically destroys large volumes of non-compliant foreign goods on a yearly basis, even though its governing law does not grant it any such authority.[34]

The JISM primarily deals with trademark enforcement, and it does not refer cases to court on its own; rather, it destroys counterfeit goods after confiscation. A court case will be filed only if the owner of the alleged counterfeit goods goes to court in order to stop the JISM from destroying the goods or to seek restitution. This explains the low number for trademark enforcement in table 5-1. It should be noted that the JISM law does not explicitly address counterfeit trademarks; rather, the JISM interprets article 30(c) of that law to allow for the destruction of counterfeit goods. Article 30(c) of the JISM law actually addresses the destruction of goods only if they do not meet the JISM standards, and the JISM seems to have adopted a *prima facie* presumption that counterfeit goods fall under the category of goods to be destroyed.[35] The JISM understands that its position is not legally supported, and consequently has declared that it is, under pressure from international donors, in the process of amending its law to reflect a clearer mandate to pursue counterfeit products.[36] Nevertheless, as it stands the activity of JISM in trademark enforcement is arguably characterized by a significant overreach of authority.

The newly proposed amendments to the current JISM law seem to acknowledge this lack of authority by proposing new language to grant the JISM authority to "confiscate or condemn to destruction goods bearing fake or forged trademarks."[37] Until that language is officially approved,

---

[33] A point underscored in interview. See appendix one.

[34] MoIT, Official Letter No. 19/2/23/5610, Annex 5.

[35] MoIT, Official Letter No. 19/2/23/5610, sec. 30(c): "If the product or material is found not to be in compliance with the applicable technical regulation issued by the Institution, the Director General shall issue a written order to seize, dispose of, or re-export the product, or alter its manufacture in such a way as to bring it into compliance with the technical regulation."

[36] The point was related to the author in interview. See appendix one.

[37] Proposed draft – Standards, Metrology and Product Safety Law, article 32(a)(15). There is no indication when this proposed draft would be presented to the Jordanian parliament.

however, there is little or no legal support for the role the JISM is currently playing in enforcing IPRs. This is not to say that JISM is never within its rights when it confiscates or condemns for destruction a counterfeit product; by law, it is allowed to do so if the product is not in compliance with an existing Jordanian standard (Institute of Standards and Metrology Law No. 22). Under the language of the current JISM law, there is no legal basis for confiscating goods bearing a fake trademark if they are in compliance with the specific Jordanian standard.

This debate about the extra authority claimed by the JISM, however, is not taking place in Jordan, and it is not clear why. Potentially its absence is the quickest and easiest way of destroying possibly infringing goods and showing the United States that the Jordanian government is fighting pirated goods. The Jordanian government is actually relying on figures drawn from the JISM's "enforcement" statistics to demonstrate to the USTR and other international agencies its efforts in combating piracy.[38] Stretching the law to cover areas it actually does not cover undermines the legislature's will and, by extension, the will of the people. Further, it weakens the concept of the orderly and reasoned progression of laws through discourse and public debate.

Industrial Property Protection Directorate (IPPD)

The IPPD registers trademarks and maintains records of active ones in accordance with the requirements of the Trademark Law, which stipulates that a trademark registrar be established to carry out those duties.[39] Similarly, the IPPD houses the registration function for patents, designs and industrial models, and layout designs of integrated circuits as mandated by those respective laws.[40]

By virtue of being the registrar for trademarks, patents, designs and industrial models, and integrated circuits, the IPPD is also responsible for managing the opposition to trademarks, patents, industrial designs and integrated circuits, as well as handling trademark cancellation requests. Tables 5-3 and 5-4 reflect the limited numbers of patent applications and patents issued, respectively. Table 5-3 shows that the majority of patent applications are international, while national patent applications are a minority. The small number of patents filed and granted raises questions about the feasibility for resource allocation for the development of a patent

---

[38] MoIT, Official Letter No. 19/2/23/5610, Annex 5.

[39] See Trademarks Law No. 33, 1952, sec. 3; Tradenames Law No. 9, 2006, sec. 3.

[40] See Patent Law No. 32, 1999, sec. 7; Integrated Circuits Law No. 10, 2000, sec. 3; Designs & Industrial Models Law No. 14, 2000, sec. 3.

administration and enforcement system, which would require considerable resources and expertise, especially if it includes the highly technical patent prosecution phase. Currently, it seems that Jordan has opted not to allocate considerable resources to a patent administration and examination system, as it is relying on the WIPO and its technical integration into the network of Western patent offices for the examination and searches of patents.[41]

Table 5-3. National and international patent applications[42]

Year	2000	2001	2002	2003	2004	2005	2006	2007	2008	2009	2010
National applications	71	52	21	25	42	49	75	59	50	60	43
International applications	127	147	117	157	141	169	428	507	535	446	431

Table 5-4. National and international patents granted[43]

Year	2000	2001	2002	2003	2004	2005	2006	2007	2008	2009	2010
National patents granted	12	0	13	8	4	9	10	23	10	11	22
Intern'l patents granted	59	0	16	39	56	46	50	40	11	40	64
Total patents granted	71	0	29	47	60	55	60	63	21	51	86

For patents filed outside Jordan, a Jordanian patent award is almost automatic, which explains the surge in the number of international patent applications, as Jordan has become an easy and inexpensive patenting venue. But filing and award times can vary, likely due to the dependency on foreign agencies for patent examination – as the Jordanian patent office has only four examiners. The discrepancy between the number of national and international patent filings, with the latter far outstripping the former, can be seen as the result of weak local research and development spending.

---

[41] This point was emphasized in interview. See appendix one.
[42] "Ministry of Industry & Trade Website," n.d., http://www.mit.gov.jo/Default.aspx?tabid=571.
[43] Ibid.

Ten years after joining TRIPS, Jordan still does not have a patent litigation practice, and the extent of the legal work done in the IPRs arena is largely limited to filing trademark registrations.[44]

The patent prosecution process governs the interaction between applicants, their representatives, and the patent office, and is divided into two parts. The pre-grant prosecution refers to negotiations with the patent office for the grant of a patent, and the post-grant prosecution refers to the amendment of a patent and any opposition filed against it. Both the pre-grant and the post-grant parts of the prosecution process represent important elements of the national patent system. They are vital for the development and cultivation of local technical and legal talent and the building of necessary skills for local examiners. A sophisticated and developed local patent prosecution staff will inevitably cause the legal practice of IP law to evolve and develop accordingly.

However, the current suboptimal situation is likely to be perpetuated, as inventors demonstrate a lack of knowledge of the elements of patent drafting and are largely unwilling to pay for its services, especially as they do not anticipate much economic gain from the patents filed as the patented products/processes are generally of poor quality. The private sector lacks a research and development base to justify the establishment of a patent prosecution legal practice, as the majority of private-sector companies either focus on using imported technology, which is protected by IPRs and therefore cannot be imitated or improved, or simply use outdated technology and see no need to invest in research and development.

Trademarks have the highest number of registration requests and court filings, as indicated by table 5-5, from which we can see that the number of filings for trademark registration is much higher than that for patents registration. The majority of the national filings come from foreign companies in Jordan.[45]

Table 5-6 shows the number of trademarks granted preliminary and final approvals, respectively; since the majority of the trademark filings were done by non-Jordanian entities, the same applies to the trademarks awarded. This discrepancy in the number of local versus foreign trademark filed and approved, ten years after accession to the WTO, poses questions as to the success of the trademark law amendments in spurring the growth of Jordanian trademarks.[46] Furthermore, there is no clear indication that

[44] This point was emphasized in interview. See appendix one.

[45] A. H. Khoury, "'Measuring the Immeasurable'—The Effects of Trademark Regimes: A Case Study of Arab Countries," *Journal of Law and Commerce* 26, no. 1/2 (2006): 11.

[46] Khoury, "Measuring the Immeasurable."

even the existing local trademarks amount to a critical economic mass, as the level of franchising of Jordanian trade or service marks is extremely low, with only a handful of brands reaching beyond the Jordanian borders. This is further supported by the fact that the major Jordanian exports come from mining industries (potash and phosphate) as well as exporting garments, vegetables, and fruit,[47] without a significant input from the service sector, which usually holds the highest weight in trade and service marks.

Table 5-5. Trademark applications[48]

Year	2000	2001	2002	2003	2004	2005	2006	2007	2008	2009	2010
National application	3307	2352	2353	2690	3206	3638	4163	4512	4484	3992	1904
International applications	3266	2623	2279	2386	3051	3078	3850	4633	4956	3741	4056

Table 5-6. Trademark preliminary and final approvals[49]

Year	2000	2001	2002	2003	2004	2005	2006	2007	2008	2009	2010
Preliminary approval	3622	5220	3720	4226	4940	4665	6490	6845	7500	5471	5715
Final approval	2612	2175	4190	5277	4444	4538	5792	6824	6710	6359	4286

Administration of authors' rights

The Jordanian copyright law (Copyright Law No. 22), which came into effect after 1992, embraces computer programs and compiled works as protected by author's rights, and designates the NL as the repository for authors' works seeking registration in Jordan. The NL still plays an important role, even though the current law no longer requires that a work be registered with it in order to attain protection (sec. 45), as the law grants the NL the authority to prevent a work not previously registered with the NL from being commercially circulated in Jordan. Similarly, no

[47] This despite the fact that Jordan is one of the poorest countries in the world when it comes to water resources; thus it is effectively exporting water through vegetables and fruits. See http://www.irinnews.org/Report.aspx?ReportId=61829 (last visited July 4, 2009).

[48] Source: Ministry of Industry & Trade Website.

[49] Source: Ministry of Industry & Trade Website.

work can be printed in Jordan until it is registered with the NL. Therefore, while the foreign work is protected from infringement in Jordan, even if it is not registered with the NL, the NL has veto power over its commercial circulation in Jordan. Similarly, the NL controls the right to publish works in Jordan by asserting its right to approve those works ahead of publication.

Both the NL and the Department of Press and Publications (DPP) can confiscate a publication and remove it from circulation (Press and Publications Law No. 8, 1998, sec. 35). Recently, the DPP has also referred to religious authorities for their opinions on the content of certain books, indicating that if the mufti[50] does not approve or condone the content of the books, they will be banned from circulation. This unofficial veto power by the mufti is not codified in any of the laws governing the work of the DPP or the NL, including the copyright law.[51]

Within the NL, the Author's Right Protection Office (ARPO) is charged with the registration of works, as well as the enforcement of the Author's rights against infringement. Its members are vested under the copyright law with law enforcement officer powers, enabling them to carry out inspection and search activities related to the enforcement of author's rights, if there is probable cause to suspect that such rights were violated or infringed (Copyright Law No. 22, sec. 36). ARPO, established in 2000, is in charge of making referrals to the courts. The number of cases referred by the NL to the Jordanian courts in the 2000–2008 period is given in table 5-7; these figures show that ARPO was quick to set about its task. The number of cases sharply increased from 2000 to 2003; since then, the numbers have slightly fluctuated but have largely stayed within the same general range since 2005. It is not clear why these numbers fluctuate or why they are not increasing, as data are not readily available and often hard to obtain. One reason might be that enforcement by the NL takes into consideration the economic and social aspects of Jordanian society. In other words, while the NL is technically charged with fighting copyright infringement, it is also aware of its limited resources and the particularities of Jordanian society. Therefore, the NL might be striking a balance between fighting piracy and accommodating the needs of citizens access to copyrighted material. The NL has yet to produce any analyses for the piracy situation in Jordan, and the situation is further compounded by the general difficulty of obtaining data in Jordan.

---

[50] The religious authority charged with interpreting religious texts to create religiously acceptable solutions to modern problems.

[51] Ranah Al-Amer, "Poet Samhan Sentenced to One Year and His Poetry Collection Referred to the Mufti," *Alghad Daily Newspaper*, June 22, 2009.

Table 5-7. Cases referred by the National Library (ARPO) 2000–2008[52]

Year	2000	2001	2002	2003	2004	2005	2006	2007	2008
Cases	6	149	298	384	218	296	285	357	354

Software piracy

With respect to software piracy, which falls within the remit of the ARPO, the official statistics might seem to show some success for the administrative system. Table 5-8 show that software piracy has been steadily declining in Jordan for the past ten years. Given the declining levels of software piracy, reaching around 66% of overall software on the market, one can argue that the Jordanian market now provides users with both original and pirated products, and the choice of one or the other is an economically rational one.

Table 5-8. Software piracy percentage[53]

Year	1994	1995	1996	1997	1998	1999	2000	2001	2002	2003	2004	2005	2006	2007	2008	2010	2011
Software piracy %	87	87	83	80	80	75	71	67	64	65	64	63	61	60	58	57	58

Unfortunately, the decline in software piracy can more plausibly be explained by reference to the economic boom of 2004–2008, which encouraged many Jordanian businesses to shed pirated software in exchange for original copies with warranties, technical support, and customer service. The economic returns from the increased economic activity in 2004–2008 justified the extra cost of original business software. This theory will be tested by the global economic downturn, which, as indicated by the post-2008 number from the above table, would cause the Jordanian businesses to reconsider their software compliance options and result in an upswing or stabilization in the percentage of business software piracy in Jordan.

This theory finds additional support from the survey of general attitudes of Jordanian college students, which indicates a significant level of apathy towards the piracy issue and the alleged losses of MNCs. As

---

[52] Source: National Library, n.d., http://www.nl.gov.jo/AR/Pages/OnlineServices .aspx.

[53] BSA, "Business Software Alliance – IDC Study," *Global Software Piracy Study*, April 27, 2010, http://global.bsa.org/idcglobalstudy2007/.

noted in chapter one, piracy is not viewed as a serious moral or legal problem, with 71.9% of Jordanian students surveyed saying that they did not think it unethical to buy counterfeit IP products (for full details of the survey, see appendix two). Students are typically the largest users of pirated products, especially software, and thus it seems would be unlikely to be moved by the expansion of criminal penalties.

Given all this, one might reasonably conclude that piracy rates will not decrease until the pricing for original products starts to make economic sense, at which point the price gradient that drives the demand for pirated products will shrink significantly. Ultimately, that point will not be reached until right-holders realize that pricing schemes designed for the developed countries do not make economic sense for developing countries like Jordan. An alternative pricing model must be introduced. Western publishing corporations have already reached that conclusion; for years now, they have offered original products at significantly lower prices for students in developing countries, with the caveat that the copies cannot be shipped in bulk outside designated geographical areas. While the application for audio-visual works might not be as straightforward, the principle is still valid, because enforcement models and mechanisms that do not make economic sense are not effective and will invariably create an underground market for the controlled product.

The Customs Department

Similar to other laws and regulations affected by the WTO accession, the Jordanian Customs Law was amended in 1998. Further, a new unit, the Intellectual Property Rights Section (IPRS) was established to deal specifically with enforcement of IPRs.

In general terms, the Jordanian Customs Department's authority to deal with IP infringements stems from Article 41 of the Customs law, which states that "The entry of foreign goods which do not meet the terms incorporated in the Laws and regulations for the protection of origin and ownership, shall be forbidden unless the relevant authorities agree to remove such prohibition" (Jordan Customs Law No 20 (1998), sec. 41). Based on that language, non-complying foreign goods cannot be admitted unless a waiver is granted. Table 5-9 presents the number of cases filed by the official commercial agent with the Jordanian courts as a result of letters from Customs to the official commercial agent informing it that it temporarily holds suspected counterfeit goods. For the years 2009 and 2010, the number of cases filed by right-holders represented 27% of the number of reports filed by the Jordanian Customs.[54] In other words, in 73% of instances, once notified by Customs that suspected counterfeit goods were impounded, the right-holder chose not to file a court action. Customs attributes the high percentage of right-holders choosing not to file an action to the small size of the Jordanian market as well as the small size of some of the confiscated shipments.[55]

Table 5-9. Number of cases filed by right-holders after notification of counterfeiting by the Jordanian Customs[56]

Year	2003	2004	2005	2006	2007	2008	2009	2010
Cases	1	5	23	17	145	109	87	96

Article 41 allows for two mechanisms to prevent counterfeit goods from entering into Jordan. First, a right-holder can file a temporary injunction request for the suspension of the suspected goods' clearance (secs. 41(a), (b), and (c)). The rules and regulations governing the request for an injunctive order include the posting of a security, the need to show a *prima facie* case of infringement, and the possibility of being sued by the importer if he or she is unrightfully damaged. The second mechanism allows the Customs to suspend the clearance procedure (sec. 41(d)). Unlike private right-holders, the Customs is not required to post a security, and the department is protected from any claims for damages by the importer (Jordan Customs Law No. 20).

Once the Customs has temporarily impounded any goods and suspended clearance, it contacts the authorized legal representative of the right-holder, informing him or her of the impounded goods.[57] The temporary impounding by the Customs is tantamount to a temporary injunctive order, and the legal representative of the right-holder has eight days to file a legal action, otherwise the suspected goods will be released. Customs, by law, bears no legal responsibility for any claims for damages by the importer of the allegedly infringing goods (sec. 41(g)).

[54] This statistic was reported in interview with the author. See appendix one.
[55] This point was conveyed to the author in interview.
[56] Customs Department, "Intellectual Property Cases Referred to Court," No. 104/4/8/45549, July 29, 2009.
[57] Instructions Governing Border Measures for IP Protection, No. 7, 2000.

The customs law and JUSFTA

The functioning of the Customs Department, as regulated by article 41, corresponds with the requirements presented under TRIPS Section 4. It is worth emphasizing that Jordanian law does meet TRIPS requirements as it stands. Table 5-10 below presents a comparison of the corresponding requirements in article 41 and TRIPS section 4, which shows that the existing law meets all of the requirements under TRIPS, including those that deal with notifying the right-holder when there is belief that goods are pirated and allowing ample time (ten days under TRIPS and eight days under Jordanian law) to start legal proceedings against the alleged infringer. Article 41 also grants the alleged infringer the right to remove the goods once the right-holder declines to press legal charges, and gives the alleged infringer the right to challenge the infringement charge before a court of law.

Article 41 of the Customs law does not require that a right-holder's case be presented before a court to obtain a temporary injunction order; rather, the right-holder can ride on the coattails of the Customs Department's impoundment order and proceed to file a legal action. Article 4(26) of the JUSFTA, however, requests that Jordan "provide, at least in cases of copyright piracy or trademark counterfeiting, that its authorities may initiate criminal actions and border measure actions *ex officio*, without the need for a formal complaint by a private party or right holder" (sec. 4(26)). This requirement is turning into a yearly sticking point in the USTR's review of Jordan's compliance with the JUSFTA. Jordan claims that its Customs Department has prepared a draft amendment to article 41 "which is in line with Jordan's international obligations and aimed at providing additional protection for [IPRs]."[58] The language used by the Jordanian government in describing the proposed amendment is very broad. This vague and non-committal language reflects the general internal struggle occurring within the various governmental agencies regarding IPRs compliance requirements.

---

[58] See MoIT, "Official Letter No. 19/2/23/5610, Annex 5," February 18, 2009, regarding Jordan's responses to the USTR's Special 301 report.

Table 5-10. JUSFTA Article 41 vs. TRIPS Section 4

Article 41 Requirements	*Section 4 Requirements*
Based on personal belief that goods are pirated, customs agents can suspend the clearance on the suspected goods and temporarily impound them. The importer of the goods and the legal representative of the right-holder are notified of the impoundment.	Members may also provide for corresponding procedures concerning the suspension by the customs authorities of the release of infringing goods destined for exportation from their territories (TRIPS sec. 51). The importer and the applicant shall be promptly notified of the suspension of the release of goods (sec. 54).
Alternatively, the right-holder can *sue sponte* file a temporary injunction with the proper court requesting, upon *prima facie* showing, the impoundment of the suspected goods, provided a security is posted and a suit is filed within eight days. Otherwise, the injunction is automatically lifted and the right-holder is subject to damages claim by the importer.	Members shall adopt procedures to enable a right-holder to lodge an application in writing with competent authorities, for the suspension by the customs authorities of the release into free circulation of such goods (sec. 51). The right-holder shall be required to provide adequate evidence that there is *prima facie* infringement (sec. 52). The applicant should provide a security to protect the defendant (sec. 53).
If within eight days the right-holder has not filed a suit, then the impoundment is lifted and the goods are cleared if there are no other issues related to the goods.	If, within a period not exceeding ten working days after the applicant has been served notice of the suspension, the customs authorities have not been informed that proceedings have been initiated by a party other than the defendant, the goods shall be released (sec. 55).
The importer of the suspected goods may challenge the temporary impoundment within eight days of being informed of the impoundment decision. The court must rule on the importer's challenge to the customs' decision within three days.	If proceedings leading to a decision on the merits of the case have been initiated, a review, including a right to be heard, shall take place upon request of the defendant with a view to deciding, within a reasonable period, whether these measures shall be modified, revoked or confirmed (sec. 55).
The Customs Department does not bear legal responsibility for damages claimed by the importer as a result of the temporary impoundment decision, or does it post any security.	Members shall only exempt both public authorities and officials from liability to appropriate remedial measures where actions are taken or intended in good faith (sec. 58).

The current official Jordanian position, however, does not challenge the analysis proffered by the United States, which is supported by compliance reports prepared by local attorneys funded by USAID. One such report concluded that the current text of article 41 does not satisfy JUSFTA obligation for the following reasons:[59]

1. It is an *ex officio* authority to suspend clearance and release of infringed goods, and does not therefore provide the right to seize goods; if the right-holder fails, within eight days after being notified of the decision to suspend release and clearance procedures, to notify the JCD that a court case has been instituted, the suspended goods are released even if JCD is aware that they are in fact counterfeit.
2. This *ex officio* authority does not include powers to initiate criminal actions.
3. This *ex officio* authority does not apply to transit goods, for which the right-holder must file a petition.

These claims, however, fail to make the case that article 41 does not meet the requirements of the JUSFTA. Point one refers to the inability of the Customs Department to "seize goods"; however, there is no mention in the language of article 4(26) of the JUSFTA that such an indefinite seizure should occur in the first place. Indeed, the language mentions authorities initiating criminal actions and border measures without a formal complaint by the right-holder, which is what article 41 provides for, as it allows for the impoundment of suspect goods either through a direct action by the right-holder, or, *sue sponte*, through the Customs Department.

The main cause of concern for the USTR, it seems, is the release of the goods if the right-holder does not file any charges. However, this course of events is not in violation of any of the requirements of article 4(26) of the JUSFTA and is in direct compliance with article 55 of the TRIPS agreement, which actually mandates such a release. What the USTR and the USAID-funded report fail to explain is why the language of article 41, which seems to be in line with JUSFTA and TRIPS, would need to be amended to force the Jordanian state to initiate a legal proceeding when the right-holder does not want to file a claim.

Point two states that article 41 is not in compliance with JUSFTA because the Custom Department's *ex officio* authority does not include "powers to initiate criminal actions," but that is not technically true; while

---

[59] Tawfiq Tabbaa, *Update on Compliance with Intellectual Property Rights in Jordan*, Improved Economic Opportunities for Jordanians (USAID – Sustainable Achievement for Business Expansion and Quality (SABEQ), February 14, 2007).

their language itself does not specify a criminal action *per se*, the copyright and trademark laws specifically provide for criminal and civilian penalties.[60] The extent of the penalty should be determined by the court. It is not clear how any amendment to article 41 would force a court to mete out criminal punishment rather than civilian fines; in fact, to do so would violate the principle of judicial independence and compromise the court's discretion, thus dangerously affecting the constitutional principle of the separation of powers. It is also a question of common fairness that not all prosecutions should be criminal, especially if the law itself allows for such a variation. The current language of article 41, which allows for a legal action, clearly includes the possibility of a criminal punishment if the court so chooses; thus, it meets the JUSFTA requirement. Furthermore, the setup of the copyright and trademark laws specifically allows for criminal or civilian penalties.

The third point in the USAID-funded report finds fault with the "ex officio authority" not applying to transit goods, yet there is no mention of such a requirement in the language of 4(26); in fact, that requirement is completely outside the scope of article 4(26).

The previous discussion raises questions as to whether some elements within the Jordanian bilateral trade agreements are turning out more to be stumbling blocks than building blocks for economic development. The JEUAA specifically calls for the applications of the "highest international standards," and while the European Union and Jordan have yet to go to the negotiating table to debate what exactly this means, it is not unlikely that their interpretations will differ. Jordan, it seems, has approached its trade agreements' IP commitments with the assumption that constant harmony will forever govern its relationship with its counterparties, whereas those counterparties have relied on calculated and enforceable rules carrying the burdens of legal liability through enforcement mechanisms.

Under the current mechanism, the customs agents have the *ex officio* authority to suspend the clearance and release of infringing goods. If a case is not filed within eight days, then the suspended goods should be released. The current mechanism is based on the presumed right-holders' vested interest in confirming that the confiscated goods are counterfeit and preventing their entry into the country by filing a legal action, which is logical and fair. Conversely, the request to amend the Customs Law to grant customs agents' *ex officio* authority to initiate criminal actions does not make economic or legal sense. On the one hand, the Jordanian Customs should not act as a private enforcement agency for right-holders,

[60] Trademarks Law No. 33; Copyright Law No. 22.

because the Customs Department would then have to shoulder the administrative, legal, and financial burden of investigation and prosecution. On the other hand, by bypassing the need to have the right-holder present his or her case before a court within the eight-day window, the owner of the alleged counterfeit goods is denied the right to due process and to present his or her case before a court. The court's role in weighing all the evidence before allowing the legal action to move forward is denied, in favour of a *sue sponte* decision by the Customs Department. The wrangling over the meaning of article 41 reflects in a particularly sharp manner the efforts of foreign governments and companies to position the Jordanian government as a proxy enforcer of their IPRs. As we have seen, such a role as a proxy enforcer promises to bring little benefit to Jordan itself, while increasing its costs in terms of institutional overload and administrative commitment.

The courts and enforcement of IPRs

Table 5-11 shows the number of IP cases decided by Jordanian courts from 2000 to 2008. The figures clearly reflect a gap between the number cases filed, as demonstrated in part by the numbers in table 5-11, and the courts' ability to resolve the disputes. Although, generally speaking, cases will not be resolved in the same year they were filed, there is evidence of considerable overload on the administrative system, and a marked lack of capacity to implement the new legal framework. However, the numbers do indicate that the number of cases resolved in 2007 and 2008 exceed the number of cases filed by the NL for the same period, which could reflect increased efficiency on behalf of the courts in handling cases turned over from previous years, as well as the increase in the number of judges appointed during that period.[61] Available statistics allow for these aggregate numbers to be further broken down into the number of cases filed with each type of court, as demonstrated by table 5-12.[62]

Under Jordanian Civil Procedure Rules, the splitting of jurisdiction between Small Claims and First Instance courts is made on two grounds.[63] The first is the general rule of monetary threshold, which specifies that general jurisdiction for cases with an estimated value of JD 7,000 ($10,000) or less falls to Small Claims Courts. Second, some types of

[61] The total number of working judges in Jordanian courts increased from 630 in 2006 to 676 in 2008, a 7.3% increase (source: 2008 Annual Court Report, issued by the Ministry of Justice).
[62] Source: Ministry of Justice.
[63] Civil Procedure Law No. 24, 1998.

cases are assigned jurisdiction based on case type, regardless of the monetary value. For example, labour disputes are always assigned to Small Claims Courts regardless of their value. Intellectual property cases are not pre-designated by type; as such, the court's jurisdiction is primarily based on the monetary threshold.

Table 5-11. Intellectual property cases decided by Jordanian courts 2000–2008 [64]

Year	2000	2001	2002	2003	2004	2005	2006	2007	2008
Cases	10	9	15	31	49	133	172	656	584

Table 5-12. Intellectual property cases per type of court [65]

Year	2000	2001	2002	2003	2004	2005	2006	2007	2008
Small claims courts	9	8	12	25	33	76	58	264	122
First instance courts	1	1	3	6	16	57	114	392	462

While the number of Small Claims Court decisions on IP issues steadily increased from 2000 to 2007, it dropped in 2008 by almost 53% from the previous year. This is in contrast to the steady increase in the number of IP cases decided by the First Instance courts, which increased by 18% during the 2007–2008 period. Given the monetary threshold rules for jurisdiction between small claims and First Instance courts, those numbers clearly point to the increased value of IP claims in excess of JD 7000 and thus explain the continued increase in the number of cases reviewed by First Instance courts.

The fact that the number of IP cases referred to courts by the Jordanian administrative agencies exceeds those filed by private citizens or companies suggests that either the Jordanian citizens do not have enough economic interest in IPRs to justify litigation, or they find the cost–benefit analysis for litigation not favourable. Keeping a close eye on the involvement of the judicial branch in enforcement is one way of measuring the future significance of IPRs in the Jordanian economy, because judicial involvement is an indicator of how much emphasis the business entity places on IPRs to justify litigation costs. To affirmatively

[64] Ministry of Justice, *Number of Intellectual Property Cases Sorted by Year & Court Type*, compiled for the author upon a written request, 2010.

[65] Ministry of Justice, *Number of Intellectual Property Cases Sorted by Year & Court Type*.

speak of an ascendancy of IPRs for Jordanian businesses one must, among other things, be able to point to a growth of IP litigation both in volume and, more importantly, in sophistication.

Progression of claims and execution of verdicts

Registration decisions for patents, trademarks, and other registrable types of IPRs are considered final governmental decisions, and as such are reviewed by the Supreme Administrative Court. First Instance courts, on the other hand, address rights and privileges arising from owning an IPR. Decisions by the Supreme Administrative Court are final.[66]

When it comes to resolving disputes, the Jordanian legislation does not set time limits on the court action, but Civil Procedure Law No. 24 does include some rules meant to limit prolonged litigation by setting time limits on presenting defences and responses. Generally, a case cannot be postponed more than fifteen days, except in extreme situations, and a case cannot be postponed more than once for a reason related to the circumstances of one of the parties. Also, a judge must render a verdict no more than thirty days after the conclusion of the trial. Overall, the Annual Courts Report for 2008 points to a very high percentage of cases being resolved by the courts less than one year from filing. The average percentage of cases resolved per the annual load of every type of court (small claims, First Instance, appeals, cassation, and special courts) exceeds 93%.[67] The real problem, however, lies with the execution of court orders, which poses a serious challenge for any enforcement effort in general, and for the enforcement of IP in particular.

Judicial civil orders are executed pursuant to Execution Law No. 36 (2002), whereupon execution departments in each First Instance Court carry out judicial orders within their respective jurisdictions. Every execution unit is headed by a judge who is assisted by one or more other judges as need be. The Judicial Council's statistics indicate that in 2008, there were 177,909 execution cases carried over from the year 2007, and an additional 70,289 were added in 2008, raising the total number of execution orders to 248,198 orders, of which only 66,164 were executed in 2008.[68] That left a total of 182,034 execution orders still outstanding, which means that 73% of the total number of execution orders in 2008 were carried over to 2009. The Amman Governorate execution units, which are the place for filing and executing the majority of the IP cases,

---

[66] Supreme Administrative Court Law No. 12, 1992, sec. 26(b).

[67] Jordanian Judicial Council, *Annual Courts Report – 2008.*

[68] Ibid.

suffer from a significant back-log in execution, with 51,560 pending execution orders, amounting to 29% of all execution orders for all of Jordan.[69] In Amman, 65% of the execution orders are carried over, annually.

While it is not clear what percentage of those cases relate to IP disputes, because the existing numbers are not broken down by case type, it is clear that execution should be a significant concern for any entity seeking resolution through judicial channels in Jordan. The numbers point to a possible systematic problem with the execution system as a whole, the mechanism by which court orders get shuffled back and forth between appellate and lower courts, and the process of giving notice to various parties in the legal dispute.

The execution of judicial criminal orders according to article 353 of the Criminal Procedure Law falls to the prosecutor at the court that issued the criminal order or verdict. In courts that do not have their own designated prosecutor, criminal execution is the responsibility of the small claims judge. The problems with civil execution seem to be shared with criminal executions, as shown in table 5-13 below.

Table 5-13. Execution of criminal orders[70]

Unit	*Rotated from 2006*	*Incoming 2007*	*Total 2006–2007*	*Executed in 2008*	*Rotated from 2008*	*Percentage execution in 2008*
Criminal Court Prosecutor[71]	637	234	871	211	660	25%
First Instance Prosecutors	163,699	70,734	234,433	75,939	158,494	32%
Small Claims Prosecutors	37,866	24,748	62,614	24,843	37,771	40%

[69] Ibid.

[70] Ibid.

[71] The Criminal Court, also known as the Serious Crimes Court, is one of a recent vintage that was created by law No. 19 (1986), and has exclusive first-instance limited jurisdiction in crimes involving murder, rape, kidnapping, and sexual assault. In effect it was envisioned to take over cases that were considered blood or honour crimes under the tribal law in Jordan, which theoretically since 1976 is no longer applicable, but still has a significant role in such crimes, in some cases forcing the relatives of the perpetrator of murder crimes to be evacuated from their homes to other areas.

As to the specific issue of courts dealing with IP, Jordan shares a similar burden with other developing countries of not having the judicial system contribute much to the evolution of IP systems. This is due to several factors, primarily:

1. The limited role of *stare decisis*, which greatly hampers the courts' ability to influence legal interpretation
2. The lack of experience and knowledge of the judicial staff in the area of IPRs
3. The limited scope of application of IPRs within the judicial system, which seems mainly concerned with trademarks to the detriment of other branches of IP.

Although a considerable amount of training is taking place for judges and Ministry of Justice staff, as indicated by the number of training seminars and conferences devoted to IPRs,[72] there does not seem to be an integrated approach towards IP enforcement, as evidenced by the number of enforcement agencies with overlapping responsibilities and duties. There is also no IP strategy other than the obligatory, but notional, governmental reference to the need to abide by and respect IP laws. The process of passing IP legislation as part of the adjustment process should have helped build the legislative capacity in that area, but in actuality it did not, as most of the amendments occurred while Parliament was suspended and were later approved by Parliament without much debate.[73]

Of course, the absence of even a semi-sophisticated IP practice contributes to the lack of such an integrated approach by the legal profession and continues to sap the energy of any efforts to elevate the practice in the area of IP.[74] Without a more sophisticated IP practice, the role that patents play in Jordan will be marginal.

Judicial reform in Jordan

Partly in response to this lack of capacity, the judicial sector in Jordan is going through a modernization and development phase, which affects the structure and functions of the Ministry of Justice and the Courts. While the judicial branch, in theory, is a separate branch of the government and should be managed exclusively by the head and members of the Judicial

[72] Jordanian Judicial Council, *Annual Courts Report – 2008*; Ministry of Justice, *First Annual Ministry of Justice Book* (Ministry of Justice, 2008).

[73] Jordanian Parliament was suspended between 2000–2002 and 2009–2010.

[74] A point emphasized in interviews.

Council, the Ministry of Justice still plays a role in the organization and setup of courts, as well as the appointment and transfer of judges. This symbiotic, albeit odd, relationship seems to have been deployed thus far for the benefit of the judicial system as a whole.

The overall effect of this trend has been a move towards expanding the authority of Small Claims Courts by expanding the financial limit that would bring a case under their purview from JD 3,000 ($4,250) to JD 7,000 ($9,900).[75] This has led to the lessening of the load on the First Instance courts, while at the same time allowing citizens to benefit from the more facilitated approach to adjudication allowed under the Small Claims Courts system. In accordance with international conventions on human rights, the court fees on criminal appeals were abolished. The impact of those reforms on IP enforcement should be tangible, as cases under an IP claim will benefit from any improvements in the litigation and adjudication process that these changes will bring about.

The number of judges has also been steadily increasing, including the number of female judges. In 2007, thirty-eight new judges were appointed, including five female judges; this raised the total number of female judges to forty-two, accounting for 6% of the total number of judges. Recently, the Ministry of Justice initiated the Future Judges Program aimed at recruiting judges; it targets high school graduates and law school students. The program intends to recruit qualified candidates and fast-track them into the judiciary by the time they are 28–30 years old. The Ministry of Justice and the Judicial Council promote the program as key to recruiting bright, young, educated judges, especially since the program involves scholarships to obtain undergraduate or graduate degrees in law.[76]

It is not clear, however, how recruiting high school and law school students will actually help enrich the level of experience of the Jordanian judicial system. Rather, the Future Judges Program threatens to make the role of the judge as that of a functionary who meets the requirements of the job by simply obtaining the requisite legal education, greatly discounting the importance of experience, which can only be obtained by working in the legal profession.

[75] Small Claims Courts Law No. 30, 2008, sec. 3.

[76] All the figures in this paragraph are taken from Jordanian Judicial Council, *Annual Courts Report – 2008*.

Specialized courts

A further proposal is that specialized courts be created specifically to address matters pertaining to IPR. The main argument presented for such courts is that the role played by them can help bridge the judges' IP knowledge gap, and thus provide a more efficient administration of justice. Furthermore, it is argued that specialized courts will provide for speedy and swift adjudication of claims. The USA's Federal Court of Appeals (Federal Circuit) is often cited as an example supporting both of these contentions. Closer scrutiny, however, reveals that the claims presented in these arguments are not strongly supported either by the history of that court or by the particularities of the Jordanian situation.

The history of the Federal Circuit began with its historic predecessor, the US Court of Customs and Patent Appeals (CCPA), which itself began as the US Court of Customs Appeals, created in 1909 and officially operational on April 22, 1910. In 1929, the US Court of Customs and Patent Appeals was created and vested with appeals from the US Patent Office. In 1982, the Federal Courts Improvement Act (FCIA) abolished the CCPA and transferred its jurisdiction, docket, and judges to the Federal Circuit. The IPRs appeals reviewed by the Federal Circuit, which are often cited as the reason behind the call for an exclusive IP court in Jordan, are only one of sixteen areas over which the Federal Circuit has appellate jurisdiction. Thus, despite the fact that patent practice in the United States is among the most vibrant and developed in the world, the Federal Circuit is not solely dedicated to patent appeals. By contrast, the IP practice in Jordan is in an embryonic stage, and patent litigation is almost non-existent. Under these circumstances, it is hard to argue that there will be any practical justification for the creation of judicial panel to exclusively review IP claims.

A more useful suggestion is the creation of a judicial body to review claims on corporate and commercial issues in general, including IP issues. The creation of such a panel or court makes practical sense because the number of cases in that area is large enough to justify the allocation of the needed resources. It also makes legal sense because it will help to create a unified body to review commercial and corporate issues, thus creating a unified body of jurisprudence that will go a long way towards the stability of the corporate and commercial environment as a whole, including IPRs.

Another argument presented to support the call for an exclusive IP judicial panel is to help bridge the judges' IP knowledge gap and thus provide a more efficient administration of justice. However, this argument does not acknowledge the reason why there is an IP knowledge gap to begin with, which is the limited scope and negligible volume of IP practice. A judge's practice and judicial knowledge are directly linked to the legal areas he or she reviews and to the type of cases presented before him or her. For example, the Federal Circuit judges can be expected to have a knowledge gap regarding tribal law in general and Jordanian tribal law in particular. Such a shortcoming will not be remedied by creating an independent judicial panel for tribal law, but rather by the independent education of those who might need such knowledge. The same, I argue, applies to the issue of Jordanian judges' knowledge gap in the area of IP law, which can be remedied by the selective training of judges in that area.

Eroding the multilateral system

This chapter has considered the ways in which the imposition of TRIPS and TRIPS-plus standards in Jordan is having a corrosive effect on Jordanian legal and administrative institutions, by increasing the disconnect between them and the Jordanian population. As a number of scholars have noted, however, the pursuit of higher IPRs is having an analogous corrosive effect at the international level. The shift away from multilateral fora, embodied by the RBT system, is having an impact on the established international institutions. Drahos directly accuses RBTs of weakening the multilateral trading system, criticizing the way in which RBTs are drafted because differences in interpretation are structured into the agreement, thus planting the seeds for future differences in expectations and obligations.[77]

A fundamental problem with RBTs is that their dispute-resolution mechanisms provide an opportunity for forum shifting which weakens the multilateral WTO dispute-resolution system. Because they are less legally sophisticated, developing countries are disadvantaged by RBT's forum shifting because it takes them away from the legal precedents under the WTO's dispute-resolution mechanism.[78] Choice of forum provisions in RBTs does not strengthen the multilateral trading system under the WTO. In particular, the dispute-settlement process within the WTO, commonly known as the DSU, has been both a victim of trade agreements and a tool for developed countries to promote the pro-intellectual-property climate.

---

[77] Peter Drahos, "Assessing the Impact of the Australia-United States Free Trade Agreement on Australian and Global Medicines Policy," *Globalization & Health*, n.d., http://www.globalizationandhealth.com/content/1/1/15; "Weaving Webs of Influence: The United States, Free Trade Agreements and Dispute Resolution," *Journal of World Trade* 41, no. 1 (2007).

[78] Drahos, "Weaving Webs of Influence."

Typically, trade agreements carry with them their own dispute settlement mechanisms, which cover potential dispute areas under those agreements, including the area of IP.[79] This has had a corrosive impact on the ability and potential for the trade agreement's contracting parties to use the DSU as they commit themselves to a new forum outside the DSU venue. The developing country is left alone in the arena against their better-prepared counterparty.

None of the dispute-settlement mechanisms under the RBTs with Jordan reference DSU cases or contemplate using them as precedents in future disputes. This dispute-settlement forum shifting occurs mostly at the expense of developing countries, which are less technically sophisticated in navigating the new venue of dispute settlement, as well as at the expense of the DSU's potential to become a universal forum for trade resolution with established precedents and uniform procedural rules that apply equally to all WTO member countries.

One obvious benefit for developed countries that seek such forum shifting is the added flexibility in managing future disputes with trading partners. Jordan, therefore, should it choose to contest any enforcement requests or interpretations similar to those issued under the Special 301 Report, is bound to address them through the JUSFTA dispute-settlement mechanism and suffer from the above shortcomings of such a forum. The JUSFTA specifically calls for the creation of a Joint Committee "to supervise the proper implementation" of the Agreement.[80] That Committee's authority is open-ended and not well defined, but its functions are broad enough to include considering and adopting amendments to the Agreement and developing guidelines and rules for its proper implementation.

That approach by developed countries, particularly the United States, is not recent or new: the United States pursued it long before the DSU system was established. US trade policy has been described as moving towards the pragmatic, ad hoc approach of dealing with trading partners on a bilateral basis and "rewarding friends."[81]

In a real-life example of the realist theory of international relations, the US Government simultaneously supported the continued evolution of RBTs and the DSU. On the one hand it became the heaviest user of the DSU system, while on the other hand it pushed for RBTs with dispute-resolution clauses that undermined the DSU system. For developed countries, trade agreements presented the opportunity to regulate the

---

[79] This applies to all US FTAs, except that with Israel.

[80] Jordan–United States Free Trade Agreement (2000), sec. 15.1.

[81] John H. Jackson, *The World Trading System: Law and Policy of International Economic Relations* (MIT Press, 1997).

unilateralist retaliation among themselves.[82] To developing countries, they also presented the opportunity for preferential access to markets. However, the increased criticisms targeting TRIPS, especially its patent provisions and their impact on access to medicines, caused US companies and their lobbyists to turn their attention to the possibilities offered by RBTs for ushering in TRIPS-plus standards and shifting the forum of dispute resolution.[83] For instance, Article 6 of TRIPS states that, for the purposes of dispute settlement, nothing in TRIPS can be used to address exhaustion issues, but the United States can use RBTs to address the issue of exhaustion.

Although these alternative fora do tend to splinter the international legal framework, it is not simply that the dispute-resolution mechanisms in RBTs supersede Jordan's rights under the DSU. Article 23 of the DSU provides that "when Members seek the redress of a violation of obligations or other nullification or impairment of benefits under the covered agreements, or an impediment to the attainment of any objective of the covered agreements, they shall have recourse to, and abide by, the rules and procedures of this Understanding."[84] The interplay between the DSU and the dispute-resolution mechanisms in RBTs, to the extent that there is any, will therefore determine whether the DSU is still considered a valid dispute-resolution mechanism between countries that have RBTs, or if the RBTs dispute-settlement processes effectively deprive parties of access to the WTO process. The flip side of this issue is whether the WTO can accept complaints initiated through the WTO dispute-settlement proceedings in possible violation of their RBT obligations.[85] To date, the WTO appellate panel has not declined any cases based on exclusive jurisdiction under an RBT. Examples include the request by the United States to review Mexico's actions against non-cane-sugar sweeteners, which Mexico argued the WTO panel should refuse to address in light of Mexico's efforts to initiate North America Free Trade Agreement (NAFTA) Chapter 20 proceedings. The Appellate Body held that the panel

82 John H. Jackson, *The Jurisprudence of GATT and the WTO: Insights on Treaty Law and Economic Relations* (Cambridge University Press, 2000). For example, both Canada and Mexico saw merits in a preferential trade arrangement that offered a way of dealing with US trade unilateralism.

83 Peter Drahos, "Intellectual Property and Pharmaceutical Markets: A Nodal Governance Approach," *Temple Law Review* 77 (2004): 401.

84 WTO, Dispute Settlement Understanding (WTO, May 1, 2010), sec. 23.1.

85 David Gantz, "Dispute Settlement Under the NAFTA and the WTO: Choice of Forum Opportunities and Risks for the NAFTA Parties," *American University International Law Review* 14 (1999): 1025.

could not decline to exercise jurisdiction and that the WTO had no basis to determine whether or not the United States had acted consistently with its NAFTA obligations.[86] That ruling offers hope that Jordan can always take any potential case to the WTO's DSU, as the DSU, it seems, would not decline to exercise to jurisdiction.[87] The problem of alternative fora, therefore, is more that they confuse the international legal framework, generating increased demands on developing countries, rather than simply abrogating it.

The position that Jordan can always take any potential case to the WTO's DSU is also supported by article 23 of the DSU, which provides that WTO violations can only be resolved through the WTO's dispute settlement mechanism even if an RBT has already adjudicated the matter.[88] This has been the case in cases involving members of the Mercado Comun del Sur (MERCOSUR),[89] which has been commonly appealed to the WTO even though a MERCOSUR panel had already adjudicated the matter.[90] This shows that the issues raised by conflicts and forum choices between the WTO and RBTs include several factors, such as disputes over jurisdiction, duplicative proceedings that can lead to conflicting rulings, various procedural issues related to the lack of *res judicata*,[91] and the preclusion of defences afforded by using the WTO as back channel to re-litigate an unfavourable RBT verdict.

---

[86] Ibid.

[87] Gantz, "Dispute Settlement Under the NAFTA"; Frederick M. Abbott, "WTO Dispute Settlement Practice Relating to the Agreement on Trade-Related Intellectual Property Rights," *SSRN eLibrary* (n.d.), http://papers.ssrn.com/sol3/papers.cfm?abstract_id=1920816.

[88] WTO, Dispute Settlement Understanding, sec. 23.

[89] A Regional Trade Agreement (RTA) among Argentina, Brazil, Paraguay, and Uruguay was founded in 1991 by the Treaty of Asunción, and later amended and updated by the 1994 Treaty of Ouro Preto. Its purpose is to promote free trade and the fluid movement of goods, people, and currency.

[90] For example, the panel in Argentina on Definitive Anti-Dumping Duties on Poultry from Brazil stated that panels are not bound to follow the rulings of RTA panel proceedings, even if the proceedings involve the same measures. See DSU Panel, "Argentina: Definitive Anti-Dumping Duties on Poultry from Brazil" (WTO, April 22, 2003). There, a MERCOSUR panel had ruled in Argentina's favour. See also DSU Panel, "Brazil: Measures Affecting Imports of Retreaded Tyres" (WTO, June 12, 2007).

[91] Meaning that a final judgment is no longer subject to appeal, and also used to refer to the legal doctrine meant to bar (or preclude) continued litigation between the same parties.

Another important concern is the impact RBT decisions can have on third parties. Hypothetically, the United States and Jordan could settle a trade dispute through the RBT mechanism, only to have one or both sued through the DSU by third parties claiming that the resolution causes its goods or services to be treated unfairly or discriminated against. This was the case, for example, when the European Commission (EC) sued Brazil through the DSU to object to restrictions on the importation of re-treaded tires, which were implemented after Brazil lost a claim to Uruguay at the MERCOSUR arbitral tribunal.[92]

The outcome of a dispute is never certain for developed countries, as shown by the outcomes of the US TRIPS disputes against India in 1996 (alleging absence of patent protections for pharmaceuticals), Argentina in 1999 and 2000 (alleging, *inter alia*, failure to protect against unfair use of undisclosed test data, and denial of certain exclusive rights for patents), and Brazil in 2000 (alleging, *inter alia*, inconsistency of measures for enjoyment of exclusive patent rights). The Indian government adopted administrative delays to lessen the impact of the dispute-settlement body.[93] Argentina still retains several provisions in its laws, and Brazil does the same, albeit agreeing to consult with the United States in the case of compulsory licensing. In the face of these obstacles, the United States deployed the Special 301 Report powers as another pressuring tool operating outside the realm of the WTO.

Although we have concentrated on the corrosive effect of RBTs on the multilateral system, it would be simplistic to describe their influence as entirely negative. Bilateral agreements can, for example, have a positive effect in promoting accession to existing multilateral agreements.[94] That is certainly true in the case of Jordan, whose accession (or promise to accede) to several international multilateral IP agreements occurred after concluding its bilateral agreements with the United States and the European Union, suggesting that the multilateral agreements were joined in order to honour bilateral commitments. For Jordan, the treaties referenced by the JUSFTA included the UPOV, which Jordan joined in 2004, as well as the Patent Cooperation Treaty and the Protocol Relating to the Madrid Agreement Concerning the International Registration of Marks, both of which Jordan has yet to join.[95] Similarly, the Budapest

[92] DSU Panel, "Brazil: Measures Affecting Imports of Retreaded Tyres."
[93] Deere, *The Implementation Game*.
[94] Ibid.
[95] Article 4.2 of the JUSFTA states that each party "shall make best efforts to ratify or accede to the *Patent Cooperation Treaty* (1984) and the Protocol Relating to the *Madrid Agreement Concerning the Registration of Marks* (1989)." In subsequent

Treaty on the International Recognition of the Deposit of Microorganisms for the Purposes of Patent Procedure was referenced by the JUSFTA, albeit without a direct requirement to join.[96]

In addition to extending the duty to abide by whole agreements, an RBT can reference certain parts of multilateral agreements that it sees fit for both parties to abide by, even if the whole agreement is not acceded to. Examples in the JUSFTA include the Joint Recommendation Concerning Provisions on the Protection of Well-Known Marks (1999), WIPO Copyright Treaty (1996), and WIPO Performances and Phonograms Treaty (WPPT, 1996).[97] The same applies to the requirements under the JEUAA to fulfil the commitments under several multilateral IP agreements, including the Berne Convention for the Protection of Literary and Artistic Works, the Convention for the Protection of Performers, Producers of Phonograms, and Broadcasting Organizations, and the Nice Agreement concerning the International Classification of Goods and Services for the purposes of the Registration of Marks (Annex VII). RBTs, therefore, can reinforce multilateral IP agreements by harmonizing the applicability of those treaties to trade and imposing additional enforcement requirements far beyond those required under TRIPS.

ACTA

A recently noted development in the scope of IP treaties is the drive for the development of a plurilateral Anti-Counterfeiting Trade Agreement (ACTA) for establishing international standards on IPRs enforcement within the participating countries.[98] ACTA's proponents describe it as a tool to provide an international framework that improves the enforcement of existing IPRs without creating a new one. They argue that ACTA will create improved international enforcement standards regarding how to act

---

FTAs with the United States, this "best efforts" language was replaced with progressively stronger language.

96 Article 4.21 of the JUSFTA states that "when it is not possible to provide a sufficient written description of the invention … each Party shall require a deposit with an 'international depository authority,' as defined in the *Budapest Treaty on the International Recognition of the Deposit of Microorganisms for the Purposes of Patent Procedure* (1980)." Note that the US bilateral treaties signed with Morocco, Australia, Bahrain, countries of Central America and Dominican Republic, Colombia, Oman, Panama, Republic of Korea, and Peru, each contain the wording: "[e]ach party shall ratify or accede to … ."

97 See article 4.1 of the JUSFTA.

98 "The Anti-Counterfeiting Trade Agreement – Fact Sheet," May 1, 2010, http://trade.ec.europa.eu/doclib/html/140836.htm.

against large-scale infringement of IPRs. The intended scope of ACTA is broad, including counterfeit goods as well as "piracy over the Internet," with a focus on counterfeiting and piracy activities that significantly affect commercial interests, rather than activities of ordinary citizens.[99] The claim that ordinary citizens are not targeted by ACTA is challenged by various groups who maintain that leaked versions indicate that ACTA will target individuals, by demanding that they prove that copyrighted material on their electronic devices does not infringe copyright law, and that internet service providers will be required to divulge information about their customers without a warrant.[100] Ascertaining the nature of ACTA is not made easier by the shroud of secrecy placed around its negotiations.[101]

Additionally, negotiations for ACTA are not part of any international organization (e.g., the WTO).[102] In October 2007, the US Government, the European Commission, Switzerland, and Japan first announced that they would negotiate ACTA; since then, countries that have confirmed their involvement in the ACTA negotiations include New Zealand, the United States, Australia, Canada, the European Union, Japan, Korea, Mexico, and Switzerland.[103] The last round of ACTA negotiations (held in Washington, D.C., July 30–31, 2008) included, in addition to the above, the United States' RBT partners such as Jordan, Morocco, Singapore, and the United Arab Emirates. On November 15, 2010, a final text of the treaty was released, further confirming that it is intended as an international legal framework that countries can join on a voluntary basis, while creating its own governing body operating independently from international institutions such as the WTO, WIPO, and the United Nations.

From a political economic perspective, ACTA is another step towards "new constitutionalism," under which "public policy is increasingly premised on the goal of increasing the security of property owners and minimizing the uncertainty of investors."[104] In effect, the goal is to

---

[99] "The Anti-Counterfeiting Trade Agreement – Summary of Key Elements Under Discussion," *ISN*, May 1, 2010, http://www.isn.ethz.ch/isn/Digital-Library/Primary-Resources/Detail/?lng=en&id=114570.

[100] Mathew Ingram, "Do we Need Copyright Cops?" *The Globe and Mail-Blogs*, May 27, 2008.

[101] See, for example, *Electronic Frontier Foundation et al. vs. Office of the United States Trade Representative* (n.d.). Filed under the Freedom of Information Act to force the USTR to divulge information about ongoing ACTA negotiations.

[102] New Zealand Ministry of Economic Development, "Anti-Counterfeiting Trade Agreement," January 23, 2010, http://www.med.govt.nz/templates/Content TopicSummary____34357.aspx.

[103] Ibid.

[104] Stephen Gill, *Power and Resistance in the New World Order* (Palgrave

"strengthen surveillance mechanisms and institutional capabilities to reinforce … market discipline at the multilateral level, and to help sustain the legal and political conditions for trans-national capital."

Conclusion

Jordan's entry into the IPRs arena has been remarkable in its intensity, consistency, and scope. One would be hard pressed to think of another country that has adopted TRIPS standards and then TRIPS-plus standards with such speed. Yet as admirable as Jordan's enthusiasm might have been, side effects and unintended consequences were to be expected from such a rapid transition, especially given the Jordanian government's lack of experience in the drafting and enforcement of IPRs legislation.

The difficulties associated with the enforcement of IP laws in Jordan stem from a disregard of its cultural, social, legal, and economic norms and how they differ from those in developed countries. Until IP laws are calibrated to those norms, enforcement will continue to be exclusively associated with the threat of punitive measures by developed countries. Establishing such a link is also important to help IPRs deliver on the so-far unfulfilled and exceedingly distant promise to boost innovation and creativity. As suggested by the data discussed above, Jordan must do more than engage in regulatory compliance to assure an equitable return on their investment in IPRs, because rewards are not guaranteed, let alone instantaneous. Jordan should definitely make more of an effort to define protection levels and strike a balance between its economic realities and its international obligations. In that regard, Jordan faces a particularly difficult task, as it is further restricted in its use of the policy flexibilities afforded under TRIPS by the more stringent standards required under the JUSFTA and JEUAA.

An understanding of the international pressures exerted on Jordan is thus doubly important, since such factors both help to explain the drive towards TRIPS and TRIPS-plus standards, as well as to account for the failures in enforcement. In the case of Jordan, the weak national political dynamics in the area of IP have diminished Jordan's ability to counter the influence of international pressures and have consequently undermined the coalescing of a national position on the adoption and enforcement of IP standards. In the absence of a national IP strategy, however, Jordan and other developing countries stand to benefit little from enforcement of

---

Macmillan, 2003).

TRIPS and TRIPS-plus standards that protect content which those countries neither produce nor possess.

The points below, drawn from the discussion in this chapter, are presented here in a more condensed form in order to set out the main impediments to the enforcement of IPRs in Jordan.

Multiple enforcement teams and poor coordination

The enforcement of IPRs faces problems due to poor coordination between the various enforcement agencies; for copyright, for example, these are the National Library, the Public Security Department, and the Department of Press and Publications. Overlapping responsibilities further compound the problems caused by the poor coordination. For example, all of the above-mentioned departments claim authority to handle counterfeited audio-visual products. Similar issues arise regarding counterfeited trademark products between the Customs Department, the Jordan Institute of Standards and Metrology (JISM), and the Public Security Department. Rather than having IP cases dealt with expeditiously, overlapping responsibilities among the multitude of agencies lead to poor cooperation and coordination.

The Jordanian authorities' efforts to harmonize the workings of its various governmental agencies are, as a result, a work in progress. A contributing factor to the confusion is the pressure exerted by various international community agencies and donor countries to ratchet up the enforcement of IPRs.

Poor drafting by the legislator and weak governmental perspective

There is a split between the legislative language and intent and the actual implementation, rooted in the inexperience of both the legislative drafters and the implementers of the IP legislation.[105]

As we saw in chapter four, poor drafting of IP legislation is evident from the inclusion of the Madrid and PCT clauses into the Jordanian trademark and patent laws, even though Jordan is not a signatory to either. For trademark law, the inclusion of the clauses was somewhat mitigated by the inclusion of language stipulating they come into force only after the Madrid Protocol is actually signed. Yet in light of Jordan's lack of progress in signing the Protocol, there is no clear justification for the addition of the language in the first place.

---

[105] This point was emphasized in interview. See appendix one.

The inclusion of language in the patent law that allows for immediate filing of international patent applications under the PCT presents a more extreme example of poor drafting, because the patent law does not even include language postponing its activation until Jordan's signing of the PCT.

The weak governmental implementation perspective is evident from the dispute over the interpretation of the JUSFTA's article 4(26), which requests that Jordan "shall provide, at least in cases of copyright piracy or trademark counterfeiting, that its authorities may initiate criminal actions and border measure actions *ex officio*, without the need for a formal complaint by a private party or right holder." The US Government's position has been to request an amendment of the Jordanian Customs law to comply with this language. The Jordanian Customs Department accepted this argument and did not present an opposing point of view (even though several are available). As argued earlier, however, the current Customs Law is in fact in compliance with the language of JUSFTA article 14(26) and, therefore, no amendment of the Customs law is necessary.

Weak governmental interpretation is also evident in JISM's destroying counterfeit goods after confiscating them, even though that is not allowed under its current law. It is up to the owner of the alleged counterfeit goods to file a claim with the court to stop the JISM from destroying the goods or to seek restitution. The work of the JISM in the area of IP enforcement is outside the scope of its law, which does not explicitly address counterfeit trademarks. The JISM interprets article 30(c) of its law to allow for the destruction of counterfeit goods, but article 30(c) actually only addresses the destruction of goods that do not meet the JISM standards.

Outsourcing and the patent prosecution system

The Jordanian patent prosecution system is centred on outsourcing the patent examination and prosecution process to the WIPO. This outsourcing allows the Jordanian patent office (which is located within the Industrial Property Department of the MoIT) to benefit from the technical capabilities of the WIPO and helps reduce the costs associated with providing the service through full-time staff in Jordan. However, this is being done at the expense of developing Jordan's own patent examination and prosecution capabilities.

In addition, the dependence on WIPO creates new lines of vulnerability as regards Jordan's capacity to develop a tailored and context-sensitive system of IP law. May criticizes WIPO for being a politicized organization that uses its capacity development and technical assistance programmes to engender, through socialisation, IPRs views similar to those under RBTs.[106] WIPO's socialization of policy makers through training and education is thought to produce advocates for enhanced IPRs protections among domestic policy decision makers.[107] Such local advocates are used to overcome local opposition for increased IPRs protections and to formulate public policy that increases the security of property owners while minimizing the uncertainty of investors.[108] This also contributes to the stigma attached to any dissenting opinions on the value of excessive IPRs, although earlier tendencies to term such voices "anti-progressive" have been tempered by the recent global economic turmoil and by the increased realization that the economic liberalization plans did not deliver the sustainability or the growth promised.

Escalating IPRs protections

By constantly attempting to extend, by both direct and indirect means, the initial IPRs protection under TRIPS, TRIPS-plus is placing further restrictions on the dissemination of knowledge and delaying the eventual placement of proprietary knowledge and know-how in the public domain. Such attempts create an atmosphere that encourages the culture of infringement because they undermine the basic tenet of the IP system, which is based on offering a *limited period* of exclusivity, after which the protected knowledge eventually reverts to the public domain.[109]

TRIPS standards, for example, resulted in the near-universal adoption of patents for pharmaceutical products, an area traditionally excluded from patent protection in developing countries, where only process patents were allowed.[110] TRIPS also assured extended protection beyond the designated

---

[106] Christopher May, "The World Intellectual Property Organization," *New Political Economy* 11, no. 3 (September 2006): 435–445.

[107] Christopher May, "Capacity Building and the Re-production of Intellectual Property Rights" *Third World Quarterly* 25, no. 5 (July 2004): 821–837; "The World Intellectual Property Organization."

[108] Gill, *Power and Resistance*; May, "The World Intellectual Property Organization."

[109] Hamed El Said and Mohammed El Said, "TRIPS-Plus Implications for Access to Medicines in Developing Countries: Lessons from Jordan–United States Free Trade Agreement." *The Journal of World Intellectual Property* 10, no. 6 (November 1, 2007): 438–475.

[110] A product patent refers to the chemical structure of a drug, regardless of its method of manufacturing. Process patents, on the other hand, offer protection for the method used to make the final product, and how the product is specifically

twenty-year patent period by introducing data exclusivity periods. Under data exclusivity pretences, drug regulatory agencies can for a limited time prevent the use of data presented to them to approve a pharmaceutical product from being used for the registration of a generic version of the same product.[111] That exclusion period is five years in Jordan, which effectively grants pharmaceutical companies a five-year protection period in addition to any patent protection they might have.[112]

The JUSFTA (art. 22) adds yet more time to the twenty-year patent period by granting an ill-defined protection to new uses of old chemicals. It is not clear what "new uses" means in this context, whether it refers to the use of the chemical entity alone or in combination with others, whether the use must be to produce something else that is desirable, or whether the new use of the material can be the desired end in itself.

In the area of copyright, the JUSFTA added significant requirements and thus higher standards of protection, giving right-holders the power to allow or deny the importation of the protected work(s), whether the work is pirated or an authorized version.[113]

The above examples represent a trend in the application of IP standards that deviates from the notion of IPRs as a limited and finite privilege granted to the right-holder for a limited period of time and meant to enhance public knowledge, not to engender monopolistic activity. This trend will ultimately serve as a catalyst for the escalation of infringing activity, because it provides an argument for the circumvention of IPRs.

As Jordan struggles through the consequences of the global economic downturn, stricter enforcement of IP laws brings with it potential economic costs to both the government and the Jordanian people. These costs can have destabilizing consequences on the social fabric and the governmental budget. The public's daily encounters with the impact of unemployment,[114] long waiting lines for public medical services, reduced

---

used to reach certain goals. A process patent is most useful if there is but one technically and financially sound way to produce the product in question.

[111] Mohammed El Said, "The Implementation Paradox: Intellectual Property Regulation in the Arab World," *Journal of International Trade Law and Policy* 9, no. 3 (2010): 221–235.

[112] Patent Law No. 32, sec. 36(d).

[113] JUSFTA article 4(11): for relevant text, see note to p. 82 of the present work.

[114] Unemployment rate: 13.5% (2009 est.), 12.6% (2008 est.), unofficial rate is approximately 30%. Source "Jordan Unemployment Rate - Economy," April 20, 2010, http://www.indexmundi.com/jordan/unemployment_rate.html.

access to medicine,[115] increased costs of goods,[116] and rising inflation,[117] along with the added cost of doing business, leave the average citizen with little alternative to pirated and counterfeit products sold by people who have no other source of income than that derived from selling them.

Despite some improvements in other areas, Jordan will remain a developing country for the foreseeable future, plagued by infringement and enforcement issues of IPRs. How to reap the full potential of administrative and judicial protection while sustaining and improving economic growth is still an open question. Even though Jordan has an IPRs legal framework that is in compliance with the international standards under TRIPS and other bilateral agreements, the resulting enforcement and implementation regime has many shortcomings, and the credibility of the Jordanian democratic and legal institutions could potentially be sapped by the obvious influence of extra-national forces.

Policy makers should formulate a coherent national policy based on an understanding that the strongest possible IPRs protection should not always be pursued. In the absence of such a reasoned mode of formulation, there is increased risk that IP will be viewed by Jordanians as hostile to their interests and needs. IPRs should be welcomed as long as they are implemented in a flexible way that meets the needs of the local economy, at reasonable social and economic costs. The current maximum-protection model is bad not only for developing countries but also, in the long run, for developed countries, yet short-sighted corporate pressures and lobbying will assure the dominance of maximum-protection models for the foreseeable future.

In general terms there is an overreliance on judicial (civil and criminal) solutions, and a neglect of economic ones. Taking economic considerations into account will allow Jordan to step away from an enforcement model that is based on balancing the economic interests of the infringer and the right-holder. Such a model would emphasize the introduction of original products at rates reasonable to the local community, thus undercutting the economic incentive for infringers. Until this occurs, the Jordanian government will continue to find itself cast as a proxy enforcer for the interests of MNCs, often at the expense of its own people.

---

[115] Mohammad Kayyali, "Cancer and Kidney Failure Medications not Available – Pharmacy Union says," *Alghad Daily Newspaper*, April 17, 2010.

[116] Jumana Ghnemaat, "Prices of Propane Gas Might Go up by 40%," *Alghad Daily Newspaper*, April 19, 2010.

[117] Inflation for 2008 was 13.9%, for 2009 –0.7%, for 2010 5%. Source "CBJ – Inflation in Jordan," April 20, 2010, CBJ website, http://www.cbj.gov.jo.

If Jordan continues to fail to raise its innovation levels, it will not place much emphasis on IP standards except to the extent necessary for window dressing. Continuing to define acceptable standards upwards might provide some easy comfort for the short term (and can generate some cheap publicity), but in the long run it is nothing short of burying one's head in the sand. In place of this, there must be a moment of reckoning when the Jordanian economic and political decision-makers answer the key question of whether they realistically see Jordan as an international, or even a regional, technological innovator and power-house. If they do not, then they must explain why Jordan has such stringent IP laws. Given the positive link between the use of imitation and increased innovation, high IP standards are actually hampering any chance that an innovative technical critical mass will ever coalesce in Jordan. Rights holders will need to focus not only on standards adopted elsewhere, but also, and primarily, on standards that accommodate the specifics of the Jordanian economic, social, and legal context. Such a novel approach will be a good start for the whole region.

The United States has an unprecedented opportunity to use its stock of knowledge to further the development of other countries in the world. With the vast knowledge within its borders, it should move to disseminate that knowledge and not succumb to the calls of multinationals to restrict its diffusion. The United States should adopt a position that considers knowledge to be part of a global intellectual commons, which, as the free software movement has shown, is not inconsistent with the development of business models. The excessive use of TRIPS-plus standards in RBTs has contributed to the anti-development reputation of the US Government, even as it seeks global support for its IP enforcement goals.

In the pursuit of IP enforcement in Jordan, there are no easy solutions to the structural enforcement problems that have been discussed in this chapter. The leading developed countries have essentially adopted the position that increasing the strength of IP systems is a means of engineering competitive advantage through regulation. Jordan must recognize the disconnect that exists at various levels between its IP laws and its economic and developmental goals, and it must move in ways that will reconcile that disconnect. Only then will enforcement be a meaningful and self-perpetuating activity, rather than one driven by foreign coercion and local half-measures.

CHAPTER SIX

NEW WAYS FORWARD

This book has set out a picture of globalization misapplied. A harmonized legal framework, designed to suit the operations of corporations with global reach, cannot be assumed to be suitable for all the markets and territories in which those corporations operate. It might be tempting to suppose that transnational corporations need care little about this mismatch, since what they really desire is hegemonic control over IPR in pursuit of wider markets and greater profits; but the argument of this book suggests otherwise. The imposition of TRIPS and TRIPS-plus standards in Jordan is creating a dysfunctional legal environment, and further alienating the population from the international norms of IP protection. The presumed corporate goals of ideological hegemony and economic profit cannot be successfully pursued within a framework which is simply unable to generate compliance, either voluntary or enforced. In the meantime, Jordanians continue to be deprived of access to IP which could be a source of innovation and development – and therefore of potential benefit to the global economy – while Jordanian legal and democratic institutions are being sapped of legitimacy. A new way forward is needed.

This new way forward must be based upon detailed legal, cultural, and economic analysis of state-level IP frameworks, such as that presented in the preceding chapters. Indeed, it has been a subsidiary argument of this book that the existing literature on IPRs pays insufficient attention to the ways in which TRIPS and TRIPS-plus systems actually play out in developing countries, particularly in the Middle East.[1] The literature is characterized by overly general statements regarding the pros and cons of TRIPS and RBTs, and pays too much attention to rules and legal provisions at a global level while neglecting country-specific analysis. While there is an abundance of literature on the origins of TRIPS and the

[1] The author has conducted a critical survey of literature on IPR and Jordan and draws on those conclusions here. See F. K. Nesheiwat, "A Critique of Intellectual Property Research." *Arab Law Quarterly* 27, no. 1 (2013): 51–69.

integration of IP into RBTs, there is a gap as regards IP policy making at state (rather than multilateral) level. A further weakness of the literature is that it makes insufficient effort to contextualize local political and cultural frameworks, or to explore the extent to which they influence IP policies. The challenge which the literature must address is to resolve the tension between the competing social objectives of encouraging innovation by recognizing private rights, and encouraging diffusion of knowledge to a broad range of people. This challenge cannot be addressed from a purely global perspective; it requires a localized approach.

This is not, of course, to deny that the literature presents considerable insights into the nature of the contemporary IP regime. Notably, however, the level of generality at which most studies are couched mirrors the generic nature of TRIPS itself. Where the global IP framework assumes that a single set of generic suppositions suffices to frame IP legal systems suitable for any developing country, the globalization literature reflects this by basing its critiques of that framework primarily on an examination of those very suppositions.

In a sense, then, the literature shares the globalizing stance which underpins TRIPS. The literature on globalization is itself globalizing in nature. In this respect, it is congenitally unable to identify the flaws in the system, since it downgrades the importance of concrete national experiences in assessing IP regimes, and it is at the national level that the flaws become evident.

The logical alternative is localized contextualization. Such analysis promises to provide the required validation or refutation of the theory that a one-size-fits-all harmonized approach to IPRs can address the tension between the social objectives just mentioned. Future research should address the question of whether country-specific knowledge and information is likely to lead to different sorts of policies. Such research should not make the mistake of confusing true and proper enforcement of IPRs with changes in laws and policies, and should recall that direct pressure on developing countries to adopt IP laws may lead to little actual change in behaviour. Such studies are likely to confirm that Jordan's approach to IP enforcement was based on acquiescence on paper to do just enough—but no more than was either possible or necessary—to free itself from US pressure.

By way of identifying new ways forward, this book has identified several central research areas that can serve as a road map for scholars. The questions sketched below draw the attention of legal scholars to outstanding questions and gaps in the existing intellectual property literature on Jordan, and can be used as a template to create future research objectives for other Arab countries as well.

1. To what extent do amendments to local laws and policies actually lead to changes in behaviour, and to what extent does international pressure to adopt IP laws automatically lead to enforcement of such laws in the developing world?
2. From a country-specific and contextualized perspective, which, if any, of the RBTs' objectives are being reached?
3. Looking beyond access to medicines, what has been the effect, if any, of TRIPS and TRIPS-plus IP laws on attracting direct foreign investments? Was the technical assistance provided to patent offices geared towards US and EU best enforcement practices at the expense of exploring flexibilities available under TRIPS and RBTs?
4. Given that the United States' and European Union's patent systems are built around allowing litigation to correct for errors in patent examination and granting, and given that developing countries generally do not have robust patent prosecution or litigation practices, are developed-world systems functionally fit for developing countries?

Speaking more generally, future research should focus on developing a more robust basis for the analysis of IP legislation. All the benefits promised by TRIPS and RBTs are based on economic factors, but to be relevant and meaningful, economic analysis should be highly country-specific, so that direct correlations can be established. And noneconomic desiderata should not be excluded from the cost–benefit analysis.

The preceding comments have been directed at shaping future studies on the impact of IP laws in developing countries. It remains to gather together the recommendations for future ways forward set out in the present work. We have seen that IP laws fail to be fully enforced in Jordan because they do not fit with its culture and level of economic development, and are therefore unable to advance the economic interests of the Jordanian people. The claims made by the developed countries that higher IPRs protection would aid and support the economic development of developing countries did not withstand closer scrutiny, at least in the case of Jordan. Such arguments failed to acknowledge the need for a national recognition of interests as the evolutionary and historically contingent context within which the development and enforcement of IPRs must be situated, as opposed to the universalist and ahistorical approach embodied in TRIPS. Jordanian national policies regarding IP were not developed in concert with wider social development dynamics, while Jordan's current stage of development indicates that the commercial interests of Jordanians lie in free access to IPRs to enable them to develop their industrial and service sectors without the restrictions of license requirements and payments. This approach is little different to that adopted by developing countries themselves in the era before they achieved high levels of industrial development and started proclaiming the reification of IPRs. The general outlines of a new approach are therefore visible. The question is, how is this new approach to be achieved?

Drahos has been especially active in the pursuit of a new way forward, elaborating a proposal for a new framework of IPRs grounded in a human rights framework which does not circumscribe the freedom of developing countries to set effective standards of IP protection.[2] However, although this is morally appealing, it does not provide the necessary tools with which to identify what limits should be applied. The question remains of whether countries should completely forsake IPRs, and if not, what new system they should accept. May has argued for jettisoning the globally harmonized IP model to allow social costs at the national level to play a larger role in determining global IPRs protections.[3] He defends that approach on the grounds that until there is a more equal global society, a global regime that attempts to treat access to knowledge in all countries and regions similarly cannot be justified.[4] The points developed in this book support his proposal to use country-specific social costs to determine the limits of each country's IPRs system; this does indeed seem to be a sound basis for an alternative to the globally harmonized IP standard.

My observations suggest that the debate on the enforcement of IPRs would best be reframed by taking into account the commercial and capitalist interests of the parties involved (developing countries, in this case Jordan, and developed countries and their global corporations), rather than in terms of the infringement of a reified natural right. Such a reframing would locate the issue of IPRs within the political domain, making it amenable to the calculus of cost and benefit, and resituating it as an issue of legitimate national concern. Current IP laws are not in sync with Jordan's economic development levels or its existing societal and cultural norms. Until that obstacle is surmounted, the public will continue

---

[2] Peter Drahos, "An Alternative Framework for the Global Regulation of Intellectual Property Rights," *Austrian Journal of Development Studies*, no. 1 (October 2005).

[3] Christopher May, "Why IPRs Are a Global Political Issue," January 2003, http://eprints.lancs.ac.uk/35544/.

[4] Ibid.

to ignore those laws and eschew their enforcement, viewing them as irrelevant to daily life, and even as detrimental to their welfare.

The current set up of patent law provides little benefit for the Jordanian people, as Jordan's industry, universities, and institutions have a low level of research and development and innovation. Consequently, they produce few if any patents or discoveries with global competitive value. At its current early stage of industrial growth, Jordan has no use for a sophisticated patent system that will hamper the imitation levels necessary to spur innovation and development by local industries and research facilities. This is especially true considering the patent law's failure to boost the transfer of technology into Jordanian industries. Had such a boost occurred it would have allowed Jordanians to gain access to advanced technology. The current patent law, with its strengthened protection system, prohibits imitation and consequently reduces the chances for innovation, leaving little room for the Jordanian public to perceive the law as meaningfully connected to its everyday needs, and thus negatively impacting the public's involvement in any enforcement effort.

At the same time, with its restrictions on the marketing of generic versions of brand-name drugs, the patent law negatively impacts the welfare of the Jordanian public by increasing the prices of medications. The exclusivity period for brand-name drugs grants up to five years of protection even if they do not have a Jordanian patent. This goes against the societal norms of the Jordanian public, which views medical treatment as above the narrow calculus of profit and loss. The current patent law must be reviewed with an eye towards those issues whereby it would benefit the Jordanian public. Until this matter is adequately addressed, Jordan should not consider joining the PCT.

The 1952 trademark law managed to establish a solid base of practical and judicial treatment and awareness. It established and emphasized concepts that were tangible and useful to the general public – associating value and quality with certain names and products which were established in Jordan and employed Jordanians, which added value to the local economy and provided impetus to the cycle of the capital movement. The amendments to the trademark law provided protection to known trademarks even if they were not registered in Jordan, giving them the same protection as those marks that are active participants in the local economy. It thus grants known trademarks rights similar to those granted under the Madrid Protocol, even though Jordan is not a party to it.

Given the relative sophistication of the trademark review and registration process in Jordan, as well as the Jordanian courts' familiarity with issues on trademark law as a result of its handling such claims for decades, Jordan should join the Madrid Protocol on trademarks. This step would give the local trademark owners a mechanism to obtain "international registration" for their trademark from the WIPO. Local trademarks will then at least have a level playing field in terms of rights granted to known trademarks under the Jordanian trademark law.

Copyright issues have real practical significance in Jordan because there is a fairly developed shadow economy based on counterfeit copyright materials. Traditionally, copyright was never acknowledged by Jordanian society at the same level as in developed countries; as a result, copyright law drastically conflicts with the Jordanian societal and social realities. The traditional view of copyright emphasizes attribution of used sources, whereas the view advocated by the current copyright law emphasizes the need for monetary compensation in return for use. Traditionally, given the humble economic realities of most of the population, copying was not seen as an issue in Jordan, as it contributed to the acquisition of knowledge. By contrast, the current law demands payment for the copyrighted material. To be enforceable, the copyright law must reflect the social and economic realities of Jordanian society, and it must provide economic alternatives to meet the interests of people who are financially dependent on what the current copyright law considers illegal commercial behaviour. Such alternatives might be in the form of reduced pricing schemes to accommodate Jordanian realities.

The chequered record for the implementation and enforcement of IP laws in Jordan should sound alarm bells and prompt an early review. The various attempts by the developed countries and other international organizations to promote strict enforcement of stringent IP laws through a coercion model that is based on framing, monitoring, capacity building, and donor funding is proving ineffectual, and thus benefiting neither party. The focus, instead, should be on the social realities and cultural values in Jordan and other developing countries, which in turn should determine what types of IP laws those societies should implement. Input from the general public, which was excluded from the process that produced the existing IPRs, must be solicited. This integrated approach will prove more effective than an ad hoc and punitive approach in securing enforcement of IPRs in Jordan. In time, such an approach may have a positive impact on the development and welfare of the local economy and consequently result in an enforcement model that is not coercion-based. For their part, multinational corporations seeking to do business in Jordan may find themselves engaging in an economy which is steadily growing more prosperous, and with a population which is more willing to purchase non-counterfeit goods. This is not a vision of globalization abandoned, but of its application for the greater benefit of all.

APPENDIX ONE

INTERVIEWS

In its assessment of the political, economic, and social aspects of the Jordanian IPR system, this book draws on fieldwork carried out by the author in the period July 26 to August 28, 2011. This fieldwork consisted of interviews with representatives of the Jordanian public and private sectors, drawn from a range of institutions. These interviews have informed the general direction of the arguments developed in this book, and are the sources for claims cited at various points in the text. This appendix identifies the institutions from which the interviewees came. The author extends sincere gratitude to all who agreed to be interviewed for this work.

Interviews were conducted with members of the following institutions:

- Ministry of Industry and Trade (MoIT)
- Jordanian Patent Office at the Department of Industrial Property within the MoIT
- Jordan Food and Drug Administration
- Jordan Customs
- Jordan Institute for Standards and Metrology
- Former governmental officials, including the head of the Jordanian delegation to the WTO and the JUSFTA negotiations
- Jordanian Association of Pharmaceutical Manufacturers
- Jordan Exporters Association.

APPENDIX TWO

IP ATTITUDES QUESTIONNAIRE

This book draws on survey information regarding Jordanian attitudes towards counterfeit products. This information was gathered via a questionnaire administered to students at Jordan University. The questionnaire was designed, prepared, collected, tabulated, and analyzed with the help of the staff of Jordan University's Center for Strategic Studies (CSS), under the supervision of Dr. Waleed Alkhateb, the head statistician of the CSS. Although students are not representative of the Jordanian population as a whole, they are highly representative of the typical Jordanian consumer of intellectual property, since students, and those with a university background, are by far the greatest users of computer software in the country.

The questionnaire consisted of four sections. The first section contained questions on perceptions of the current prevalence of counterfeit products among university students. The second section contained questions on the respondents' attitudes towards counterfeit products based on their religious beliefs; these questions were intended to examine whether students' ethical orientations affected their behaviour towards counterfeit products. The third section, consisting of six items measured on a two-point (yes or no) scale, contained questions on the respondents' ethical attitudes towards counterfeit products. The fourth section elicited the following demographic information:

- Respondent's age
- Marital status
- Monthly income of the respondent's family
- Respondent's college
- Respondent's country of birth
- Respondent's place of residence (province)
- Source of respondent's tuition fees.

Sample

Jordan University students from several colleges were chosen as the sample for the questionnaire because college students represent a large segment of copyright violators.[1] Jordan University is the oldest and largest campus in Jordan, and its location in Amman attracts students from various parts of the country, unlike provincial universities where the student composition tends to be more local.

The total sample was 381 students. Of the 362 valid responses, 177 (46.5%) of respondents were male and 199 (52.2%) were female, with 5 (1.3%) not reporting their gender. The respondents represented a cross-section of majors taught at the university, and was representative of the various colleges at the University of Jordan (table A2-1 gives the distribution by faculty):

Table A2-1. Survey sample distribution

Faculty	Frequency	Per cent
Engineering	109	28.6
Education	35	9.2
Science	43	11.3
Islamic Law (*sharia*)	17	4.5
Agriculture	4	1.0
Information Technology	33	8.7
Business Administration	71	18.6
Arts	50	13.1
Total	362	100

Analysis and findings

The first group of questions explored the current state of digital piracy among Jordan University students. A total of 89.9% of the respondents had knowingly engaged in buying counterfeit products or using cracked software on at least one occasion. This finding confirms widespread beliefs about the high level of use of counterfeit goods among young people in Jordan.

[1] See Steven Lysonski and Srinivas Durvasula, "Digital Piracy of MP3s: Consumer and Ethical Predispositions," *Journal of Consumer Marketing* 25, no. 3 (2008): 167–178.

Table A2-2. Have you engaged at least one time in knowingly buying counterfeit products?

		Frequency	Per cent	Valid percent	Cumulative percent
Valid	1 Yes	342	89.8	89.8	89.8
	2 No	39	10.2	10.2	100.0
	Total	381	100.0	100.0	

When respondents were asked if they had any original software installed on their computers, the responses were: none (26.5%), one to two software products (59.6%), three or more software products (13.1%); none of respondents claimed that all of their software was original. When asked if they were likely to continue buying counterfeit products or using cracked software, 53% said they would, indicating that buying counterfeit products is an acceptable social norm for the majority of the respondents. The economic factor was a major incentive to buy counterfeit products, as 64.3% of the respondents said that they would not buy counterfeit goods if they could afford to buy the original versions. It is a measure of the inappropriate pricing levels of original products that even in rich countries like Kuwait, with a GDP nine times that of Jordan, the economic factor plays an essential role in the purchase of counterfeit products for 51.9% of respondents to a similar question.[2]

Dedicated shops were the source for buying counterfeit products for 24.7% of the respondents, while 55.9% of the respondents said they bought the counterfeit products from dedicated shops as well as other places, and 19.2% of the respondents indicated that friends and relatives were their source of counterfeit products.

The second group of questions explored the respondents' attitudes towards counterfeiting based on their religious beliefs. This examined whether students' ethical orientation affected their choice to buy counterfeit products. Ethical orientation was tested using responses to scales which measured ethical cases. A majority of the respondents (65.9%) believed that counterfeit products are not prohibited by religion, while only 28.6% of the respondents thought that religion prohibited counterfeit products, and 4.7% did not know whether such a religious prohibition existed.

[2] Salah Al-Fadhli, "The Ethical Dilemma of Software Piracy in Islamic Societies: The Case of Kuwait," *The Electronic Journal of Information Systems in Developing Countries* 39 (2009).

Table A2-3. If you knew that counterfeit products were prohibited by religion, would you continue to buy and use such products?

		Frequency	Per cent	Valid percent	Cumulative percent
Valid	1 Yes	66	17.3	17.3	17.3
	2 No	309	81.1	81.1	98.4
	6 I don't know	4	1.0	1.0	99.5
	9 Missing	2	0.5	0.5	100.0
	Total	381	100.0	100.0	

Table A2-4. If you knew that state law prohibited counterfeit products, would you continue to buy and use such products?

		Frequency	Per cent	Valid percent	Cumulative percent
Valid	1 Yes	132	34.6	34.6	34.6
	2 No	247	64.8	64.8	99.5
	6 I don't know	1	0.3	0.3	99.7
	9 Missing	1	0.3	0.3	100.0
	Total	381	100.0	100.0	

The results from tables A2-3 and A2-4 show that the majority of the respondents (81.1%) would stop buying counterfeit products if they knew that Islam prohibits it, while 64.8% of them said that they would stop buying counterfeit products if prohibited by state law. But given that IP is not a matter dealt with directly by religion, and given the decentralized and non-hierarchical nature of the Islamic faith practised by the vast majority of Jordanians,[3] it may be misleading to take answers based on religious belief without further scrutiny. In the interest of such scrutiny, two more questions were posed. First, respondents were asked to identify what they considered to be their source of religious authority, and then they were asked to identify the degree to which they were inclined to follow the opinion of that religious authority on matters related to counterfeit goods. Tables A2-5 and A2-6 show the results for these questions.

[3] "Guide: Christians in the Middle East," *BBC*, December 15, 2005, sec. Middle East, http://news.bbc.co.uk/2/hi/middle_east/4499668.stm. This estimates that only 3–4% of Jordanians are Christian.

Table A2-5. What is the main source of your Islamic actions and decisions?

		Frequency	Per cent	Valid percent	Cumulative percent
Valid	1 The Mufti	157	41.2	41.2	41.2
	2 The Cleric in my neighbourhood	60	15.7	15.7	57.0
	3 Parents	65	17.1	17.1	74.0
	4 Other	96	25.2	25.2	99.2
	6 I don't know	2	0.5	0.5	99.7
	9 Missing	1	0.3	0.3	100.0
	Total	381	100.0	100.0	

Table A2-6. If the source of your religious guidance deemed counterfeiting to be prohibited by religion, to what extent would you abide by such an edict?

		Frequency	Per cent	Valid percent	Cumulative percent
Valid	1 Always	201	52.8	52.8	52.8
	2 Sometimes	148	38.8	38.8	91.6
	3 Never	30	7.9	7.9	99.5
	6 I don't know	1	0.3	0.3	99.7
	9 Missing	1	0.3	0.3	100.0
	Total	381	100.0	100.0	

The mufti (a Muslim legal expert and adviser on the law of the Qur'an) was considered the source of religious authority by 41.2% of respondents; however, only 52.8% said they would always follow the guidance of their main religious authority on the prohibition of counterfeit products, while 46.7% said they would either never or only sometimes follow such guidance, indicating that the effect of religion on the respondents' choice to use counterfeit products may not be as strong as it first appeared. This validates the earlier conclusion that the suggestion that Muslims will abide by IPRs laws if piracy is prohibited by Islam should be interpreted within the context of the lack of treatment of IPRs under Islamic law, and the fact that any Islamic legal opinion on piracy holds little or no universal jurisprudential weight.

The third group of questions focused on the respondents' ethical attitudes towards counterfeit products. The results showed that 71.9% of the respondents believed that buying counterfeit products is an ethical act, because counterfeit products provide people with limited income with access to goods, software, and books, while only 27.3% of respondents believed that buying counterfeit products is an unethical act. Oddly, 75.1% of the respondents believed that counterfeit products infringed on the rights of companies, while 63.5% indicated that they personally did not care about the companies' losses because of counterfeiting, which shows that a majority of the respondents do not see the intrusion on the rights of companies because of counterfeit products as a personal issue for them to care about. To the probable satisfaction of the IP scholar and opponent of IP reification Christopher May, the reification of IPRs in Jordan has a long way to go.[4]

Although 27% of the respondents indicated that they would continue to buy counterfeit products even if they could afford to buy the original, 49.3% indicated that they felt uncomfortable when buying counterfeit products. It is worth noting that 45.5% of the respondents did not believe that buying counterfeit products causes any harm to Muslim people, likely because the companies that produce the original goods are located in the West.

[4] Christopher May, "The Denial of History: Reification, Intellectual Property Rights and the Lessons of the Past," *Capital & Class* 30, no. 1 (Spring 2006): 33–56.

BIBLIOGRAPHY

Abbott, Frederick M. "WTO Dispute Settlement Practice Relating to the Agreement on Trade-Related Intellectual Property Rights." *SSRN eLibrary* (n.d.). http://papers.ssrn.com/sol3/papers.cfm?abstract_id=1920816.

ACTA. "The Anti-Counterfeiting Trade Agreement: Fact Sheet," May 1, 2010. http://trade.ec.europa.eu/doclib/html/140836.htm.

Addor, Felix, and Alexandra Grazioli. "Geographical Indications Beyond Wines and Spirits." *Journal of World Intellectual Property* 5, no. 6 (2002): 865–897.

Al-Amer, Ranah. "Poet Samhan Sentenced to One Year and His Poetry Collection Referred to the Mufti." *Alghad Daily Newspaper*, June 22, 2009.

Al Arab Alyawm Daily Newspaper. "CBJ Issues Import Export Numbers." *Al Arab Alyawm Daily Newspaper*, October 25, 2009.

Al-Dajani, E. M. "Post-Saddam Restructuring of Intellectual Property Rights in Iraq Through a Case Study of Current Intellectual Property Practices in Lebanon, Egypt, and Jordan." *J. Marshall Rev. Intell. Prop. L.* 6 (2006).

Al-Fadhli, Salah. "The Ethical Dilemma of Software Piracy in Islamic Societies: The Case of Kuwait." *The Electronic Journal of Information Systems in Developing Countries* 39 (2009).

Al-Qasem, Anis. "The Injurious Acts under the Jordanian Civil Code." *Arab Law Quarterly* 4, no. 3 (August 1989): 183–198.

Al Sharari, S. "Intellectual Property Rights Legislation and Computer Software Piracy in Jordan." *Journal of Social Sciences* 2, no. 1 (2006): 7–13.

Alghad Daily Newspaper. "Agreement to Supply Software Programs at Discount." *Alghad Daily Newspaper*, April 25, 2007.

—. "Engineering Offices Demand IP Law Postponement." *Alghad Daily Newspaper*, January 23, 2007.

—. "Engineering Offices Protest Union's Decision." *Alghad Daily Newspaper*, September 12, 2007.

—. "Head of NL: IP Key for Investments." *Alghad Daily Newspaper*, April 10, 2006.

—. "Joint Jordanian USAID Media Campaign Promoting IP." *Alghad Daily Newspaper*, October 2, 2005.

—. "Jordan to Receive $150 Million More in Military Aid." *Alghad Daily Newspaper*, February 15, 2010.

—. "Launching of the IP Arab Day." *Alghad Daily Newspaper*, December 6, 2009.

—. "Ministry of Environment Signs an MoU with U.S. Embassy." *Alghad Daily Newspaper*, October 23, 2008.

—. "NL Warns Public From Buying Pirated Products." *Alghad Daily Newspaper*, November 9, 2005.

—. "Pharmaceutical Exports Rise by 15% in 10 Months." *Alghad Daily Newspaper*, January 17, 2009, 1607 edition.

—. "USAID Supports AmCham Paper on Jordan's IP Laws." *Alghad Daily Newspaper*, February 21, 2009.

Amara, Jomana. "Military Industrialization and Economic Development: Jordan's Defense Industry." *Review of Financial Economics* 17, no. 2 (2008): 130–145.

Anani, Jawad. "Intellectual Property Rights." *Alghad Daily Newspaper*, November 1, 2009.

Astorino, M. "Obviously Troublesome: How High Should the Standard Be for Obtaining a Patent." *J. Pat. & Trademark Off. Soc'y* 89 (2007): 239.

Attaran, A, and L. Gillespie-White. "Do Patents for Antiretroviral Drugs Constrain Access to AIDS Treatment in Africa?" *JAMA: The Journal of the American Medical Association* 286, no. 15 (October 17, 2001): 1886–1892.

Bagchi, K., P. Hart, and M. F. Peterson. "National Culture and Information Technology Product Adoption." *Journal of Global Information Technology Management* 7, no. 4 (2004): 29–46.

Baradei, Dana. "The Right Prescription." *Jordan Business*, January 10, 2007.

Barnett, Michael, and Raymond Duvall. *Power in Global Governance*. Cambridge: Cambridge University Press, 2004.

Barons, Lisa. "Amending Section 337 to Obtain GATT Consistency and Retain Border Protection." *Law and Policy in International Business* 22 (1991).

Binley, M. "Intellectual Property Rights: A Strategic Instrument for Developing Countries." Working Paper No. 46, University of Toronto, 1992.

Boyle, James. "Manifesto on WIPO and the Future of Intellectual Property." *Duke Law and Technology Review*, no. 9 (2004).

Braithwaite, John. "Responsive Regulation and Developing Economies." *World Development* 34 (2006).

Bräutigam, Deborah. "Foreign Aid and the Politics of Participation in Economic Policy Reform." *Public Administration and Development* 20, no. 3 (August 1, 2000): 253–264.

—. "Governance, Economy, and Foreign Aid." *Studies In Comparative International Development* 27, no. 3 (September 1992): 3–25.

BSA. "Business Software Alliance - IDC Study." *Global Software Piracy Study*, April 27, 2010. http://global.bsa.org/idcglobalstudy2007/.

Burqan, Nedal. "Ministry of Culture Conference: Jordanian Drama in Danger." *Addustour Daily Newspaper*, March 5, 2010.

de Carvalho, Nuno Pires. *The TRIPS Regime of Trademarks and Designs*. Kluwer Law International, 2006.

Chellappa, Ramnath K., and Shivendu Shivendu. "Managing Piracy: Pricing and Sampling Strategies for Digital Experience Goods in Vertically Segmented Markets." *Information Systems Research* 16, no. 4 (December 1, 2005): 400–417.

Chiang, T. J. "Cost-Benefit Approach to Patent Obviousness, A." *John's L. Rev.* 82 (2008).

Chow, Daniel. "Counterfeiting as an Externality Imposed by Multinational Companies on Developing Countries." *Virginia Journal of International Law* 51, no. 4 (2011).

Cleveland, William L. *A History of the Modern Middle East*. 2nd ed. Boulder: Westview Press, 1999.

Cohen, A. "The Relationship Between Multiple Commitments and Organizational Citizenship Behavior in Arab and Jewish Culture." *Journal of Vocational Behavior* 69, no. 1 (2006): 105–118.

Commission on Intellectual Property Rights (UK). *Integrating Intellectual Property Rights and Development Policy*. London: CIPR, 2002.

Correa, Carlos. "Intellectual Property Rights and the Use of Compulsory Licenses: Options for Developing Countries." Trade-Related Agenda, Development and Equity (T.R.A.D.E.) Working Papers 5. South Centre, October 2001.

—. *Intellectual Property Rights, the WTO, and Developing Countries: The TRIPS Agreement and Policy Options*. New York: Zed Books, 2000.

Correa, Carlos, and S. Musungu. "The WIPO Patent Agenda: The Risks for Developing Countries." South Center, November 2002.

Correa, Carlos, and Abdulqawi Yusuf. *Intellectual Property and International Trade*. Alphen aan den Rijn: Kluwer Law International, 2008.

Coulson, N. J. "The State and the Individual in Islamic Law." *The International and Comparative Law Quarterly* 6, no. 1 (January 1, 1957): 49–60.

—. *A History of Islamic Law*. Edinburgh: Edinburgh University Press, 1995.

Council of the European Communities. *Council Directive 2001/29/EC*, n.d.

—. Council Directive 92/100/EEC, 1992.

Customs Department (Jordan). "Intellectual Property Cases Referred to Court." Customs Department No. 104/4/8/45549, July 29, 2009.

Deere, Carolyn. *The Implementation Game: The TRIPS Agreement and the Global Politics of Intellectual Property Reform in Developing Countries*. Oxford: Oxford University Press, 2008.

Deere-Birkbeck, Carolyn. "Reforming Governance to Advance the WIPO Development Agenda." In *Implementing the World Intellectual Property Organization's Development Agenda*, ed. J. de Beer. Waterloo, ON: Wilfred Laurier University Press/Centre for International Governance Innovation/International Development Research Centre, 2009.

Depken, C. A., and L. C. Simmons. "Social Construct and the Propensity for Software Piracy." *Applied Economics Letters* 11, no. 2 (February 10, 2004): 97–100.

Directorate General of Trade. *Strategy for the Enforcement of Intellectual Property Rights in Third Countries*. Brussels: European Commission, 2004.

Drahos, P. "An Alternative Framework for the Global Regulation of Intellectual Property Rights." *Austrian Journal of Development Studies*, no. 1 (October 2005).

—. "Assessing the Impact of the Australia-United States Free Trade Agreement on Australian and Global Medicines Policy." *Globalization & Health*, n.d. http://www.globalizationandhealth.com/content/1/1/15.

—. "Biotechnology Patents, Markets and Morality." *European Intellectual Property Review* 21, no. 9 (1999): 441–449.

—. "A Defence of the Intellectual Commons." *Consumer Policy Review* 16, no. 3 (May 2006): 101–104.

—. "Expanding Intellectual Property's Empire: The Role of FTAs." International Centre for Trade and Sustainable Development, April 22, 2010. http://ictsd.org/i/ip/24737/.

—. "Four Lessons for Developing Countries from the Trade Negotiations Over Access to Medicines." *Liverpool Law Review* 28, no. 1 (May 2007): 11–39.

— ."Global Property Rights in Information: The Story of TRIPS at the GATT." *Prometheus* 13, no. 1 (1995): 6–19.

—. "Information Feudalism in the Information Society." *The Information Society* 11, no. 3 (July 1995): 209–222.

—. "Intellectual Property and Pharmaceutical Markets: A Nodal Governance Approach." *Temple Law Review* 77 (2004): 401.

—. *A Philosophy of Intellectual Property*. Aldershot: Dartmouth Publishing Co. Ltd., 1996.

—. "Trust Me: Patent Offices in Developing Countries." *American Journal of Law & Medicine* 34 (2008): 151.

Drahos, Peter, and Ruth Mayne, eds. "Negotiating Intellectual Property Rights: Between Coercion and Dialogue." In *Global Intellectual Property Rights: Knowledge, Access and Development*, ed. Peter Drahos and Ruth Mayne, 161–182. Basingstoke: Palgrave Macmillan and Oxfam, 2002.

—. "Weaving Webs of Influence: The United States, Free Trade Agreements and Dispute Resolution." *Journal of World Trade* 41, no. 1 (2007).

Dunoff, Jeffrey. "Free Trade or Fair? The Softwood Lumber Dispute and Beyond." *Alberta Law Review* 45 (2007): 319–356.

Dutfield, Graham. *Intellectual Property Rights, Trade and Biodiversity*. London: Earthscan Publications Ltd., 2002.

El Said, Hamed, and Mohammed El Said. "The European Trips-Plus Model and the Arab World: From Co-Operation to Association—A New Era in the Global IPRS Regime?" *Liverpool Law Review* 28, no. 1 (2007): 143–174.

—. "TRIPS, Bilateralism, Multilateralism and Implications for Developing Countries: Jordan's Drug Sector." *Manchester J. Int'l Econ. L.* 2 (2005): 59.

—. "TRIPS-Plus Implications for Access to Medicines in Developing Countries: Lessons from Jordan–United States Free Trade Agreement." *The Journal of World Intellectual Property* 10, no. 6 (November 1, 2007): 438–475.

El-Said, Mohammed. "The Implementation Paradox: Intellectual Property Regulation in the Arab World." *Journal of International Trade Law and Policy* 9, no. 3 (2010): 221–235.

—. "From TRIPS-minus to TRIPS to TRIPS-plus: Implications of IPRs for the Arab World." *The Journal of World Intellectual Property* 8, no. 1 (2005): 53–65.

Endeshaw, Assafa. *Intellectual Property Policy for Non-Industrial Countries*. Hants: Dartmouth Publishing Group, 1996.

Farakas, L. Peter. "Trade-Related Aspects of Intellectual Property." In *The World Trade Organization: Multilateral Trade Framework for the 21st Century and U.S. Implementing Legislation*, ed. Terence P. Stewart. American Bar Association, 1996.

Fordham, Benjamin, and Victor Asal. "Billiard Balls or Snowflakes? Major Power Prestige and the International Diffusion of Institutions and Practices." *International Studies Quarterly* 51, no. 1 (2007): 31–52.

Frankel, Jeffrey A., Ernesto Stein, and Shang-Jin Wei. *Regional Trading Blocs in the World Economic System*. Institute for International Economics. Washington, DC: Peterson Institute, 1997.

Gantz, David. "Dispute Settlement Under the NAFTA and the WTO: Choice of Forum Opportunities and Risks for the NAFTA Parties." *American University International Law Review* 14 (1999): 1025.

Ghazal, Mohammad. "Investments Benefiting from Incentives Hit Record High in First Two Months." *Jordan Times*, February 28, 2010.

Ghnemaat, Jumana. "Prices of Propane Gas Might Go up by 40%." *Alghad Daily Newspaper*, April 19, 2010.

Gill, Stephen. *Power and Resistance in the New World Order*. London: Palgrave Macmillan, 2003.

Ginarte, J. C., and W. G. Park. "Determinants of Patent Rights: A Cross National Study." *Research Policy* 26 (1997): 283–301.

Glass, Amy Jocelyn. "Imitation as a Stepping Stone to Innovation." *OSU Working Paper No. 99-11* (July 14, 1999). http://papers.ssrn.com/sol3/papers.cfm?abstract_id=170879.

Gleditsch, Kristian Skrede, and Michael D. Ward. "Diffusion and the International Context of Democratization." *International Organization* 60, no. 4 (2006): 911–933.

Global Integrity. *Jordan: 2009*. Global Integrity, 2009.

Goldschmidt, Arthur, and Lawrence Davidson. *A Concise History of the Middle East*. 9th ed. Westview Press, 2009.

Gruber, Lloyd. *Ruling the World: Power Politics and the Rise of Supranational Institutions*. Princeton University Press, 2000.

Gurry, Francis, and Debora Halbert. "Globalization, Development, and Intellectual Property: New Challenges and New Opportunities." *American Society of International Law Proceedings* 99 (2005).

Habib, Randa. "Unconditional Aid." *Jordan Times*, March 4, 2010. http://www.jordantimes.com/index.php?news=24531&searchFor=budget%20deficit.

Hafner-Burton, Emilie M., and Kiyoteru Tsutsui. "Human Rights in a Globalizing World: The Paradox of Empty Promises." *American Journal of Sociology* 110, no. 5 (March 1, 2005): 1373–1411.

Haggard, Stephan. *Developing Nations and the Politics of Global Integration*. Brookings Institution Press, 1995.

Hair, Joseph F., Bill Black, Barry Babin, Rolph E. Anderson, and Ronald L. Tatham. *Multivariate Data Analysis*. 6th ed. Upper Saddle River, NJ: Prentice Hall, 2005.

Halbert, Debora. "Feminist Interpretations of Intellectual Property." *American University Journal of Gender, Social Policy & the Law* 14 (2006).

—. "Mass Culture and the Culture of the Masses: A Manifesto for User-Generated Rights." *Vanderbilt Journal of Entertainment and Technology Law* 11 (2009/2008).

Hatch, Orrin G. "Better Late than Never: Implementation of the 1886 Berne Convention." *Cornell International Law Journal* 22 (1989): 171.

Haunss, Sebastian, and Kenneth C. Shadlen. "Introduction: Rethinking the Politics of Intellectual Property." In *Politics of Intellectual Property: Contestation over the Ownership, Use, and Control of Knowledge and Information*, ed. Sebastian Haunss and Kenneth C. Shadlen, 1–12. Cheltenham: Edward Elgar Publishing Limited, 2009.

Heald, Paul J. "Misreading a Canonical Work: An Analysis of Mansfield's 1994 Study." *Journal of Intellectual Property Law* 10 (2003).

Hofstade, Geert, and Michael Bond. "The Confucius Connection: From Cultural Roots to Economic Growth" 16, no. 4 (1988): 5–21.

Hofstede, Geert, Michael H. Bond, and Richard H. Franke. "Cultural Roots of Economic Performance." *Strategic Management Journal* 12, no. S1 (1991): 165–173.

Hovenkamp, Herbert, Mark D. Janis, Mark A. Lemley, and Christopher R. Leslie. *IP and Antitrust: An Analysis of Antitrust Principles Applied to Intellectual Property Law*. Wolters Kluwer Law & Business: Aspen Publishers, 2001.

Husted, Bryan. "The Impact of National Culture on Software Piracy." *Journal of Business Ethics* 26, no. 3 (2000): 197–211.

ICG. "The Challenge of Political Reform: Jordanian Democratisation and Regional Instability." International Crisis Group, 2003.

Idris, Kamil. "Intellectual Property—A Power Tool for Economic Growth." World Intellectual Property Organization, 2003.

Ikenberry, G. John, and Charles A. Kupchan. "Socialization and Hegemonic Power." *International Organization* 44, no. 3 (1990): 283–315.

IEO [Independent Evaluation Office of the IMF]. "Evaluation Report IMF Support to Jordan, 1989–2004." April 14, 2010. http://www.imf.org/External/NP/ieo/2005/jor/eng/index.htm.

Ingram, Mathew. "Do We Need Copyright Cops?" *The Globe and Mail-Blogs*, May 27, 2008. http://www.theglobeandmail.com/blogs/ingram-2_0/do-we-need-copyright-cops/article687387/.

IPW [Intellectual Property Watch]. "Clash Continues on U.S.-Central America Trade Deal." *Intellectual Property Watch*, March 1, 2005. http://www.ip-watch.org/weblog/2005/03/01/clash-continues-on-us-central-america-trade-deal/.

ILO [International Labour Organization]. "Forced Labour and Trafficking In Jordan—A Pilot Programme on the Qualified Industrial Zones." Project, March 1, 2009. http://www.ilo.org/sapfl/Projects/lang--en/WCMS_104023/index.htm.

ISN [International Relations and Security Network]. "The Anti-Counterfeiting Trade Agreement - Summary of Key Elements Under Discussion." *ISN*, May 1, 2010. trade.ec.europa.eu/doclib/docs/2009/november/tradoc_145271.pdf.

Issawi, Hiba. "Values of Projects Benefitting from Investment Promotion Laws Do Not Reflect Improvement in Data." *Alghad Daily Newspaper*, April 8, 2010, sec. Markets & Finance.

Jackson, John H. *The Jurisprudence of GATT and the WTO: Insights on Treaty Law and Economic Relations*. Cambridge: Cambridge University Press, 2000.

—. *The World Trading System: Law and Policy of International Economic Relations*. Cambridge, MA: MIT Press, 1997.

Jordan Times. "Gov't Issues JD160m Budget Supplement." *Jordan Times*, March 3, 2010.

Jordanian Judicial Council. *Annual Courts Report—2008*. Jordanian Judicial Council, 2008.

JUSFTA. "Memorandum of Understanding on Issues Related to the Protection of Intellectual Property Rights Under the Agreement Between the United States and Jordan on the Establishment of a Free Trade Area," 2000. www.jordanusfta.com/documents/memo_property .pdf.

Kayyali, Mohammad. "Cancer and Kidney Failure Medications Not Available—Pharmacy Union Says." *Alghad Daily Newspaper*, April 17, 2010.

Khaleej Times. "Bahrain Defends Right to Sign FTA with US." *Khaleej Times Online*, November 29, 2004. http://www.khaleejtimes.com

/DisplayArticle.asp?xfile=data/business/2004/November/business_November412.xml&section=business.

Khoury, A. H. "'Measuring the Immeasurable'—The Effects of Trademark Regimes: A Case Study of Arab Countries." *Journal of Law and Commerce* 26, no. 1/2 (2006): 11.

Khresat, Mohammed. "More Foreign Aid Expected." *Alghad Daily Newspaper*, May 16, 2009.

Kurman, J. "Why Is Self-Enhancement Low in Certain Collectivist Cultures?" *Journal of Cross-Cultural Psychology* 34, no. 5 (2003): 496–510.

Kwong, T. C. H., and M. K. O. Lee. "Understanding the Behavioral Intention to Digital Piracy in Virtual Communities—A Proposed Model." In *IEEE International Conference on e-Technology, e-Commerce and e-Service, 2004. EEE 2004*, 223–226. Taipei, 2004.

Laswi, Rasha. "Effect of Technology Transfer Contracts on the Growth of the Pharmaceutical Sector (Jordan-Case Study)." Master's diss., Jordan Institute of Diplomacy, 2002.

Lawrence, Robert Z. *Regionalism, Multilateralism, and Deeper Integration*. Washington, DC: Brookings Institution Press, 1996.

Lesser, W. "The Effects of TRIPS-Mandated Intellectual Property Rights on Economic Activities in Developing Countries." WIPO, 2001.

Lippman, Matthew, Sean McConville, and Mordechai Yerushalmi. *Islamic Criminal Law and Procedure: An Introduction*. Praeger Publishers, 1988.

Lu, Jia. "Chinese Culture and Software Copyright." *New Media & Society* 11, no. 8 (December 1, 2009): 1372 –1393.

Lysonski, Steven, and Srinivas Durvasula. "Digital Piracy of MP3s: Consumer and Ethical Predispositions." *Journal of Consumer Marketing* 25, no. 3 (2008): 167–178.

Machin, N. "Prospective Utility: A New Interpretation of the Utility Requirement of Section 101 of the Patent Act." *Cal L. Rev.* 87 (1999).

Machlup, Fritz, and Edith Penrose. "The Patent Controversy in the Nineteenth Century." *The Journal of Economic History* 10, no. 1 (1950): 1–29.

Mackenzie, Simon. "Counterfeiting as Corporate Externality: Intellectual Property Crime and Global Insecurity." *Crime, Law and Social Change* 54, no. 1 (July 2010): 21–38.

Malkawi, Bashar H. "The Intellectual Property Provisions of the United States–Jordan Free Trade Agreement: Template or Not Template." *The Journal of World Intellectual Property* 9, no. 2 (March 1, 2006): 213–229.

Malkawi, B. H., and H. A. Haloush. "Intellectual Property Protection for Plant Varieties in Jordan." *The Journal of World Intellectual Property* 11, no. 2 (2008): 120–138.

Mandel, G. N. "Patently Non-Obvious: Empirical Demonstration that the Hindsight Bias Renders Patent Decisions Irrational." *Ohio St. LJ* 67 (2006): 1391.

Marron, Donald B., and David G. Steel. "Which Countries Protect Intellectual Property? The Case of Software Piracy." *Economic Inquiry* 38, no. 2 (2000): 159–74.

Maskus, Keith Eugene. *Intellectual Property Rights in the Global Economy*. Institute for International Economics. Washington, DC: Peterson Institute, 2000.

Masterson, John T. *International Trademarks and Copyrights*. ABA Web Store, 2004.

Matthews, Duncan. *Globalising Intellectual Property Rights: The TRIPS Agreement*. London: Routledge, 2002.

—. "NGOs, Intellectual Property Rights and Multilateral Institutions." *SSRN eLibrary* (December 2006).

—. "TRIPS Flexibilities and Access to Medicines in Developing Countries: The Problem with Technical Assistance and Free Trade Agreements." *European Intellectual Property Review* 27, no. 11 (2005).

Matthews, Duncan, and Viviana Munoz-Tellez. "Bilateral Technical Assistance and TRIPS: The United States, Japan and the European Communities in Comparative Perspective." *Journal of World Intellectual Property* 9, no. 6 (November 1, 2006): 629–653.

May, Christopher. "Between Commodification and 'Openness': The Information Society and the Ownership of Knowledge." *The Journal of Information, Law, and Technology* 2005, no. 2–3 (2005).

—. "Capacity Building and the Re-production of Intellectual Property Rights." *Third World Quarterly* 25, no. 5 (July 2004): 821–837.

—. "The Denial of History: Reification, Intellectual Property Rights and the Lessons of the Past." *Capital & Class* 30, no. 1 (Spring 2006): 33–56.

—. *A Global Political Economy of Intellectual Property Rights*. 1st ed. London: Routledge, 2000.

—. "The Hypocrisy of Forgetfulness: The Contemporary Significance of Early Innovations in Intellectual Property." *Review of International Political Economy* 14, no. 1 (2007): 1–25.

—. "Why IPRs Are a Global Political Issue." *European Intellectual Property Review* 25, no. 1: 1–6.

—. "The World Intellectual Property Organization." *New Political Economy* 11, no. 3 (September 2006): 435–445.

—. *The World Intellectual Property Organization: Resurgence and the Development Agenda*. Abingdon: Taylor & Francis, 2007.

May, Christopher, and Susan K. Sell. *Intellectual Property Rights: A Critical History*. Boulder, CO: Lynne Rienner, 2005.

Mayne, R. "The Global Campaign on Patents and Access to Medicines." In *Global Intellectual Property Rights: Knowledge, Access and Development*, ed. Peter Drahos and Ruth Mayne, 244–259. Basingstoke: Palgrave Macmillan and Oxfam, 2002.

MSF [Medecins Sans Frontieres]. "MSF: Doha Derailed: Technical 'Assistance'—A Case of Malpractice?" January 11, 2010.

Mertha, Andrew, and Robert Pahre. "Patently Misleading: Partial Implementation and Bargaining Leverage in Sino-American Negotiations on Intellectual Property Rights." *International Organization* 59, no. 3 (2005): 695–729.

MoIT [Ministry of Industry & Trade, Jordan] Website. n.d. http://www.mit.gov.jo/Default.aspx?tabid=571.

—. "Official Letter No. 19/2/23/5610, Annex 5," February 18, 2009.

Ministry of Justice. *First Annual Ministry of Justice Book*. Jordanian Ministry of Justice, 2008.

—. Number of Intellectual Property Cases Sorted by Year & Court Type. Compiled for the author upon a written request, 2010.

Moores, Trevor T., and Jasbir Dhaliwal. "A Reversed Context Analysis of Software Piracy Issues in Singapore." *Inf. Manage.* 41, no. 8 (November 2004): 1037–1042.

Moran, W. "Rural Space as Intellectual Property." *Political Geography* 12, no. 3 (1993): 263–277.

Morin, Jean-Frederic. "Multilateralizing TRIPs-Plus Agreements: Is the US Strategy a Failure?" *The Journal of World Intellectual Property* 12, no. 3 (2009): 175–197.

Musungu, Sisule. *Designing Development-oriented Intellectual Property Technical Assistance Programmes*. ICTSD-UNCTAD Dialogue, 2nd Bellagio Series on Development and Intellectual Property, 2003. http://ictsd.org/i/ip/24504/.

Nawafleh, A. "Development of Intellectual Property Laws and Foreign Direct Investment in Jordan." *Journal of International Commercial Law and Technology* 5, no. 3 (2010): 142–153.

Neimat, Khalid. "Half of Foreign Grants to Support Budget." *Jordan Times*, February 23, 2010.

Nesheiwat, F. K. "The Adoption of Intellectual Property Standards Beyond TRIPS—A Misguided Legal & Economic Obsession by Developing Countries?" *Loyola of Los Angeles International and Comparative Law Review* 32 (2010).

—. "A Critique of Intellectual Property Research." *Arab Law Quarterly* 27, no. 1 (2013): 51–69.

New, William. "India Joins Opposition to Casablanca Patent Meeting Outcome." Intellectual Property Watch, April 10, 2005. http://www.ip-watch.org/weblog/2005/04/10/india-joins-opposition-to-casablanca-patent-meeting-outcome/.

—. "US 'Pulls Out All Stops' as UNESCO Backs Culture Treaty." *Intellectual Property Watch*, October 17, 2005. http://www.ip-watch.org/weblog/2005/10/17/us-pulls-out-all-stops-as-unesco-backs-culture-treaty/.

—. "WIPO Launches New Agenda On IP And Development." Intellectual Property Watch, 2007. http://www.ip-watch.org/weblog/2007/09/29/wipo-launches-new-agenda-on-ip-and-development/.

New, William, and Kaitlin Mara. "WHO Session on IP and Health Clashes on Vision, Practicalities." *Intellectual Property Watch*, 2007. http://www.ip-watch.org/weblog/2007/11/09/who-session-on-ip-and-health-clashes-on-vision-practicalities/.

New Zealand Ministry of Economic Development. "Anti-Counterfeiting Trade Agreement," January 23, 2010. http://www.med.govt.nz/templates/ContentTopicSummary____34357.aspx.

Noland, Marcus. "Chasing Phantoms: The Political Economy of USTR." *International Organization* 51, no. 3 (1997): 365–387.

Obeidat, Omar. "Income Tax Revenues to Drop in 2010." *Jordan Times*, March 1, 2010.

—. "Jordan Should Do More to Combat Piracy." *Jordan Times*, February 14, 2010.

USTR [Office of the US Trade Representative]. "USTR Team Holds Meetings in Jordan," September 30, 2009. http://www.ustr.gov/about-us/press-office/press-releases/2009/september/ustr-team-holds-meetings-jordan-discuss-labor-ri.

Ordover, J. A. "A Patent System for both Diffusion and Exclusion." *The Journal of Economic Perspectives* 5, no. 1 (1991): 43–60.

Oxfam. "All Costs, No Benefits: How TRIPS-plus Intellectual Property Rules in the US-Jordan FTA Affect Access to Medicines." Briefing Paper. Oxfam, March 2007.

DSU Panel. "Argentina: Definitive Anti-Dumping Duties on Poultry from Brazil." WTO, April 22, 2003.

—. "Brazil: Measures Affecting Imports of Retreaded Tyres." WTO, June 12, 2007.

Pengelly, T. "Technical Assistance for the Formulation and Implementation of Intellectual Property Policy in Developing Countries and Transition Economies." *UNCTAD/ICTSD*, Issue Paper 11 (2005).

PhRMA. "PhRMA 'Special 301' Submission," 2005. www.cptech.org/ip/health/trade/2005phrma301.pdf.

Price, David. "The U.S.–Bahrain Free Trade Agreement and Intellectual Property Protection." *Journal of World Intellectual Property* 7, no. 6 (2004): 829–850.

Pugatch, Meir Perez. *The Intellectual Property Debate*. Northampton, MA: Edward Elgar, 2006.

Rapp, R. T., and R. P. Rozek. "Benefits and Costs of Intellectual Property Protection in Developing Countries." Working paper No. 3. White Plains, NY: National Economic Research Associates, 1990.

Rawashdeh, Ahmad. "IP Cornerstone of New Economic World Order." *Alghad Daily Newspaper*, June 17, 2009.

Reichman, Jerome H. "From Free Riders to Fair Followers: Global Competition Under the TRIPS Agreement." *New York University Journal of International Law and Politics* 29 (January 1, 1996): 11–93.

Robbins, S. S., and A. C. Stylianou. "A Study of Cultural Differences in Global Corporate Web Sites." *Journal of Computer Information Systems* 42, no. 2 (2002): 3–9.

Robinson, Mary. "Opening Address by Mr. Brian Burdekin on Behalf of Mrs. Mary Robinson, United Nations High Commissioner for Human Rights." *WIPO*, 1998. http://www.wipo.int/tk/en/hr/paneldiscussion/papers/opening-unhcr.html.

Roffe, Pedro and David Vivas-Eugui. "A Shift in Intellectual Property Policy in US FTAs?" *Bridges* 11, no. 5 (International Centre for Trade and Sustainable Development, August 2007). http://ictsd.org/i/news/bridges/4128/.

Samahon, Tuan. "TRIPS Copyright Dispute Settlement after the Transition and Moratorium: Nonviolation and Situation Complaints Against Developing Countries." *Law and Policy in International Business*, Spring 2000 (April 1, 2000).

Scheuerman, William E. "False Humanitarianism? US Advocacy of Transnational Labour Protections." *Review of International Political Economy* 8, no. 3 (2001): 359–388.

Schrank, A. "The Software Industry in North America: Human Capital, International Migration, and Foreign Trade." In *Industrial*

Agglomeration: Facts and Lessons for Developing Countries, ed. M. Kagami and M. Tjusi. Chiba: IDE International Joint Research Project Series No. 7, 2003.

Schwartz, Bryan. "The Fate of Section 337 Litigation after the Uruguay Round Agreements Act." *Law and Policy in International Business* 27 (1995).

Scotchmer, S., and J. Green. "Novelty and Disclosure in Patent Law." *The RAND Journal of Economics* (1990): 131–146.

Sell, Susan K. "Intellectual Property Protection and Antitrust in the Developing World: Crisis, Coercion, and Choice." *International Organization* 49, no. 2 (1995): 315–349.

—. *Power and Ideas: North–South Politics of Intellectual Property and Antitrust*. Albany, NY: SUNY Press, 1998.

—. *Private Power, Public Law: The Globalization of Intellectual Property Rights*. Cambridge: Cambridge University Press, 2003.

Sell, Susan, and Christopher May. "Moments in Law: Contestation and Settlement in the History of Intellectual Property." *Review of International Political Economy* 8, no. 3 (September 2001): 467–500.

Shadlen, Kenneth C. "Exchanging Development for Market Access? Deep Integration and Industrial Policy Under Multilateral and Regional-Bilateral Trade Agreements." *Review of International Political Economy* 12, no. 5 (2005): 750–775.

—. "Globalisation, Power and Integration: The Political Economy of Regional and Bilateral Trade Agreements in the Americas." *Journal of Development Studies* 44, no. 1 (January 2008): 1–20.

—. "Intellectual Property for Development in Mexico." In *The Future of North American Trade Policy: Lessons from NAFTA*, 53–59. The Frederick S. Pardee Center for the Study of the Longer-Range Future. Boston University, Boston, 2009.

—. "Intellectual Property, Trade, and Development: Can Foes Be Friends?" *Global Governance* 13 (2007): 171.

—. "The Politics of Patents and Drugs in Brazil and Mexico: The Industrial Bases of Health Policies." *Comparative Politics* 42, no. 1 (2009): 41–58.

—. "Policy Space for Intellectual Property Management: Contrasting Multilateral and Regional-bilateral Arrangements." *Econômica* 10, no. 2 (2008): 55–81.

—. "The Puzzling Politics of Patents and Innovation Policy in Mexico." *Law and Business Review of the Americas* 16 (2010): 823.

—. "Resources, Rules and International Political Economy: The Politics of Development in the WTO." In *The World Trade Organization and*

Human Rights: Interdisciplinary Perspectives, ed. Sarah Joseph, David Kinley, and Jeff Waincymer, 109–132. Cheltenham: Edward Elgar Publishing Limited, 2009.

Shadlen, Kenneth C., Andrew Schrank, and Marcus J. Kurtz. "The Political Economy of Intellectual Property Protection: The Case of Software." *International Studies Quarterly* 49, no. 1 (2005): 45–71.

Sharabati, Abdel-Aziz Ahmad, Shawqi Naji Jawad, and Nick Bontis. "Intellectual Capital and Business Performance in the Pharmaceutical Sector of Jordan." *Management Decision* 48, no. 1 (September 2, 2010): 105–131.

Simmons, Beth, and Zachary Elkins. "The Globalization of Liberalization: Policy Diffusion in the International Political Economy." *American Political Science Review* 98, no. 1 (2004): 171–189.

Sirhan, A. A. "Intellectual Property and Copyright Laws and Their Impact on Digital Resources in Jordan." Manuscript (n.d.). www.informationstudies.net/images/pdf/120.pdf.

Solis, Hilda, et al. "Leter from 12 Members of Congress to President Bush on Intellectual Property Provisions in CAFTA," 2004. http://www.cptech.org/ip/health/trade/cafta/congress09302004.html.

Strikwerda, Robert A., and John Minor Ross. "Software and Ethical Softness." *Collegiate Microcomputer* 10, no. 3 (1992): 129–36.

Su, Evelyn. "The Winners and the Losers: The Agreement on the Trade-Related Aspects of Intellectual Property Rights and Its Effects on Developing Countries." *Houston Journal of International Law* 23 (2003): 169.

Sykes, Alan O. "Constructive Unilateral Threats in International Commercial Relations: The Limit Case for Section 301." *Law & Policy in International Business* 23, no. 2 (1992): 263–330.

Tabbaa, Tawfiq. *Update on Compliance with Intellectual Property Rights in Jordan*. Improved Economic Opportunities for Jordanians. USAID – Sustainable Achievement for Business Expansion and Quality (SABEQ), February 14, 2007.

Tang, Jih-Hsin, and Cheng-Kiang Farn. "The Effect of Interpersonal Influence on Softlifting Intention and Behaviour." *Journal of Business Ethics* 56, no. 2 (January 1, 2005): 149–161.

Tansey, Geoff, and Tasmin Rajotte, eds. *The Future Control of Food*. Ottawa: Earthscan, 2008.

Tarawnah, Naseem. "Steal This Article!" *Jordan Business*, May 2008.

Tareq Deajah. "Abiding by Intellectual Property Conditions is key for Attracting Foreign Investments." *Alghad Daily Newspaper*, July 15, 2009.

Trebilcock, M. J., and Robert Howse. *The Regulation of International Trade*. New York: Routledge, 2005.

US Government Accountability Office. *International Trade: Four Free Trade Agreements GAO Reviewed have Resulted in Commercial Benefits, but Challenges on Labor and Environment Remain.* 2009. http://www.gao.gov/products/GAO-09-439.

UNCTAD. UNCTAD Least Developed Countries Report 2007. Chapter 3: Intellectual Property Rights and Other Incentive Mechanisms for Learning and Innovation. 2007.

UNESCO Institute for Statistics. Measuring Educational Participation: Analysis of Data Quality and Methodology Based on Ten Studies. UNESCO Institute for Statistics, 2010.

Wang, Fang, Hongxia Zhang, Hengjia Zang, and Ming Ouyang. "Purchasing Pirated Software: An Initial Examination of Chinese Consumers." *Journal of Consumer Marketing* 22, no. 6 (January 10, 2005): 340–351.

Weintraub, Sidney. "The Politics of US Trade Policy," *BBC News Online*, February 15, 2010. http://news.bbc.co.uk/2/hi/business/3169649.stm.

WHO [World Health Organization]. "Trade, Intellectual Property Rights and Access to Medicines," January 12, 2010. http://www.who.int/medicines/areas/policy/globtrade/en/index.html.

Wikileaks. Cables pertaining to "Embassy," "Amman," n.d. Wikileaks website. http://wikileaks.org/origin/187_0.html.

Wiktorowicz, Quintan. *The Management of Islamic Activism: Salafis, the Muslim Brotherhood, and State Power in Jordan*. Albany, NY: SUNY Press, 2001.

WIPO [World Intellectual Property Organization]. "Proposal by Argentina and Brazil for the Establishment of a Development Agenda for WIPO," January 11, 2010. http://www.wipo.int/meetings/en/doc_details.jsp?doc_id=31737.

Wong, Tzen, and Graham Dutfield. *Intellectual Property and Human Development: Current Trends and Future Scenarios*. Cambridge: Cambridge University Press, 2010.

World Bank. Global Economic Prospects 2005: Trade, Regionalism, and Development. World Bank, 2004.

—. Preventing HIV/AIDS in the Middle East and North Africa: A Window of Opportunity to Act. World Bank, 2005.

World Economic Forum. *Global Competitiveness Report 2009–2010*. World Economic Forum, 2010.

WTO [World Trade Organization]. "Dispute Settlement Understanding." WTO, May 1, 2010.

—. *Trade Policy Review, 10 and 12 November 2008—Jordan*. Minutes of Meeting. World Trade Organization, December 19, 2008.